WE PROMISED YOU A GREAT MAIN EVENT

Bill Hanstock

WE PROMISED YOU A GREAT MAIN EVENT

An Unauthorized WWE History

HARPER

An Imprint of HarperCollins*Publishers*

FIRST EDITION

Designed by Bonni Leon-Berman
Illustrations by Lauren Moran

Library of Congress Cataloging-in-Publication Data
Names: Hanstock, Bill, author.
Title: We promised you a great main event : an unauthorized WWE history / Bill Hanstock.
Description: First edition. | New York City : Harper, An imprint of HarperCollins Publishers, [2020] | Includes index. |
Identifiers: LCCN 2020030713 (print) | LCCN 2020030714 (ebook) | ISBN 9780062980847 (hardcover) | ISBN 9780062980854 (ebook)
Subjects: LCSH: World Wrestling Entertainment, Inc.—History. | Wrestling—United States—History. | Wrestlers—United States.
Classification: LCC GV1196.25 .H35 2020 (print) | LCC GV1196.25 (ebook) | DDC 796.8120973—dc23
LC record available at https://lccn.loc.gov/2020030713
LC ebook record available at https://lccn.loc.gov/2020030714

20 21 22 23 24   LSC   10 9 8 7 6 5 4 3 2 1

To Kristen, who has loved and supported me all these years despite my obsession with pro wrestling.

And to Archer: may you never grow up to be a wrestling fan.

CONTENTS

WE PROMISED YOU A GREAT MAIN EVENT

INTRODUCTION
YOU KNOW IT'S ALL FAKE, RIGHT?

et's go ahead and get this out of the way right up front:
yes, professional wrestling fans know it's fake.

The truth is that for the vast majority of pro wrestling fans, we've lived most of our lives being told that our pastime isn't actually real—the implication being, of course, that a perceived lack of "authenticity" means it isn't worth our time, attention, and passion. It's a very strange social and pop cultural stigma that is unique to wrestling, and it's one that every single wrestling fan has encountered. Yes, it's fake. And we really don't care, because that isn't the point.

For one thing, the athleticism and artistry of the performers and the consequences of the pro wrestling lifestyle couldn't be more real, but for another, no one goes up to someone excited about the latest *Star Wars* movie and says, "You know that Darth Vader isn't real, right? Yep. All made up. You big dummy." Few (if any) people will cut someone off in the middle of gushing about a particular Meryl Streep performance to tell you that she didn't really have to choose which of her children would be killed, or that she wasn't really Julia Child.

It doesn't matter that wrestling is "fake." In fact, it is that very artifice that makes it so enthralling and watchable. Consider this: "Legitimate" sports are in fact so random that our narrative-driven brains aren't able to perceive them as the objective and random collection of moments that they really are. Our brains and our broadcasters and analysts and columnists and other assorted talking heads try to awkwardly staple a narrative to a given game, sport, or athlete: the Yankees always win; LeBron fades in the fourth quarter; the refs were biased against us; Matt Ryan isn't clutch. We look for a story in sports when there usually isn't one. Wrestling gives us that story we crave.

Of course, wrestling also goes above and beyond by giving us backstage skits and exploding cars and witch doctors who make bodybuilders throw up. But face it: wouldn't you be a lot more likely to tune in to a typical Thursday night NFL game if you knew Roger Goodell was going to show up beforehand and tell his archnemesis Aaron Rodgers that he'll have to take on the Vikings using only seven players on offense all night? You'd watch the ever-living hell out of that. And even if it was fake, you'd probably enjoy it just the same.

We want to suspend our disbelief. We love doing it. Just like when we take in any other form of a narrative, we pay attention to the stories that are being told. Maybe these two combatants in the ring aren't really trying to defeat one another in unarmed combat for realsies, but if we're lucky, the story that they tell inside that ring is going to transport and elevate our emotions as only the best combination of art and sport is capable of doing.

Pro wrestling's "fakeness" isn't a liability. It's a storytelling device—one that wrestlers employ now with more self-awareness than ever. Fans have been in on the joke to varying degrees all along, but these days wrestlers are more than happy to make metacommentary on their own sport, from The Rock's hyper self-aware heel to CM Punk's pipe bomb promo.

The world of The Rock and CM Punk is a wildly different one from that of Bruno Sammartino. For the first time in the sport's hundred-year-plus history, most of the people plying their trade as wrestlers are not members of a sworn brotherhood or society, invested in keeping kayfabe at all costs and keeping outsiders at arm's length. The people performing as wrestlers now are—nearly exclusively—fans of wrestling in all its forms. These aren't mostly former amateur wrestlers or former football players or street fighters or bodybuilders or models pressed into service because of their legitimacy and look and physique and told to protect the business and make sure the marks don't peek behind the curtain; these are people who have grown up knowing about the artifice of wrestling and loving it with their entire hearts not just in spite of, but *because of* its postmodern, metatextual idiosyncrasies. These are fans of wrestling who loved the show so much that they became wrestlers, in an age when it's never been easier to find credible wrestling schools. They've emerged and entered the business (or adapted their craft) in the age of social media and YouTube. They've practiced and distributed their promos and matches on the internet, posted on message boards, traded tapes, written letters to fan magazines, and promised themselves they'd have their very own WrestleMania moment. Not because they want to be rich, but because they want to be artists—and their medium is wrestling.

(It's not all pathos and high art, of course. Due to the very nature and sheer ridiculousness of the reality of the "reality" of professional wrestling, there are going to be some kitschy or hokey aspects on *some* level. You cannot completely separate the hokeyness of wrestling from all of wrestling.)

So yes, fans aren't idiots. We are even well aware of the long history of problematic, racist, and bigoted characters and story lines, and the shady business practices that have plagued the industry in general and World Wrestling Entertainment in particular.

Not that we get any credit for that. The condescension that pro wrestling fans experience doesn't just extend to daily interactions with nonwrestling fans. I have had to wade through a good amount of biographies and memoirs and explainers and long-form articles that spend a lot of time trying to explain pro wrestling terms that most fans already know, while simultaneously having been through an editor who doesn't know there was a person named Lou Thesz, or why that person existed, or why he might have a move named after him. Or how his name is spelled. We've had to deal with good but uninformed writers talking down to us, or (far more often) extremely knowledgeable fans and documentarians whose strong suit isn't entertaining or, sadly, legible writing. Generally, these histories are either dry to a fault or talk down to the audience.

Even so, we'll snatch up any piece of content that we can find if we think we'll get some quality wrestling-based entertainment or information out of it—or just a shot of that pure, sweet, delectable pro wres nostalgia. In my decade of writing about wrestling on the internet, I've learned two fundamental truths about wrestling fans: we'll click on and read absolutely anything we can about wrestling, and we'll never, ever be able to get enough of it.

What I'm hoping to accomplish over the course of this book is a delicate balancing act. An informative history of the largest professional wrestling company in history (and by extension, a history of professional wrestling in the United States) that doesn't insult the intelligence of hardcore fans, doesn't alienate the uninitiated, and remains entertaining throughout. I'm excited to take on the challenge, and I'm excited that you're coming along with me.

The story of WWE—formerly the World Wrestling Federation (WWF)—is a drama for the ages. Real-life backstabbing; all the drugs, booze, and sex you could possibly imagine; cutthroat business takeovers; and actual murder. What has happened over the course of Vince McMahon and his company's ascendancy is every inch the "soap opera for men" that the on-camera pro wrestling product is constantly derided for aspiring to.

From the very beginning of the company, long before it was WWE, the McMahon family has been behind the scenes, steering the ship, and for forty years, since the company set its sights on national, and then global, expansion, they've had to deal with purists crying loudly that they're murdering the very sport in which they ply their trade.

NFL fans hate Roger Goodell. NBA fans hated David Stern. Soccer fans hate everything about FIFA. NHL fans hate the rules that have made the league "soft." But no sport has ever despised a despot more than the wrestling industry loathes the McMahon family.

PART I

THE MCMAHON FAMILY AND THE EARLY YEARS

1

GENETIC JACKHAMMERS AND ACTUAL SLEDGEHAMMERS

An Introduction to the McMahon Family

Jim Browning, a rough-and-tumble brawler with a face like Jack Dempsey on a bad day and a thick midsection that, even in clothes, would warn bystanders not to start trouble, sends a roar up through the Coney Island crowd on a summer day in 1933.

Decades later, Hulk Hogan whipped the crowd into a frenzy when, at a given point in a match, he would channel the positive vibes of his Hulkamaniacs into a short period of imperviousness and "Hulk up," vibrating his eye-popping 24-inch pythons* and marching in a spasmodic circle before pointing an accusatory finger at his challenger—almost invariably a barrel-chested monster from whatever country the United States happened to be feuding with or distrustful of at the time.

One year before the new millennium, a smug billionaire stands in a wrestling ring with his family and his chosen corporate wrestling champion: a well-over-6-foot-tall specimen known only as The Rock, a third-generation pompous ass with a penchant for silk Versace shirts and cocking an eyebrow beneath his rapidly dwindling hairline. This group's moment of serenity would come to a screeching halt when the sound of breaking glass fills the arena, and a crazed redneck in a camouflage jacket drives a Coors beer truck to the ringside area. This lunatic hillbilly stomps out of the truck in jean shorts and proceeds to blast everyone standing in the ring—and most fans at ringside—with a torrent of beer sprayed directly out of a fire hose. Apparently, that's a function of beer trucks, although it's likely seldom used.

But all these scenes, from ankle-booted hourlong exchanges of amateur wrestling holds, to beer hoses, to flips and cakes, have been presided over (in one form or another) by one family: the McMahons.

---

* By all accounts, Hogan's bicep circumference was much closer to 22 inches, a spectacular achievement in its own right, but as with everything else around Hulk Hogan, why settle for the well-above-average truth when you can fudge the numbers to claim to be the biggest and most impressive of anyone who has ever lived?

The McMahon family are the central figures behind the scenes (and usually smack-dab in the middle of the scenes), a group that is about as self-made as a batch of American moguls can get—at least in the carny-ass industry that is pro wrestling.

The current and reigning patriarch, Vince McMahon, is hailed as perhaps the most brilliant wrestling mind of all time, *and* as the main source of problems that fans, peers, and onlookers have with WWE in particular, and, fair or not, with wrestling at large. As the driving force of the WWE machine, the architect of its monopolization of the industry, and the sole person who determines what makes it onto every television show, pay-per-view, house show, website article, coffee table book, press release, or program, he reaps the lion's share of the credit for anything that gains acclaim, and is the person to blame if things are received poorly. In more recent years, WWE's successes are largely considered by fans to happen in spite of Vince rather than because of him, almost as if the company has produced something worthwhile by sheer accident.

The McMahons' power in the New York sports universe started a long time ago. Jess McMahon, born Roderick James McMahon in 1882, was the youngest child of Roderick and Elizabeth McMahon, hoteliers who had recently emigrated from County Galway in Ireland to Manhattan, New York. Jess's main contribution to the family dynasty was building a good reputation in the boxing world in the Northeast, and by extension, making his last name notable in New York combat circles. Wrestling promotion wouldn't pick up until his middle child, Vincent James McMahon, took over the family business.

Vincent (eventually referred to as "Vince Sr." by the entire world following his death) shared his father's love of promoting and talent for innovation. McMahon partnered with Toots Mondt to turn the Capitol Wrestling Corporation into a true powerhouse in the Northeast. The CWC was later renamed the World Wide Wrestling Federation—possibly to take advantage of infighting in the National Wrestling Alliance at the time or to set up an unaffiliated company in the event the Department of Justice decided to pursue a rumored antitrust suit against the NWA. Strangely, a large point of contention in the NWA squabble was whether television would be a negative to the business, as the relatively new medium threatened to air in certain territories within the markets of a rival. But McMahon understood the power of television as a marketing tool.

For one thing, wrestling could be adequately produced for television on a (relatively) tiny budget. Pro wrestling had been airing on the DuMont Network in some form since 1940, and in the late forties the small screen helped turn personalities like Gorgeous George into national phenomena. Television would entice fans to come out to Madison Square Garden and other venues for the big cards and the showcase matches. McMahon was hardly the first to put wrestling on TV, but he was one of the first to lean into it as an integral part of the business. Television needed programming, and McMahon was eager to oblige.

Within a year of assuming control of the company, McMahon's CWC arranged a deal to air a weekly show on the DuMont Network. Since sporting and concert venues were in no way set up to allow for television taping at the time, McMahon arranged for a ring and studio to be constructed in a barn in

Washington, D.C. The CWC would air every Wednesday on DuMont until 1956 and would move to New York's WABD and air on Saturday evenings every week until the 1970s.

Unlike his father, Vincent settled on professional wrestling promotion as his primary venture, and he worked hard to utilize television and continue his father's tenure in New York and Madison Square Garden. As the popularity of the now-named World Wide Wrestling Federation grew, McMahon developed a stranglehold on wrestling in the Northeast, and McMahon's jurisdiction was soon just referred to as "New York" among people in the business. (That Vince Sr. was purportedly one of the very first promoters to begin splitting a percentage of the gate with the in-ring performers didn't hurt "New York's" reputation as a great place for wrestlers to work.) As the WWWF separated from the National Wrestling Alliance, there was a shift in aesthetics and ethos. By 1971, pro wrestling in the United States could be distilled into Southern wrestling (or Southern rasslin', if you want to be more accurate and/or rile up and/or inspire fans) and New York.

Which brings us to Vincent Kennedy McMahon, the Vince McMahon you're likely familiar with. Vince is a singularly fascinating individual, perhaps one of the most perplexing humans who has ever graced the face of the Earth. Stories about his proclivities and peculiarities—both apocryphal and verified—could fill their own book: he hates sneezing and considers it a sign of weakness. He was in his forties or later when he first learned what a burrito was, and that Asian porn existed. He's been known to deliberately step on a person's feet or make a personal verbal attack on them in order to try and get them to stick up for themselves. He believes you can eat an entire box of Oreo cookies in one sitting with no ill effect; it's having a few every day that will make you fat. He finds farts the most hilarious thing in the world, unless it's a day when he's tickled by poop. He yelled at a prospective screenwriter for using the phrase "to tell you the truth"—the implication being in Vince's mind that the individual must have been lying to him during the rest of the conversation.

He once tried to pitch his daughter two separate story lines involving incest: one that implied she was in a romantic relationship with her brother, and one where she was sleeping with him. She declined both. Howard Cosell, perhaps the most famous sportscaster of all time, told a story in his autobiography of McMahon calling him in 1984 to offer him a job as the WWF's lead announcer. Cosell laughed, incredulous, and told Vince that he didn't want to finish up his illustrious career "calling phony wrestling matches." He said Vince must be crazy and turned him down cold. McMahon, in an instant, turned furious, yelling, "Fuck you, Howard! You're making the biggest mistake of your life." Howard recalled, "After I hung up, I thought McMahon was a real kook. I still do. But he's an incredibly successful one." A more succinct appraisal of McMahon would be difficult to find.

Vince is ruthless both personally and professionally. If he feels a perceived slight, he has a long history of enacting his revenge fantasies on the air within his programs and inside the ring. When Rosie O'Donnell ran afoul of his good friend Donald Trump, he booked a match on *Raw* between a Rosie impersonator and a Trump impersonator (neither of which looked much like their real-life counterparts, apart from the Trump wig), with Trump going over. He booked a similar match between "Barack Obama" and "Hillary Clinton." He cast geriatric actors to portray Hulk Hogan, Randy Savage, and "Billionaire Ted" when his two former top stars decided to sign with Ted Turner's World Championship Wrestling (WCW). He's hired former longtime opposition stars and paid them big money just to make them look foolish and diminish their value elsewhere. The many regional bookers, promoters, and adversaries who went up against McMahon hated his guts long before he eventually drove them all out of business. He has at one time or another employed just about every dirty trick in the wrestling *and* the promoter business in order to gain an upper hand, although that's pretty much what you'd expect from any billionaire. Vincent Kennedy McMahon has kept an iron grip on his empire against all odds, but he wasn't necessarily the born-into-this golden child you might expect given his promoter-family lineage.

Vince Jr. was the younger of two boys born to Vince Sr. and his first wife, Victoria. Vince Jr. was born in 1945 in North Carolina, but Vince Sr. divorced Victoria in 1946 and departed with his eldest son, Roderick McMahon III. As a result, Vince Jr. didn't meet his father until adolescence, instead growing up with several fathers and being raised under the name Vinnie Lupton. Vince Jr. said in a 2001 *Playboy* interview that the stepfather from who he took this surname, Leo Lupton, abused his mother, and subsequently beat Vinnie when he once tried to intervene on his mother's behalf. Of Leo, Vince later said, "It is unfortunate that he died before I could kill him. I would have enjoyed that." He also said in that same interview that he was sexually assaulted or molested as a child by someone very close to him. "You said the sexual abuse in your childhood 'wasn't from the male,'" said interviewer Kevin Cook. "It's well known that you're estranged from your mother. Have we found the reason?" After a pause,

McMahon nodded and offered, "Without saying that, I'd say that's pretty close."

Vince told *Forbes* that he grew up "dirt poor" and lived in a trailer park before finally meeting his biological father at the age of twelve. By all accounts, Vince was instantly hooked on the wrestling business, even wanting to become a pro wrestler himself before Vince Sr. forbade it.* After meeting his father, Vince would regularly make trips to MSG to watch the shows by his father's side behind the scenes. Vince graduated from military school in Virginia, then got his bachelor's degree at East Carolina University in 1968.† He quickly came aboard his father's business, eager to learn, and debuted in the World Wide Wrestling Federation as a ring announcer in 1969. It was off to the races at that point, as he became a play-by-play man in 1971 and continued to work hand in hand with his father. They clashed at times, as Vince Sr. was a traditionalist. Among other disagreements, Vince Sr. believed the role of a booker and promoter was to be behind the scenes and unseen at all costs—something Vince Jr. would eschew for the bulk of his time in the wrestling business.

Linda Marie Edwards met Vince Jr. when she was thirteen years old and Vince was sixteen, as their mothers worked in the same building. Victoria McMahon became good friends with the Edwards family, and Vince and Linda dated throughout high school. The Edwardses' stable home life was a balm

---

* In retrospect, Vince wanting to be a wrestler first and foremost makes a lot of otherwise-baffling decisions over the years make way, way too much sense.

† Vince has a business degree, and at this point you should just go ahead and stamp his face on all business degrees handed out in the United States. Give it time; I'm sure we'll get there.

to Vince, and he spent most of his free time there until heading off to college. He proposed to Linda after she graduated from high school, and they married in August 1966, when Linda was seventeen years old. Linda attended East Carolina University alongside her husband, and finished college with a French degree and her teaching certification in just three years, so that she could walk in the same graduation ceremony as Vince. After Vince joined his father's company, Linda worked as a receptionist and paralegal in Maryland, translating documents for a law firm and studying IP law, which would definitely come in extremely handy for the couple's future in professional wrestling.

In 1970, Linda gave birth to their son, Shane McMahon, and Stephanie McMahon was born in 1976. In 1980, Linda and Vince founded Titan Sports, which would eventually orchestrate the buyout of Vince Sr.'s wrestling company. Linda would make her way onto WWE television—most notably as a wheelchair-bound zombie drugged by her real-life husband and evil business partner, and recipient of some of the most gingerly applied wrestling holds in history. Outside of pro wrestling, Linda took part in various entrepreneurial and philanthropic efforts, and along with the success of WWE, the McMahons were real movers and shakers in Connecticut, their adopted home state ever since putting down the proverbial Titan Sports stakes (which eventually found its permanent home in Stamford*).

---

* According to Shane McMahon, Vince settled on Connecticut because the Greenwich area would be the "last place on earth" people would expect a pro wrestling company to be based. The other finalist for Titan Sports' home base was allegedly Beverly Hills.

In 2009, Linda became a member of the Connecticut State Board of Education, appointed by then-governor Jodi Rell, and stepped down from that post the following year to begin the first of two attempted U.S. Senate campaigns. Running as a Republican, she was handed defeats in the 2010 and 2012 senatorial elections, reportedly spending tens of millions of dollars of her own money on the campaigns. After seeing her general-election political hopes dashed in two straight elections, McMahon became heavily involved as a donor and fundraiser for the GOP. Not surprisingly, the McMahons have donated several million dollars to Donald Trump and his various personal and political exploits, including a $6 million donation to a Trump campaign super PAC in 2016. Equally not surprisingly, Linda was one of the first people earmarked for a spot in Trump's cabinet following his election. On February 14, 2017, Linda became the head of the Small Business Administration, and despite the subsequent mind-boggling picture of her and Vince in the Oval Office with their pro wrestling children and their children, she would eventually become one of the least controversial and least scandal-plagued members of the entire Trump administration.*

So now we really must talk about the McMahon-Trump relationship. Linda and Vince have a long-standing personal friendship with Donald Trump, dating back to the 1980s. The earliest notable on-screen collaboration between the Trumps and the McMahons came in 1988, when Wrestle-Mania IV was referred to on-screen as being held at the

---

* Admittedly, this is not a particularly sparkling distinction.

Trump Plaza Hotel and Casino.* Trump also appeared on-camera at ringside during the event, schmoozed backstage with wrestlers, and did it again the following year, when WrestleMania V was held at the same venue and Trump was interviewed at ringside by announcer Sean Mooney midway through the event. These were the formative events in the McMahon-Trump alliance, and the family have been friends with Donald ever since.

Much has been written about the relationship between the McMahons and Donald Trump over the years, but the underlying sentiment and belief is that the two showmen tend to have a lot in common in terms of showmanship under the guise of business—or vice versa. A sizable chunk of the American populace views the two men as billionaire hucksters of a sort, and huckster one-percenters tend to stick together. Personally, I believe the relationship is a bit more nuanced than that.

Donald Trump and Vince McMahon see something in the other man that they desperately wish they could obtain for themselves. Vince McMahon has accomplished everything there is to be accomplished in a specific niche, but all his other ventures have met with limited success or pointed failure over the years, especially when he's tried to court a more mainstream audience. He's always desired validation from the mainstream press and has either subtly or overtly wanted to be seen as something other than a carny wrestling

* In actuality, both WrestleManias IV and V were held at the Historic Atlantic City Convention Hall, but as the adjacent Trump Plaza was a primary sponsor of the events, that's what the venue was called, exclusively, throughout the broadcast.

promoter. He's hailed as a genius, visionary, and the largest mogul his field could ever imagine, but he desires nothing more than to be thought of as a self-made billionaire and genius, period, without the "wrestling" label appended to any of his superlatives. In Donald Trump, McMahon sees someone with his same mindset and mentality (to varying degrees) and his same love of bombast and showmanship, but someone who has always managed to convince the world at large of his business acumen, celebrity, and personality— someone who is Vince McMahon viewed from a different angle, but a Vince McMahon who has managed to attain the ultimate validation of mainstream acceptance: the office of the presidency of the United States.

Similarly, when Trump looks at McMahon, he sees what he's always imagined in himself: someone who has scrapped and clawed for every inch of his personal success and wealth; someone who has conquered his corner of industry and is hailed as an innovative genius, visionary, and ruthless businessman; and someone who is a big, strong, macho guy—a swaggering manifestation of excess and masculinity that Trump has always been single-mindedly focused on in endless interviews and speeches and braggadocio. Trump was handed immense wealth by his father and got a family doctor to write a note to avoid joining the military. He reportedly gorges on fast food and watches television most of the day, seething at people who call him out for what he perceives as petty slights. Vince McMahon, meanwhile, grew up in a trailer park, bought out his own father's business, and has spent the past few decades working out hours a day, growing his business, and barely having time for sleep—not that he'd claim to need sleep, anyway. Vince has a full head of hair and bulging muscles and minuscule body fat. He fancies himself as being in control at all times, to the point where he has nearly mastered his own body's compulsion to occasionally sneeze. That sure ain't Trump. The two men recognize their ruthless showmanship nature in the other, but their yearning for what the other has is what drives them. If they weren't friends, they'd be bitter enemies. If one of them didn't exist, the other would create a hypothetical image of him in their mind to motivate them and propel them forward.

Vince is seemingly motivated by this raging desire to break into a more respected business. Every time a nonwrestling website or publication spills any amount of positive ink or devotes any amount of space to something WWE did, the weekly shows will dedicate a short bumper to showing the headlines on screen, while lead announcer Michael Cole explains why the noteworthy news item was important. In the 1980s and 1990s, McMahon tried to start a movie production company, a bodybuilding league, a supplement company, and get into the boxing game (among other ventures). In the 2000s, he tried to start a mainstream football company (twice) and actually *did* start a movie studio. It's his continued insistence that his company is an entertainment company, not a wrestling company. It rankles him that he'll never get the mainstream respect he craves due to the societal stigma associated with the fundamental nature of pro wrestling—and yet he is unable to break free from his status as a self-made billionaire who became rich and powerful by being better at promoting pro wrestling than anyone else in history.

2

A BRIEF HISTORY OF KAYFABE AND THE TERRITORIES

Wrestling is probably the most carny-ass business on Earth, especially given how the origins of the business lie in—you know—carnivals.

Between the 1830s and 1850s, pro wrestling evolved as a circus and carnival sideshow attraction, one that eventually developed a set of loose rules. From its inception, the fix was in: in order to put on a good show for spectators (this was the circus, after all), the performers needed to be certain that it would go as planned. And the carny promoters and showmen realized that a staged competition, under the guise of authentic sport, really made for the best possible adrenaline rush. You could make sure the hero prevailed after a prolonged struggle, or that the dastardly villain took advantage of a weakness or utilized unscrupulous tactics.

By the mid-nineteenth century, promoters of wrestling contests were savvy enough to realize that they could maximize their profits and the enjoyment of the paying audience by ensuring the proper person emerged victorious. Thus, the performers began to **work** the crowds—make them believe what they were seeing was real. (The opposite of a work, as every good fan knows, is a **shoot**—something that is actually, really real. No, really.) By the time the 1900s rolled around, traveling carnivals had created a brotherhood of **kayfabe**: the insistence on the artifice of legitimacy where pro wrestling was concerned.

It was in the twentieth century that wrestling became a global business, dominated by trusts and charismatic billionaires. And the exact strictures of kayfabe, major wrestling companies, and the narratives that those companies create were developed during the 1930s.

Georg Hackenschmidt and Frank Gotch were the first international ultrasuperstars in the world of professional wrestling, but their careers wound down around the time the sport suffered a drastic decrease in popularity: during World War I, when there was a dearth of strapping young lads to grip one another roughly about the waist, because they were all in foxholes in Europe trying not to die.

The business was dying, and something had to be done. Enter the team of Billy Sandow, Ed "Strangler" Lewis, and Joseph Raymond "Toots" Mondt, three "meat tossers" who had the wherewithal to do two important things: give the public a reason to line up to buy a ticket, and essentially form a cartel to ensure people watched their wrestling shows instead of anyone else's.

Toots Mondt, like all the other biggest pro wrestlers and promoters of his generation, made it his business to befriend and eventually have in his pocket an assortment of newspapermen and other journalists. As such—like many other pro wrestling promoters and companies before and after him—much of what we understand as Mondt's backstory is likely hooey, but the fact remains that he's one of the most influential men in the evolution of what we recognize as professional wrestling today, and his importance may be largely due to his foresight of controlling his own narrative. It was an important lesson that the McMahon family paid close attention to, and a trick that has served well every wrestling promoter to venture into the business since.

A brief history of Toots Mondt, as presented by people friendly with Toots Mondt, is as follows: Mondt, inspired by wild brawls at the lumber camp where he worked, the best of the Greco-Roman and catch styles, and a liberal dose of various carny-assery, trained up a cadre of wrestlers, innovated some amazing-looking (but relatively safe) moves of his own devising, stuck the whole damn thing inside a boxing ring, and called it "Slam Bang Western-Style Wrestling." We should still be calling it that, and the fact that we're not is a crime.

A brief history of Toots Mondt by people *not* so friendly to him would highlight his financial irresponsibility. He nearly (or by some accounts, completely) ran the wrestling scene in the Northeast into the ground with his failure to live up to promises and his failure to pay his wrestlers what they were owed.

Mondt is credited with coming up with the idea that every

match should have a recognizable **finish** that the crowd could follow—that is, a clearly defined conclusion. Building on that, he also came up with the **fuck finish**, an unsatisfying or controversial end that would guarantee a return match—one that would theoretically draw an even bigger crowd and a much larger gate. And of course, there was the **double countout** and the planned **time limit draw**—the latter another innovation of Mondt's, because somehow no one had thought to put a hard time limit on what had previously been an interminable sport. Mondt and his partners never let one match be enough when there was any possibility people would pay to see a second. As another famous carny once said, always leave them wanting more.

Mondt, Sandow, and Lewis were given the name "The Gold Dust Trio" in a 1937 tell-all book by Marcus Griffin called *Fall Guys: The Barnums of Bounce*. That book was filled to the brim with details about exactly how and why the wrestling business was all a sham, even though—as was the journalistic convention at the time—it was also filled with its own outright fabrications, boosting numbers, exaggerating paydays, and the like.

That book's existence just goes to show that as long as there has been professional wrestling, there have been critics, journalists, and nonfans continually blowing the lid off the fact that it was all rigged. Every five or ten years or so, a newspaper story, magazine article, or book would come along and shine a bright light on the scandal that negatively impacted business to varying degrees—until the public forgot about it and just wanted to have a good time going to see the matches. A few years later, it would start all over again.

Despite semiregular exposés, pro wrestling was able to

keep up the ruse for decades due to the extremely close-knit fraternity developed by those inside the business. Kayfabe became the rule of the day: you don't tell anyone about what really goes on here unless they're one of us. Even into the 1990s, fans (and even people actively training to be pro wrestlers) weren't "smartened up" until and unless it was deemed absolutely necessary.

Pro wrestling still requires some level of kayfabe, even today, for any of it to work at all. Take a nonfan to any independent wrestling show and by midway through, they'll probably ask you if some move or some result was real. The illusion of the dance is intoxicating. Thanks, kayfabe!

The bottom fell out of pro wrestling in the 1930s, but after World War II, the influx of commerce (and the advent of television) led to business picking up once again. In 1948, the National Wrestling Alliance (NWA) was formed by a half-dozen promoters, largely from the Midwest. They created a unified NWA World Heavyweight Champion, who would serve as a touring national champion, shared between territories, traveling the country and allowing not only for a quasi-universally recognized world champ for the sport, but for all NWA promoters to share in the profitability of promoting the "real" world's champion.

It's important to note that in those days—and all the way up until the late 1990s in some respects—wrestling was regional. This was partly due to logistics and infrastructure (like the local news, the local television station, the local newspaper, and the concept of a local versus a long-distance call). The country was carved up into "territories," many affiliated with the NWA, and those unaffiliated were considered "outlaw" promotions. Some NWA promoters wouldn't book you if you went and worked an outlaw show; but then again, if there was money in it, both sides were always plenty willing to do business. Some wrestlers were exclusive to certain promoters or territories, but many big-name main-event players and other upper-card guys (especially the heels) would join up with Georgia Championship Wrestling for a few months, finish up all their story lines, then move somewhere else in the country (or the continent, or the world) like Championship Wrestling in Florida, or Mid-South Wrestling in Oklahoma, Louisiana, Mississippi, and Arkansas, or Pacific Northwest Wrestling. All this helps explain why finally having one agreed-upon national champion was a big deal.

Orville Brown was the first man to hold the national NWA title, but in 1949 the man who would become synonymous with it—Lou Thesz, former protégé of Ed Lewis—kicked off a prosperous six-year reign. Thanks to the NWA, pro wrestling for the first time ever had an official, agreed-upon champion in all of the English-speaking world.

In the midst of Thesz's first run as world champion, Toots Mondt formed and incorporated his own official wrestling promotion in 1952: the Capitol Wrestling Corporation. In 1953, the CWC joined the NWA and was able to pull not just from the NWA pool and its fighting champion, but from the very deep well of the New York territory and the nearby cities of Philadelphia and Boston.

In 1954, Vince Sr. joined up with the CWC, and McMahon and Mondt proved to be an unparalleled team in the promotion game—at least in the Northeast. They ramped up booking of NWA talent and its champion even more as the center of the pro wrestling world began to tilt heavily toward New York.

The boom of wrestling broadcast on television caused endless infighting among NWA members. While Thesz was usually the consensus pick to hold the world title and represent the NWA, some felt his time had passed and wanted to go with a new, flashier, and more modern champion—one who was either matching or surpassing Thesz's popularity and drawing power in many markets. "Nature Boy" Buddy Rogers, like fellow heel Gorgeous George a decade earlier, captured the imaginations and assorted hatreds of viewers via his televised antics as an unabashed blowhard infatuated with nothing other than himself. His bleached-blond hair, gaudy robes, in-ring strut, and nickname were all eventually adopted by a much more famous "Nature Boy": Ric Flair.

Rogers became NWA World Heavyweight Champion in 1961 and although he lacked the pure grappling acumen of many of the other champions who had preceded him, his abundance of personality (particularly suited to getting people to hate his rotten guts) made him a supernova. But as his calendar filled up, the NWA brain trust was dismayed to find he was being primarily booked in the New York metropolitan area, with Mondt and McMahon's CWC taking the majority of the haul from the gates.

By 1963, NWA wanted to switch the world title back to their tried-and-true guy, Lou Thesz. Rogers lost to Thesz in a one-fall match on January 24, 1963.

The one-fall match was a strange anomaly, borne of the Alliance's distrust of Rogers. Typically, world heavyweight title matches were contested under two-out-of-three-falls rules (the better to allow for both champion and challenger to look good and save face—even in defeat—as much as the situation dictated). The NWA wanted to get the match over quickly to allow for the slightest possible chance that Rogers might fuck them over (despite the fact that Thesz could have shot on Rogers during the match and handled him with ease, should the issue have arisen). But the safeguard ended up biting the NWA in the ass, as it allowed Rogers to continue to claim he was still the rightful world champion, given he did not lose the title under traditional rules as was custom. He had a point!

The perfect storm of circumstances presented a golden opportunity to Mondt and McMahon. Thesz was nowhere near the draw in the New York area that Rogers was; Rogers had a mostly legitimate claim to be world champion; and Verne Gagne had already proven a non-NWA promotion could succeed (more on Gagne later). The two men promptly withdrew from the NWA and founded a brand-new promotion: the World Wide Wrestling Federation, or WWWF.

Thus the company was born, and Rogers became its first star, in a coup for McMahon and Mondt. Rogers was introduced as the first WWWF World Heavyweight Champion a few short months after losing his NWA title to Thesz. As the story went, Rogers secured the world championship after winning a grueling tournament in Rio de Janeiro filled with top-level talent from every corner of the globe. Oh, you should have seen the thing! But you couldn't have, because it never happened. The "tournament in Rio de Janeiro" became a favorite of the WWWF, as inaugural WWE Intercontinental Champion Pat Patterson won a startlingly similar tournament in 1979 to introduce that secondary title. It's a real shame that the internet exists now, because "I won a tournament; don't worry about it" is one of the best things pro wrestling has ever given to the world.

Rogers and the WWWF were a success right out of the gate. As is always the case with a despised heel (and the reason that heels exist as a draw), people loved flocking to see the possibility of a Rogers loss, and his claim of being the real, legitimate world champion was an enticing one. Unfortunately, Rogers, now in his forties, was plagued with a litany of heart issues. After being hospitalized multiple times, it was clear that Mondt and McMahon needed to find a new top draw. Luckily, they happened to have the man who would soon become known as "The Living Legend," Bruno Sammartino, already in their employ. And he ended up being a better choice than the WWWF could have ever hoped for.

Sporting a perpetual grin outside the ring and a no-nonsense look any time he stepped inside the ropes, Italian-born Sammartino was built like two adjacent brick shithouses, with a thick mat of chest hair completing the perfect look of what a "real man's man" looked like in the 1960s. Sammartino's adopted hometown of Pittsburgh loved him, and he spent his early years traveling to territories with huge Italian-American populations, rising to the top in short order in each of them. (By the 1950s, promoters had hit upon a winning formula: heavily promote heroes of certain ethnicities while playing up negative stereotypes of villainous foils.) Mondt and McMahon agreed this would be their guy, and on May 17, 1963, Sammartino defeated the ailing Rogers in just forty-eight seconds. Fans were elated at Rogers being unseated, and the lightning-quick defeat of the world champion further served to make Sammartino look like a true force of nature.

Sammartino's reign was an unequivocal success. He drew massive crowds everywhere, but especially in Pittsburgh and in Madison Square Garden. The tried-and-true formula of cycling in challengers, building them up and feeding them to Bruno, worked every time, so the WWWF just kept the gravy train running. Sammartino's first title reign became the longest in the long history of the WWWF, which became the WWF and then WWE. Long, multiyear championship reigns were the norm for the larger part of pro wrestling's history, but it's safe to say that given the nature of the business since the 1990s (at least), Bruno's 2,803-day first championship run (seven years, eight months, and a day) will never be equaled.

Naturally, Italian hero Sammartino's first title run was ended when he ran up against an ethnic opposite: the villainous "Russian Bear" Ivan Koloff. Koloff was a fearsome Soviet monster who played into wrestling fans' worst Cold War fears about the Red Menace. In reality, Koloff was a native Quebecois named Oreal Perras who grew up on a dairy farm in rural Ontario. Hilariously, the Koloff character wasn't Perras's first bite of the ethnic stereotype apple: he broke into the wrestling business as an eyepatch-wearing Irish ne'er-do-well by the name of Red McNulty. Once adopting the Koloff persona, however, he never went back. His top rope knee-drop put a stunning end to Sammartino's historic reign as world champion. In doing so, Koloff became another historic first in the WWWF: he became the company's first **transitional champion**: someone who's simply there to hold the title while the real hero builds up steam.

It's a fact of the wrestling business that there should always be another champion waiting in the wings. But occasionally, that *next* star's position on the hero/villain alignment scale is the same as your existing star's, and you don't want to dilute the fan base's support by running a babyface vs.

babyface title match—or damage your potential gate by running a heel vs. heel match. (And in those days, a heel vs. heel match, especially for a title, was nearly unheard of.) Koloff's role as champion was to hold it just long enough to drop it to the next ethnic hero tabbed to be the company's top star: Pedro Morales.

Morales, a native Puerto Rican, was adored by Latino and Hispanic fans from coast to coast. He held the world title for the better part of three years before it was time for Bruno—who had continued to wrestle at the top of cards and to sell out Madison Square Garden whenever he was in the main event—to take center stage once again.

During the end of Sammartino's first run as world champion, Mondt parted ways with the WWWF. Sammartino himself said late in life that the relationship had been souring for years, possibly due to how quickly the decision had been made to move on from Rogers as their top star. Mondt sold his half of the company to McMahon, who then re-sold Mondt's half to Arnold Skaaland, Phil Zacko, and 400-pound pro wrestler (and Sammartino opponent) Gorilla Monsoon. During Morales's reign in 1971, McMahon quietly rejoined the NWA, once again availing himself of the deep talent pool and national web of connections the Alliance afforded him.

McMahon set about securing better and wider-ranging television deals and began utilizing his best talkers to get fans to buy tickets to live events. One of McMahon's strokes of brilliance was to take Lou Albano—a lower-card wrestler who was no great shakes in the ring and boasted nothing in the way of an impressive look or fearsome stature or physique, but had a peerless ability to run his mouth nonstop—

and convert him from pro wrestler to pro wrestling manager. Almost invariably, Albano would bring a new challenger for Sammartino's title into the WWWF, run his mouth about everything, and get fans to show up in droves to see Sammartino kick the snot out of Albano's charges.

Until well into the Hulkamania era, the company employed a clever tactic to further goose ticket sales at the box office. At the live events at Madison Square Garden, Boston Garden, and other of the territory's big strongholds, the advertised main event would not run at the end of the evening, but as the final match prior to intermission. Often, the world title match would have some sort of controversial finish or an angle indicating there would be a return match, but nearly always after the main event, the following month's main event for the return to the building would be announced—with tickets on sale at the box office, beginning at intermission. After the main event, fans would spend the intermission in line at the box office, contributing to next month's gate ahead of time. Now that's some good carny-ing!

For a decade, it seemed nothing could slow down Sammartino and his unparalleled drawing power. But that was before Stan Hansen came into town. Hansen was the real-life equivalent of Mongo from *Blazing Saddles*: a big, violent, terrifying cowboy who was nice as hell outside the ring and absolutely beat the shit out of his opponents inside it.* In

---

* Hansen's brutality in the ring was owed in part to his awful vision when not wearing glasses. Since everything in the ring was a blur to him, he eliminated the possibility of whiffing on moves by just absolutely clobbering the holy bejesus out of whoever was unlucky enough to be in a program with him.

April 1976, Hansen legitimately broke Sammartino's neck, and although a broken freakin' neck only ended up keeping Bruno out of action for two months, that injury in addition to the constant toll of his schedule had added up. By 1977, Sammartino told McMahon that his time as champion and face of the company was up. Thus the decision was made for Sammartino to lose the title to the biggest heel in the company, who could hold the world championship while the WWWF spent the better part of the next year building up another stalwart, upstanding hero who could hopefully live up to the long, long shadow cast by Sammartino.

But by the time Sammartino ended his legendary run, McMahon and the WWWF understood what they believed was a magic formula of sorts: have a vaguely ethnic babyface who still appeals to a wide (but predominantly white) audience, make sure he's a physical specimen with a lot of personality, and make sure he's *just vulnerable enough* that a loss can seem possible, while still being a superhuman among mortals. Simple, right?

The essential tropes seemed to have been established. The same went for the "real life" story line, as central visionaries like Toots Mondt "singlehandedly" built a sport empire. The Vinces McMahon would embrace that narrative going forward as well—particularly Vince Jr., whose love of self-promotion many times eclipsed his love of wrestling promotion.

When he finally hung up his boots, Sammartino main events had sold out Madison Square Garden an astounding 188 times over the course of his career. No one ever came close to matching Sammartino's stature in New York, nor as a dominant world champion for the McMahons, although many would try—and are arguably still trying to this very day.

3

HOWDY DOODY
MUST DIE

Standing 6 feet 4 inches and tipping the scales at 275 pounds of pure, Dianabol-assisted muscle, "Superstar" Billy Graham was quite unlike anything the 1970s pro wrestling world had ever seen. A former competitive bodybuilder, Graham made the transition to professional wrestling and instantly set about getting paid to piss people off for a living. While Gorgeous George was arguably the first pro wrestler made for that fantastic new medium of television, Superstar Billy Graham leapt right off the screen. His promos were electrifying and infuriating, and he looked superhuman in a way that heroes like Bruno never did—because Bruno never used the gas. Graham brought something far edgier to wrestling—he was sex, drugs, and rock 'n' roll all rolled up into one enormous, larger-than-life package. As the 1970s turned into the 1980s, he was threatening to the old-timers and the traditionalists in a whole new way. His emergence caused a disparity between himself and the lingering top-level babyfaces of the previous generation. Next to Graham, all the heroes seemed stodgy and stuffy. That worked for the older audience, but the writing was on the wall: the good guys would have to start gaining a similar edge—or at the very least, relating just a little bit more to the younger generation.

With a personality that was equal parts Gorgeous George, Muhammad Ali, and his own cocky, ornery disposition, Graham (real name Wayne Coleman) was interested in having the best body in the business and being the most successful. He swept through the territories like a supernova, but he seemed destined for New York, where his long hair and rippling physique could stand under the brightest and gaudiest spotlight. Graham popped into the WWWF in 1975 but departed again soon after for other NWA territories. After Vince McMahon Sr. received word from Bruno Sammartino that his champion wished to relinquish the title, it didn't take long for Graham's name to come to mind.

Graham returned to the WWWF in April 1977 and was immediately booked into a title match against Sammartino. On April 30, Superstar Billy Graham became the WWWF World Heavyweight Champion, defeating Bruno in Baltimore. Graham then held the title for nine and a half months while McMahon got his ducks in a row, building his next champion, who turned out to be Bob Backlund, another in a long line of exemplary amateur and professional wrestlers from Minnesota. (The Hennig family, Sean Waltman, the Gagnes, Rick Rude, Backlund, Nikita Koloff, Barry Darsow, Jesse Ventura, Tom Zenk, Gene and Ole Anderson, Chad Gable, Scott Norton . . . there must be something in the water.)

After being an All-American in both wrestling and football in high school, Backlund won the NCAA Division II amateur wrestling championship at North Dakota State University before turning pro. He started off in the American Wrestling Association (AWA) (as all good Minnesota boys should) and quickly developed a reputation as a thoroughly stand-up guy and a legitimately skilled wrestler, capable of going toe-to-toe with anyone in the ring.

Shortly after entering the WWWF in 1976, Backlund was paired with Arnold Skaaland as a manager and marketed as a wholesome, all-American boy. The next year, he began to be groomed for the world title. On paper, it all made perfect sense: he was the antithesis of everything that Graham stood for: a natural physique; a hardworking and skilled wrestler who was no frills and no nonsense; a God-fearing and authority-respecting goody two-shoes who operated as a throwback type of "proud American" in the increasingly cynical late 1970s. He was popular, but crowds were slower to warm to him than the WWWF would have liked. As time wore on, Backlund picked up steam, and fans especially grew increasingly desperate to see someone, *anyone*, end Graham's reign as world champion.

On February 20, 1978, Backlund defeated Graham for the world title at Madison Square Garden, kicking off a 2,135-day run as champion*—to this day second only in length to

* The officially recognized number of unbroken days in Backlund's reign is 2,135. In actuality, there were a few very brief blips—Antonio Inoki won the title at a house show in Japan (to strengthen the WWF's relationship with New Japan) for a week before Backlund returned home with the belt; the title was later held up for a month starting in October 1981 due to a fuck finish against Greg Valentine. WWE considers the Inoki reign to have never happened and the Valentine incident to not have caused a gap in the lineage.

Sammartino's first reign. During his five-plus years as champion, fans waxed and waned with their tolerance and support of Backlund. Sometimes his Pollyanna, hokey attitude toward things struck fans as earnest and endearing; other times, it grated. But by the end of his reign, they had mostly soured on him. They chanted "Howdy Doody" at him (due to the fact that he looked a great deal like Howdy Doody, which most people can agree is not his fault) and began booing him outright at times. Like John Cena many years later, WWF fans had a love-hate relationship with Bob Backlund, but there was one thing everyone could agree on: Bob Backlund was fundamentally, irreparably uncool. As a new decade set in, the last thing anyone wanted from the face of their company was for him to be viewed as an unrepentant and unsalvageable square.

It was clearly time for a new type of babyface—one who suited the glorified and celebrated excess of the neon-bright 1980s.

Two other vital things happened during Backlund's time as world champion. The first is that, in 1979, the World Wide Wrestling Federation became the infinitely more marketable and easier-to-talk-about World Wrestling Federation, dropping one of their time-consuming Ws and becoming the WWF.

The other is that Vince McMahon's son, Vincent Kennedy McMahon, or Vince McMahon Jr., started to become a key part of the company, both backstage learning in the footsteps of his father and in front of the camera as an interviewer and commentator. (Vince Jr. first joined the company as on-screen talent in 1971.) Vince Jr. joining the business may have been the single most momentous occurrence in pro wrestling history, as he would shape everything that came after.

Vince Sr. commanded respect from his employees and the wrestlers he booked, partly because of his no-nonsense approach to the business. He believed that bookers and promoters should be strictly behind the scenes and should be focused on getting the job done. Vince Jr. did not feel *exactly* the same way. But both father and son enjoyed the same type of professional wrestling: heavy on character and story and—true to Vince Sr.'s partnership with Mondt—slam bang wrestling. The New York style was focused on bombast, huge bodies, and flash. (André the Giant made the WWWF a favorite haunt for much of his career in the United States prior to the 1980s, and the two parties were a perfect fit.) As such, the WWWF had drawn a much different type of wrestling fan than the wrestling in the Midwest (which was focused on grappling and legitimate athletes like Thesz and Gagne) and especially—*especially*—in the South, where pro wrestling was all about raw emotion, blood and guts, and men fighting tooth and nail to best one another and knock a hated rival's dick in the dirt.

But Vince Jr. believed his father still wasn't going as far as he could with his company or with his cartoonish characters and over-the-top productions. He set his sights and his designs on creating something massive, something that may very well change the world. And something that aspired to be more than pro wrestling as the populace had always known it—for better or for worse.

PART II

HULKAMANIA, STEROIDS, AND THE NEW GENERATION

4

BLACK SATURDAY

Vince Jr. Runs the Territories Out of Town

By the time Vince Sr. passed away on May 24, 1984, his son had established all-out war—a decision he has long acknowledged his father would have disliked. Vince Sr. always remained cordial with rivals and respectful of territories, old-school to the very end—in line with his belief that a promoter should be a backstage presence and no more. Furthermore, he hadn't even wanted his son to enter the business. Vince Jr. recalled in his *Playboy* interview that his father always tried to steer him away from wrestling whenever he could. "He remembered the bad years he'd had,"

Vince said. "He'd say, 'Get a government job, so you can have a pension.'"

The first step in the takeover came in 1980, when Vince Jr. and his wife, Linda, founded Titan Sports, Inc. McMahon recognized the power of nationally syndicated television and set his sights far beyond the Northeast region that Vince Sr. had held sway over for many years.

Knowing that his father had no interest in going national, let alone global, and also knowing that his father owned only 50 percent of the company, Vince Jr. understood he had to assume complete control of the enterprise in order to carry out his vision. This was the beginning of Vince Jr.'s war to dominate the entire world of wrestling, by any means. The first major shot fired in this war would be his hostile takeover of a major competitor, a date later known in wrestling infamy as "Black Saturday."

Vince Jr. orchestrated a sale to Titan Sports of the other owners' shares of the WWF in June 1982. Skaaland's 10 percent and Zacko's 20 percent came easily, and he made a sweetheart deal to Gorilla Monsoon for the remaining 20 percent, one that would employ Monsoon for life and help make it possible for the onetime mindless brute to become the voice of a generation of wrestling fans and one-half of a beloved and indispensable commentary team.*

---

* Monsoon's 20 percent, in addition to the buyout itself, included a ten-year contract as an announcer (and later as an on-screen authority figure), as well as 1.5 times what opening match wrestlers were making on *every* WWF house show for the duration of his contract. Given that this contract was signed just before the absolute height of the 1980s wrestling boom, at a time when the WWF was sometimes running three house shows a night, nearly every night of the year, Monsoon spent a good number of years earn-

With 50 percent of the WWF in Vince Jr.'s hands, Vince Sr. agreed to sell the remaining 50 percent to his son. Senior would remain behind the scenes, helping to smooth along the transition to his son and continuing to act as the company's ambassador to Antonio Inoki and New Japan, given the long-standing relationship there. In 1983, the McMahons and the WWF attended the annual meeting of the National Wrestling Alliance solely in order to announce their promotion would be withdrawing from the agreement. This ended some twelve years of good standing with the NWA and was Vince Jr.'s first shot across the bow of the old guard.

Immediately upon wresting control of the WWF from his father and his father's former partners, Vince set about cultivating a promotion that he felt had the best possible viability not only in being a national television product, but in capturing the eyeballs and imaginations of a *potential* casual wrestling audience, rather than merely catering solely to the wrestling fan base that was already long established. In McMahon's mind, the casual viewer wanted broad comedy, absolutely enormous and freakish physiques, and larger-than-life characters who weren't just tough guys in plain trunks with normal names. Not coincidentally, those happened to be the things that Vince himself was most interested in.

That made for quite a change from the norm. From the inception of pro wrestling until around the advent of the 1970s, the average wrestler's physique was somewhere between peak Charles Atlas and your dad. Georg Hackenschmidt, a

---

ing an average of $3,000 a week just off house shows that he never had to attend, in addition to his announcer's salary. Gorilla Monsoon might just be the smartest man in wrestling history.

strongman and one of the greatest wrestlers who ever lived, ended his in-ring career in 1911 and had an absolutely unbelievable body—especially considering anabolic steroids didn't exist at all back then. He had enormous legs, shoulders, and arms, with a V-taper down to a trim waist, but he was a freak of nature and an exception to what most wrestlers looked like at the time. His biggest rival, Frank Gotch, was absolutely fit and fighting trim, but his physique was always somewhere between 1990s George Clooney (not in the Batsuit) and the third-fittest guy on your office softball team.

Buddy Rogers was considered one of the best body guys in the business in the 1950s and 1960s, but he was never really *big*. Combatants like The Destroyer and The Crusher—while having perfect wrestling names describing how they would ruin someone's body—were barrels of men.

Which brings us to steroids. Steroids didn't really enter the sports conversation until Dr. John Ziegler (a weightlifting enthusiast who was eventually nicknamed Montana Jack, which must be noted simply for how fucking righteous that is) developed the oral muscle-building steroid Dianabol in the mid-1950s. He pumped every member of the 1960 United States Olympic weightlifting team full of DBOL, although they were still unable to take home the gold in Rome that year. From there, word of the drug's effectiveness (and by extension, other anabolic steroids) began to spread, catching on with bodybuilders and weightlifters before trickling out to NFL players and to other sports from there. As a large percentage of pro wrestlers in the 1960s and 1970s came from bodybuilding and weightlifting circles, it's no shock that fake fighters were at the forefront of the steroids game. Montana Jack would later express profound regret for his role in the ubiquity of anabolic steroids for cosmetic purposes, but that swole-as-fuck cat was out of the bag, and it never, ever skipped leg day.

Two of the first men to really display superhuman, steroid-aided physiques were Superstar Billy Graham and "Superfly" Jimmy Snuka. Not coincidentally, both men were heavily involved in the 1960s and 1970s bodybuilding scenes, respectively, before transitioning to wrestling. Billy Graham stood in stark contrast to his greatest rival, Bruno, who was solidly in the "barrel-shaped dad" camp. Even more impressively, since Graham and Snuka had that bodybuilding background, they combined enormous muscles with very little body fat and a ton of definition, and fans found themselves unable to look away. Their looks added to the mystique of both men, and steroids began spreading throughout locker rooms quickly, becoming the rule rather than the exception by the 1980s. Since a majority of wrestlers lacked the bodybuilding background or the dieting discipline of Graham and Snuka, the average wrestler using steroids tended to have huge arms, shoulders, and pecs, but with a noticeable or sizable gut to go along with them. Even Hulk Hogan, prior to the steroids scandal of the 1990s, was mostly an arms guy, and rarely had visible abs until after he slimmed down in WCW. (And often, not even then.)

The NWA and Southern promotions (on average) tended to focus on headliners and main-eventers who were capable of impressing fans with their wrestling prowess more than with their bodies or costumes, but McMahon was fascinated by big, big, big. It's what he loved, and it's what he wanted to stock his company with. A bodybuilder and narcissistic body guy himself, he tended to think the television audience

would be just as agog by these specimens of *beef* as he was—
and he was largely correct.

He began poaching a mixture of main-event and just plain
enormous wrestlers from vulnerable promotions all over the
country, hoping to snag not only guys he was interested in
and who would be eye-popping to people flipping through
channels, but who might upset the apple cart enough that a
territory might flounder due to the loss of a key star. While
wrestlers cycling through territories was a fact of life (and
in fact necessary to keeping promotions fresh and relevant),
both the NWA affiliates and outlaw territories alike knew
what McMahon was attempting, and they didn't like it one
bit. Before the inaugural WrestleMania made its bow in
1985, the WWF had signed away regional top draws Junkyard Dog, Roddy Piper, Ricky Steamboat, and of course Hulk
Hogan, and had brought aboard huge, juiced monsters like
Snuka, John Studd, Dynamite Kid and Davey Boy Smith,
Don Muraco, Paul Orndorff, Hercules Hernandez, and many
more.

After his first pass at raiding territories, McMahon began his relentless pursuit of having weekly WWF television
programs syndicated nationwide. For many in the NWA alliance, this was the unforgivable act in the WWF's monopolization play. There had been a long-standing agreement
dating back to the advent of televised wrestling that no territory would encroach into the local television broadcast jurisdiction of another, and each territory's weekly television was
vital to drawing crowds to house shows, which was by far the
most important revenue stream for any pro wrestling company in those days. But McMahon's stated goal was to be the
biggest—if not the only—wrestling empire in the world, and

that necessarily meant breaking these unwritten traditional rules to achieve his goals. He would broker deals with local stations, many of which already had existing deals with existing wrestling companies, and promise the stations increased ratings and better production values. As he honed the perpetual hype machine of the WWF that he would later perfect, stations were drawn to his bombast. In many situations, McMahon would outright pay to snipe TV slots from rival promotions if they failed to be seduced by his full-throated sales pitch. (This was not a foolproof methodology, as some regional fans refused to tune into WWF programming, which meant some television stations relented and dropped the WWF, returning the time slots to their previous territory owners.)

As the WWF continued to ramp up its national expansion, McMahon also began coming up with ways to freeze rivals out of major cities. By 1986, the WWF had locked a staggering number of big arenas into exclusive deals that prevented any non-Titan entity from running a wrestling show in the building within 30 days before or 30 days after a WWF event. Since the WWF would make sure to book a show in those buildings at least once every 90 days, other promotions were forced to either run in smaller buildings or scramble for other alternatives. (McMahon also liberally employed other tactics for killing towns, just to fuck over the other guy. The WWF in the mid- to late 1980s was notorious for booking last-minute shows the day before or the day of NWA or Jim Crockett Promotions shows in the same town, or running a show that went until the wee hours of the morning in a town that had a rival show the next day, in the interest of burning out the fans and reducing the walk-up gates for the competition. They would run their own shows close together in the same area, or top load a star-studded card. If they absolutely had to, the WWF was willing to kill a town for wrestling events for years, just so the other guy couldn't profit.)

McMahon was one of the few pro wrestling promoters to understand the potential of diversification and alternative revenue streams. Beginning in 1985, the WWF began going full-bore into both the nascent pay-per-view market and the spectacularly lucrative home video market. Starting with the VHS version of the first WrestleMania in 1985, the WWF partnered with Coliseum Video domestically (which was a subsidiary of the primarily porn-focused Evart Enterprises, Inc.), and Silver Vision in the U.K., to begin regularly releasing condensed versions (topping out at two hours and forty minutes for a one-tape release) of the PPVs a few months after they first aired, as well as compilation tapes of big wrestlers, big feuds, title matches, or gimmick matches. The WWF did so well in the home video market that when they finally decided to split from Coliseum in 1997 and bring the home video department in-house, Coliseum quickly folded altogether.

McMahon's syndicated programming relied predominantly on sizzle, which accompanied increasingly weighty steaks. The colorful costumes and outlandish characters, along with the freak-show physiques, had droves of casual fans—and children especially—tuning in. When Hogan came aboard (much more on him in the next chapter), there was an easily identifiable, endlessly charismatic superhuman face of the company that anyone could latch on to. For the new or young fan, or the nonfan, the WWF product was an easily palatable, easily enjoyed junk food product, a simple pleasure you could let wash over you in digestible chunks, with short matches that didn't risk trying the patience of anyone who happened to be tuning in.

Wrestling elsewhere was different. The majority of many territories—in particular Jim Crockett Promotions, Jerry Lawler and the Jarretts in Memphis, the Grahams and Dusty Rhodes in Florida, the Von Erichs and the Funks in Texas, and others both domestically and abroad—were about hard-scrabble grown men who had personal beefs with each other and wanted to fight and hurt them. There was very much a mentality of "red equals green," so many matches up and down the cards every night involved no small amount of blood, and many main events in the territories ended with both men wearing the crimson mask. Wrestling magazines throughout the 1970s and 1980s were emblazoned with garish color photographs of Dusty or Abdullah the Butcher or Ric Flair or the Sheik or Bruiser Brody with their faces covered in thickening, bright red blood.

By contrast, while McMahon certainly allowed his wrestlers to bleed when the situation demanded in the 1980s, he considered the wanton bloodshed to be a bit too barbaric for the casual fan—and he was probably right. But what the WWF considered an audience-limiting freak show, the rasslin' fans considered a vital part of a gritty sport that *should* have a very real and visceral element of danger and horror.

To new fans, the World Wrestling Federation was a romp and a lark. To longtime, hardcore fans—especially those outside the Northeast, who weren't previously exposed to any of McMahon's rosters or booking and were used to the more reality-based, mat-focused athletes and technicians—it was anathema, and McMahon's WWF instantly became the enemy. This promotion was, in the eyes of the traditionalist and Southern rasslin' fans, making an outright mockery of their sport. If they never liked the cartoon characters Vince Sr. presented, they outright loathed the product his son was now churning out. When the WWF began encroaching on TV slots and counterprogramming their beloved weekly shows, it was us vs. them. And the biggest uppercut to the family jewels came on July 14, 1984—a day that became known to wrestling fans forever after as "Black Saturday": the day Vince McMahon took over his first rival company.

The Atlanta-based, Ted Turner–owned TBS (at that time WTBS, a self-stylized SuperStation due to its national cable and satellite broadcast reach) had, by 1984, been the home to Georgia Championship Wrestling for twelve years. The flagship weekly show of GCW was a two-hour program called (beginning in 1982) *World Championship Wrestling*, which aired Saturdays on "Turner Time" beginning at 6:05 p.m., and is still considered by many fans to be one of the pinnacles of weekly pro wrestling television. In 1984, GCW was owned by a cadre of eight men, including wrestlers Jack and Gerald Brisco and Ole Anderson. McMahon was eager to find a second national cable deal to go along with his programs popping up several times a week on the USA Network and on WWOR in New York City. He approached Ted Turner directly about buying GCW's time slot on TBS, but Turner had no interest in selling. McMahon wouldn't let the idea go, however, and found a way to circumvent that stumbling block.

McMahon learned of discord behind the scenes at GCW

when Jack Brisco phoned him to check on Roddy Piper, as Brisco had heard rumors the Hot Rod had suffered a horrific hand injury. The conversation turned to business, and in short order the Briscos helped to gather the other shareholders interested in selling their stakes in GCW. McMahon gleefully bought them out.

McMahon, now armed with a 52 percent controlling interest in GCW, had obtained his TBS time slot via hostile takeover—or at the very least, hostile toward Ole and Turner. The fans, of course, had no idea about these backstage machinations. Then, on July 14, 1984, Freddie Miller, standing in front of the World Championship Wrestling logo and backdrop, opened the show by introducing fans to Vince McMahon and the World Wrestling Federation on behalf of WTBS. Vince stepped into the frame, shook Miller's hand, and took the microphone and center stage. In the most bizarre sight wrestling fans would experience until 2001, the owner of the WWF stood in front of GCW's World Championship Wrestling logo and gave a rundown of the WWF matches the audience would be seeing on this episode, before tossing to an animated graphic and a narrator breathlessly telling people all the places they could catch live World Wrestling Federation shows over the next week. Needless to say, fans tuning in expecting to see the normal World Championship Wrestling roster were horrified, and angry calls and letters began flooding into TBS.

No one had ever seen anything like it before. Wrestling shows had been canceled, companies had gone out of business, but never before had a rival company owner barged onto the airwaves to passive-aggressively boast that the old wrestling show was being replaced by *his* wrestling show, which was *better.* For Southern wrestling fans, this was their darkest day.*

While some accounts claim the ratings for the new show immediately went into the toilet, the WWF format was actually a success for a while, at least as far as raw viewership was concerned. Southern fans were incensed, and Turner himself was irate not only because McMahon had orchestrated an end-around of his wishes, but because the WWF had promised original in-studio matches and shows but continued to run compilations of previously aired matches and house show clips. As fans continued to complain, Turner searched for a way to punch back against McMahon.

Ironically, McMahon's takeover of GCW and the TBS time slot not only didn't help his national expansion all that much, it directly led to several other territories and promotions obtaining national television deals. Turner gave a Sunday afternoon time slot on TBS to Bill Watts's Mid-South Wrestling and organized a separate Saturday morning time slot to Ole Anderson's new venture, the *totally creatively distinct* Championship Wrestling from Georgia. Both shows immediately began outperforming the WWF's TBS show, and McMahon was furious, since he had assumed the WWF would be exclusive to the SuperStation. McMahon saw the

---

* McMahon would return to the Black Saturday well in 1993, when he appeared at the beginning of a broadcast of USWA wrestling in Memphis and unbuttoned his enormous, bespoke, powder-blue WWF blazer to reveal the USWA world title around his waist. In a four-years-early preview of his soon-to-be-famous heel persona, McMahon actively taunted the Memphis fans and mocked Jerry Lawler to kick off an interpromotional feud. It's less well remembered but was no less of a "fuck you" to the USWA faithful than Black Saturday had been to fans of Crockett.

writing on the wall and was also in need of money to help fund national tours and a new deal with NBC, so he asked Jim Barnett to help orchestrate a sale of the time slot. Jim Crockett Promotions bought the 6:05 p.m. slot from McMahon outright for $1 million, although Vince never sold the GCW name and trademarks, folding them in 1986. With the all-valuable time slot in hand, Crockett immediately brought the NWA back to TBS under the old World Championship Wrestling banner.

But this was just a momentary setback. McMahon barreled full speed ahead with his shows on USA Network and NBC, in addition to his myriad regional syndication deals, but his big takeover had only proven that multiple, disparate wrestling programs could succeed on a national level. The WWF was now in prime position to turn wrestling into a pop culture phenomenon. And it would do exactly that thanks to one man: Hulk Hogan.

5
THUNDERLIPS, THE ULTIMATE MALE

On March 29, 1987, tens of thousands of flashbulbs sparkled as Hulk Hogan, his body glistening with sweat, all the muscles in his back either torn or strained, hefted André the Giant over his head and slammed him to the mat. He had done the impossible: in front of 93,173 fans at the Pontiac Silverdome, he became the first man to ever slam the Giant (who was a full foot taller than Hogan and weighed in at nearly 600 pounds), and the event was the culmination of Vince McMahon's master stroke—transporting professional wrestling out of smoky bingo halls and into the mainstream, triggering a global phenomenon known as Hulkamania. Seconds after the body slam, Hogan dropped the big leg and pinned André, ending the fifteen-year undefeated streak of the Eighth Wonder of the World. Tragically,

André the Giant would die a short time after this, his final match, his body already breaking down.

It's a timeless story, and one of the most iconic, lasting, and pop culturally relevant moments in the history of what is professional wrestling. The only problem is that the above paragraph is the official company line about what transpired at WrestleMania III, with a little bit of Hulk Hogan's personal hyperbole thrown in for good measure. (Sometimes, the way the Hulkster tells it, André died almost immediately after the match—whether he's insinuating that André's death is the result of his Herculean body slam is something he generally sort of lets just hang there in the ether.)

The truth is, a lot of the aspects of the story have been fudged, in good old-fashioned carny style, the way WWE wants you to hear them. There weren't really 93,173 fans in the Silverdome that night (although there were plenty); it was far from the first time André had been slammed; André's record, although stellar, had involved multiple losses in the fifteen years prior; Hogan's back was just fine; André wasn't more than a few inches taller than Hogan; "smoky bingo halls" prior to WrestleMania III included such venues as the Omni in Atlanta, Madison Square Garden in New York City, the Cow Palace in San Francisco, the Grand Olympic Auditorium in Los Angeles, Shea Stadium, and multiple 10,000-seat arenas all over the world. The height of Hulkamania was far from the first time pro wrestling became a national pop cultural phenomenon, but it was the catalyst that eventually allowed Vince McMahon to consolidate power, drive all of the other territories in North America out of business, and ultimately gain a virtual monopoly on professional wrestling in the English-speaking world—and, for that matter, most non–English speaking countries as well.

Looking back at the early days of Hulkamania sometimes seems like viewing footage beamed in from another planet. Especially when viewed through the lens of what we now know about the Hulkster—such as the racist tirades on his leaked sex tape that eventually bankrupted the Gawker Media empire—it might be befuddling to parse what made him a worldwide phenomenon. But even when Hogan was at his most fever-pitch nigh-incoherent in the mid-1980s—eyes popped, nostrils flared, his oiled and swollen arms and torso threatening to explode all over backstage interviewer "Mean" Gene Okerlund as he ranted about Trump Plaza crumbling to the ground and pulling Donald Trump from the wreckage and dog-paddling him to safety in the waters of the Atlantic Ocean—it was impossible to keep your eyes off him. He had an undeniable charisma that few others in wrestling before or since have matched. Combine that with his then-superhero-like physique and his gimmick—that he couldn't be hurt when feeding off the power of his fans, like a coke-fueled, roided-up Tinkerbell—and it was absolute lightning in a bottle for the pro wrestling business. Vince McMahon's stroke of genius was recognizing this comic book character come to life when other rival promoters were unable to, and the P. T. Barnum of wrestling finally had his prize pachyderm. Only in Vince's case, this jacked-to-the-gills elephant would do a rail of coke, jump through a ring of fire, pulverize the fuck out of a 400-pound man, and then show his muscles to every last screaming fan in the building for fifteen minutes to send them home happy as his theme song gave everyone a rock-hard boner for America.

McMahon understood that squeaky-clean Bob Backlund wasn't the man who would take his company nationwide. He didn't need a Glenn Miller number the whole family could enjoy; he needed a combination of Alice Cooper, KISS, and Bruce Springsteen. In short, he needed a garish, screaming American flag that loved to fuck.

Hogan's character was the perfect crossover star for the MTV generation, and was such a real-life cartoon character (and later, a literal cartoon character) that channel surfers were all but guaranteed to stop and watch when he was on the screen. The effect on children was even more pronounced, as Hogan was larger than life in every respect, and, on the surface, at least, the perfect role model and patriot for the 1980s youngster. The Hulk way of life was a simple one: you just need to live by his three "demandments" (a thunderously aggressive positive affirmation, in hindsight): train, say your prayers, and eat your vitamins, and you can be as jacked and as virtuous as the main man himself, DUDE. (Hogan would add an *all-new* fourth demandment in 1990, which was "believe in yourself," but most Hulkamaniacs had already inferred that.)

Hulk Hogan, born Terry Bollea in Georgia in 1953, was actually a product of both Vince Sr. and Vince Jr. Hogan became a wrestling fan at age sixteen, but by the time he was in college, he was more focused on playing bass in Tampa Bay–area bands. If you've ever seen footage of Hogan playing the bass, you know that the visual is absolutely hilarious. Hogan stood over 6 feet 5, and by the time he dropped out of college to focus on his band, Ruckus, he had begun swelling out his physique, making even a fretless bass look puny in his hands. It's no surprise that when Jack and Gerald Brisco saw Hogan play a gig in 1976, they knew they had to try to get this guy into the biz. Fast-forwarding past his training, which may or may not contain some serious fibs as Hogan tells it,* Bollea wrestled in Florida for a bit before moving on to Alabama, where under the name Terry Boulder he formed a tag team with his best friend, Ed Leslie. Jerry Jarrett, impressed by the Boulder Brothers, offered them (according to Hogan and Hogan alone) a 100 percent pay raise (all the way up to $800 each per week) to come wrestle in his Memphis-based territory.

As befitting his cocky heel persona at the time, Terry Boulder added "Hulk" as a sobriquet. (After departing Memphis for Georgia, he also wrestled as "Sterling Golden," which is the best pro wrestler name he ever had—except for Thunderlips, probably.)

In 1979, Bollea was brought to the attention of Vince Sr., who quickly decided to bring Hulk to New York. As Hogan tells it, Vince Sr. was the person who insisted he take the new surname of Hogan to further his fixation on having ethnic heroes and villains. While the Hulkster balked at Vince's supposed request to dye his hair red, he acquiesced to being officially rechristened Hulk Hogan. As a cocky heel with a thick mat of black chest and stomach hair contrasting with his bleach-blond locks, Hogan began terrorizing the WWF roster alongside manager and mouthpiece "Classy" Freddie Blassie.

Although WWE would officially deny it for many years—in order to better sell and then to build the legacy of their "first

---

* One of Hogan's favorite stories is that his trainer, Hiro Matsuda, broke Hogan's leg on the first day of his training. Upon healing, Hogan returned to continue his training, thus proving to Matsuda that he was serious about the craft. This is probably not true.

meeting ever" at WrestleMania III, Hogan's first run in the WWF included a lengthy feud all across the country with André the Giant that did big business. André, in this iteration of their feud, was the conquering hero, while Hulk was the dastardly and underhanded villain. Their first series of matches would come to a head with a blow-off match at the third Showdown at Shea on August 9, 1980, where André would defeat Hogan in under eight minutes in front of over 36,000 fans at Shea Stadium in Flushing, New York. The match was the tenth on a thirteen-match supercard headlined by a cage match between Bruno Sammartino and his protégé-gone-bad Larry Zbyszko.

Hogan likely would have stuck around in the WWF past 1981, but he caught the eye of Sylvester Stallone, who was gearing up to make *Rocky III* and needed a wrestler for a sequence in the film inspired by—in an absolute bundle of ironies and coincidences—an absolute fiasco of a match from the *second* Showdown at Shea, where André the Giant faced boxer Chuck Wepner in a mixed-discipline match. Wepner, who was the journeyman-turned–title contender who inspired the Rocky Balboa character in the first place, wasn't fully smartened up to the inner workings of worked matches and popped André a little bit too hard over the course of the freak-show match. Eventually, André got fed up and simply picked up Wepner and unceremoniously dumped him over the top rope to the outside. With the exception of Gorilla Monsoon and other WWF officials blocking Wepner's corner from tossing him back in the ring to avoid a count-out, the scene in *Rocky III* played out nearly the same way, with Rocky being tossed into the crowd by an irritated goliath.

Coincidentally, Hogan took his leave from WWF at around

the same time. According to Hogan, his departure was due to his foresight of becoming a massive worldwide star, but McMahon was too stodgy to understand the value of cross-over appeal. In the Hogan legend, the Hulkster knew what a big deal the Rocky franchise was by that point, and eyeing a star-making role in a surefire blockbuster, he told Vince Sr. of his plans to accept the role. McMahon's belief (again, according to Hogan) was that his wrestlers shouldn't be movie stars—they should be wrestlers. McMahon disagreed with Hogan's decision, and so Hogan left the WWF.

Hogan shot his part in the film as Thunderlips and settled into his permanent partnership with New Japan Pro-Wrestling, where he had begun working shows over six months prior to leaving the WWF. He would continue working for New Japan off and on until the year 2003. Discovering Hogan's work in Japan tends to be a rite of passage for all fans who get deep into wrestling. Finding lengthy, competitive matches with Hogan holding his own against work-rate legends like the Great Muta and Masa Chono without relying on his signature showmanship tricks and minimal effort tends to be mind-blowing for wrestling fans who have only known his cookie-cutter superhero work in the States. He was an instant sensation in Japan, this enormous, tanned specimen who radiated personality and was unlike anyone the Japanese crowd—or any wrestling audience, for that matter—had ever seen.

Hogan headed to Verne Gagne's Minnesota-based AWA in 1981, and although he entered the company as a heel, he landed like a warhead and overnight, the AWA was regularly drawing crowds of 16,000 in the Twin Cities.

AWA, a powerhouse at that time, had been the first major

NWA defection back in 1960. Verne Gagne, an unparalleled draw near his hometown base of Minnesota, had lobbied hard to be given the NWA vote of approval to take the world title from Thesz. The NWA governors were uninterested, so Gagne took his ball and literally went home, withdrawing from the Alliance and forming his own promotion, based out of Minnesota: the American Wrestling Association.

The Hogan fever that began in Japan really caught fire in the AWA, and the seeds of Hulkamania began to blossom long before Hogan returned to the WWF. It was in the AWA that Hogan first began entering the ring to the strains of the *Rocky III* theme song, "Eye of the Tiger," which he would carry over to the WWF. By 1982, around the same time that large banners reading HULKAMANIA began appearing regularly in AWA buildings, Hogan had honed the promo style he would later perfect, which was cultivated by borrowing liberally from his teenage wrestling heroes, Superstar Billy Graham and Dusty Rhodes. Also key to Hogan's time developing his character in the AWA was his pairing with backstage interviewer "Mean" Gene Okerlund. Hogan's promos began kicking off with the words "Well you know something, Mean Gene," which became one of his earliest and most enduring catchphrases.

Also by 1982, Hogan had developed a key part of his gimmick, also borrowed liberally from the Incredible Hulk's core tenet of "the madder Hulk gets, the stronger he gets." Later tweaked to be fueled by the power of Hulkamaniacs rather than sheer rage, a signature Hulk Hogan match would involve him being pushed to a limit, then tapping into an inner reserve that would make him Hulk up and briefly be impervious to any pain, in addition to receiving a significant boost in power. As this reserve tended to be tapped into very late in a given match, Hogan was usually able to pick up the win shortly thereafter, hitting his finisher (which was the bear hug for a time, before everyone came to their senses and realized that his setup move, a running leg drop, was far more visceral a climax and more visually compelling than slowly squeezing a beefman until he nodded at the referee), then celebrating by treating the crowd to a gander at his "24-inch pythons." (Which, if you happen to have been made aware of Hulk Hogan in the post-Gawker era, actually referred to his arms.*) The gimmick was the absolute perfect thing for the new or casual wrestling fan, and since Hogan's matches were usually short, they were perfectly suited to television, which the industry was increasingly reliant upon.

(Hogan eventually became loathed even by his own fans for a strict adherence to his match formula, which always ended so predictably that audiences were able to *chant along* with his *moves*. But it might surprise fans to go back and look at how long it took for him to really settle into coasting on this formula. Many early pay-per-views are devoid of a comeback, and it wasn't until the late 1980s and early 1990s that the infamous cookie-cutter Hulk Hogan match became the norm.)

AWA head Gagne, a former member of the U.S. Olympic

---

* There probably isn't going to be a more appropriate place to include this particular footnote, so let us thank and/or curse the memory of Gawker for leading to this tidbit: while on the stand for his defamation trial, Hogan was for some reason forced to clarify that while the real-life person *portraying* Hulk Hogan, Terry Bollea, does *not* have a 10-inch penis, the *character* of Hulk Hogan *does*. Hulk Hogan has a 10-inch penis. It's canon. Or a cannon. Whichever you prefer. (Please say "neither.")

wrestling team and a dyed-in-the-wool old-school shooter, considered Hogan to be a soft bodybuilder who was all flash. But he sure loved the money that Hogan was bringing in. While Gagne and Hogan didn't get along—on at least one occasion, the two got into a backstage scuffle, where Hogan ended up on top of the much older Gagne—the promoter realized Hogan was bringing in a boom period that he'd never seen before and, once Hulk departed, would never see again.

Unfortunately for Gagne, when Vince Jr. bought out the WWF from his father in 1982 and immediately set his sights on national expansion, the AWA's top draw was the WWF's top target. McMahon knew his plan was to court the new and casual fan with pomp (and, depending on how things went, circumstance), and he knew he needed a big damn star to be the face of the brand. When McMahon came calling, Hogan was eager to take big checks to become a big damn star. Over the years, it's become something of a myth that Gagne's shortsightedness and inability to change or work with Hogan led to McMahon "stealing" him. But the truth was, everyone involved saw the writing on the wall, and with Hogan already drawing white-hot crowds in the more traditionalist AWA, there was no reason for him to not transfer to McMahon's more ambitious WWF.

After the Iron Sheik captured the WWF Championship from Backlund, many expected Backlund would get a series of rematches. Instead, Hogan steamrolled the Sheik at Madison Square Garden less than a month after making his return to the WWF. The roof blew off the building as Hogan brought the title "home" from the evil Iranian, and while Hulkamania unofficially began in Japan in 1980, and continued in the

AWA for two years, the sensation officially kicked off on January 23, 1984, with Hogan's very first WWF world championship. Hogan and the WWF were off and running.

Hogan's star was ascending and about to go supernova, and thanks to his role in *Rocky III*, which was a pop culture touchstone and smash hit, pretty much everyone knew who he was. However, it ended up being a parallel stroke of synergistic genius that put the WWF and the pro wrestling boom over the top: the WWF's partnership with Cyndi Lauper.

It started when "Captain" Lou Albano, who had become one of the best talkers and personalities in the business by 1983, got to know Lauper on a flight to Puerto Rico. Albano was a onetime wrestler converted to a manager thanks to his gift of gab and unique look. She instantly became a fan and asked him to portray her father in the video for "Girls Just Want to Have Fun." Lauper, a pop sensation on par with Hulkamania (relative to their respective mediums) at that time, bonded with Albano and became fascinated with the wrestling business. Albano, who shared Vince Jr.'s ability to know a good thing when he saw it, wasted no time in bringing her into the fold, and she soon appeared on WWF television, getting into a war of words with Albano on an installment of "Rowdy" Roddy Piper's *Piper's Pit* segment.* Lauper came to blows with Albano, and a challenge was laid out in which she and Albano would each corner a woman

---

* Wrestlers hosting fake talk shows is nothing new. *Piper's Pit, The Body Shop, The Snake Pit, The Flower Shop, The Barber Shop, The Brother Love Show, The Funeral Parlor*—the WWF has had a long fascination with giving a wrestler a microphone and a backdrop and having them interview other wrestlers in the hope that it will lead to someone getting hit with food and sparking a blood rivalry.

wrestler in some sort of brawl. Perhaps a brawl that would strive to achieve, say, an end to the entire kerfuffle. As luck would have it, MTV agreed to broadcast a live special on July 23, 1984, which just so happened to be called *The Brawl to End It All*. This special ended up comprising a good number of famous firsts, including the first live wrestling match on cable TV, and the first live women's wrestling match to be broadcast on television of any sort. Albano chose the Fabulous Moolah as his proxy, who was in the midst of a purported twenty-eight-year reign as the WWF Women's Champion (which, as with all claims of this sort in wrestling, wasn't true, although she had been holding the title for over five years at that point, and had held it for ten straight years from 1956 to 1966), while Lauper selected Wendi Richter as her champion. Richter was seen as the perfect woman wrestler for the 1980s: young, athletic, beautiful, stylish, and with a lion's mane of Aqua Netted hair. She was positioned as the female equivalent of Hogan for a brief, shining moment, although her run with the WWF would shortly come to an ignominious end. (We'll catch up with Richter's last days in the company in the next chapter.)

Lauper got involved in the finish of the match, bashing Moolah with her loaded purse and allowing Richter to get the win and the title.

Lauper became thoroughly entrenched with pro wrestling, bringing in many wrestlers (including both Richter and Moolah) to take roles and cameos in her videos over the next year. A second MTV live special, *The War to Settle the Score*, followed in February 1985 and, like *The Brawl to End It All*, was a spectacular success. Hulkamania was a sensation, but the Rock 'N' Wrestling Connection formed by Lauper's involvement with the sport and the synergy with MTV was a vital part of the cocktail that led to the largest pro wrestling boom the world had ever seen at that point in time. Depending on what metrics you're using, it may have been the absolute height of pro wrestling's popularity, full stop.

In the year between the two MTV specials, Hogan was doing the heavy lifting as the face of the company* and the reigning world champion. He battled a string of fearsome foes from 1984 to 1985, and as Hogan's star rose, Roddy Piper came into his own as the biggest and hottest heel in the company. Piper allied himself with "Mr. Wonderful" Paul Orndorff (whose name Hulk Hogan has never once pronounced correctly, despite doing sellout business with the man all over the world for a couple of years) and their enforcer, "Cowboy" Bob Orton, who was also a medical oddity, possessed of a broken arm that refused to heal for years on end.

With live events selling out all over the country and the MTV specials doing gangbusters ratings, NBC became the first television network desperate to do business with the company. As McMahon continued to build toward national expansion, he began planning a closed-circuit spectacular from Madison Square Garden to follow on the heels of *The War to Settle the*

---

* Hogan's fame became so great in 1984 that Marvel Comics finally realized that the biggest pro wrestler in the world was running around using the name of one of their trademarked characters. The WWF's parent company, Titan Sports, reached a licensing agreement with Marvel that paid the comics publisher quite handsomely over the course of the next twenty years, so long as Hogan was never billed solely as "Hulk," was never advertised as being "Incredible" (something promoters in Memphis and in AWA were never afraid to lean into), and never appeared in a costume that was purple and green. Stop for a moment and consider a Hulk Hogan who wears purple and green, and you'll see why this was an easy agreement to sign.

Score. Envisioned as a Super Bowl of pro wrestling, and given a name by ring announcer Howard Finkel, McMahon took a big gamble and broke the bank to bring in celebrities and loads of press for the first-ever WrestleMania on March 31, 1985. The legend goes that Vince wagered absolutely everything on the success of WrestleMania, and the WWF was in danger of going under if it was a flop, but once again, that isn't entirely true.

After all, before WrestleMania bowed, McMahon was able to close a lucrative deal with NBC to create *Saturday Night's Main Event*, an infrequently aired regular series that would air when *Saturday Night Live* had its scheduled breaks throughout the season. McMahon closed several other deals around this time, and the gates were so phenomenal at WWF live events that the company could have easily coasted for some time, even if WrestleMania was such a catastrophic failure that it ruined future closed-circuit deals *and* killed off New York as a viable market forever.

While other companies had run wrestling supercards and stadium shows many times over the years, no one had gone quite as all in on the glitz and glamour, with the express purpose of attracting as large a casual crowd as possible.

Hogan was also key to the WWF's international ventures. The World Wrestling Federation made its first televised foray into the United Kingdom in January 1984, when it was one of the few exclusive, first-run programs on the slate for Rupert Murdoch's newly launched Sky Channel. That channel, at launch, was only available in a few areas in England, but was only the *fifth* available television channel in the country at the time, excluding the very few houses that owned the enormous satellite dishes of the early 1980s. Airing in prime time, this was the first glimpse most Britons had of American wrestling. Until then, the art form for television viewers had been limited to the British wrestling featured on Saturday morning's *World of Sport* program on ITV. The British style placed an emphasis on holds, reversals, and pinning combinations, and used a rounds system. This strain of wrestling was not without its numerous charms and featured world-class talents like Jim Breaks and Rollerball Rocco, whose innovations would not be fully appreciated until decades later. But the biggest stars in England for decades were chief villain Giant Haystacks (whose image you can probably conjure just from his name) and the supremely anachronistic Big Daddy. These two just couldn't compare to the top of the WWF slate.

Big Daddy was well into his midfifties at the time the WWF came to England and still positioned as the biggest star in the country and at the top of every card (opposite his eternal rival, Giant Haystacks). A 350-pound man with no physique to speak of, clad in a discomfortingly ill-fitting leotard and wearing a sparkly gold top hat to the ring, Big Daddy was beloved among the British wrestling audience—but they had never gotten an eyeful of Hulk Hogan or his accompanying WWF menagerie.

The Sky Channel viewers were stunned by the American version of what they knew as pro wrestling. The WWF brought them fast-paced matches, finishing moves, story lines, interviews, promos, backstage segments, vignettes, blood feuds, and matches that resolved the narrative—all of these were new concepts. Compared to the parade of lackadaisical in-ring rounds-system chess matches on *World of Sport*, the WWF was basically breakneck-speed action and mayhem, with enticing drama and tawdry intrigue thrown in. And Hogan was the glowing golden god at the center to capture the eye. He similarly anchored ventures into television elsewhere in Europe. Italian television, French television—it didn't matter; the language of Hulkamania was universal.

By this time, not even two years into Vince Jr.'s takeover of the company, the hardcore and longtime fan of pro wrestling already hated McMahon's guts, and everything that they perceived he was doing to wrestling. They hated the pomp, they loathed the flash, and they spat on what they viewed as an untalented joke of a roster, especially compared to the territories and NWA, which were carried on the backs of Ric Flair, Harley Race, the Funks, and other "legitimate" mat heroes. Not surprisingly, the Southern rasslin' fans and the die-hard, longtime pro wrestling fanatics absolutely loathed the majority of the WrestleMania card, but many of those onlookers begrudgingly acknowledged the event was entertaining and looked good, at the very least. And no one could question the impressiveness of Vince McMahon's hype machine, which made WrestleMania national news and an honest-to-goodness event of note.

Another important aspect of the McMahon-Hogan partnership is the perfect storm of the two men's ability to inflate any claim to hype themselves and the product they were presenting. Hucksterism is a key component of the promotion business, no matter what you're promoting, and kayfabing things to hype up yourself, your opponent, and the card is one of the very building blocks of professional wrestling, but Vince and Hogan displayed a willingness to bend and stretch the truth—any truth—in the name of getting even one more set of eyeballs on themselves. It was a level of exaggeration and bombast that even wrestling fans had never seen before, and it drove the traditionalists absolutely up the wall.

Muhammad Ali, Billy Martin, Liberace, and a coterie of Rockettes were among the celebrities who took part in the festivities, but the central celebrity was Mr. T, right in the thick of his own pop cultural moment as the household-name star of *The A-Team*. A friend of Hogan's, T was pressed into the fold to team with the Hulkster in the main event, facing off against Piper and Orndorff. It didn't hurt that Mr. T and Piper had legit and sustained issues with one another. The main event of WrestleMania also solidified Hogan as *the* reason for the average (casual) fan to watch the WWF and also cemented his iconic in-ring look: yellow and red. Hogan would wear those colors at WrestleMania for the next eight years in a row, with few exceptions, in the main event.

WrestleMania was here, Hulkamania was here, and business looked like it was only about to pick up.

6

HULKAMANIA
RUNS WILD

McMahon continued to raid talent from territories and amp up the cartoon antics of already-outrageous acts. He also continued his tactics of attempting to muscle various promotions out of their existing television time slots. Amazingly, Jim Crockett would officially file a lawsuit against the WWF in December 1985, seeking $1 million from McMahon for violating antitrust acts. The case never went anywhere, and the irony of the largest member of the NWA—an organization referred to at various times as "The Trust" and formed *literally to unite all of professional wrestling under one governing body*—suing for antitrust violations must not have been lost on anyone.

Hulk Hogan and Hulkamania ended up being either a central or integral aspect of WrestleMania for the first *nine* years of its existence. However, in contrast to the lengthy reigns on top by stars of the past—from Hackenschmidt to Thesz to Sammartino and even Backlund—Hogan had the misfortune of straddling the shift from cable television to the twenty-four-hour news cycle and beyond, remaining on top (although not with the WWF, at first) well into the age of the internet. While Hulkamania was custom-made for cable television and the louder-bigger-faster MTV Generation, constant national exposure made his act wear thin sooner than it would have in decades and generations past. Luckily for Hogan, McMahon shared a zeal to be the biggest—the best—the *only*. They wanted to crush everyone else and make the WWF synonymous with anything involving wrestling. Hogan was firmly in McMahon's pocket, as his positioning and the WWF hype machine were making him far and away the richest pro wrestler of the modern era. Meanwhile, McMahon wasn't about to give up his golden goose for anything—until and unless something better came along. He put all his eggs in the Hogan basket, but never stopped looking for other, better baskets to move those eggs into.

Hogan did tremendous business as the WWF house shows crisscrossed the country. McMahon leaned even more heavily into branding, licensing, and merchandising. T-shirts, magazines, buttons, and other souvenirs had been part of the wrestling business for a good long while, but McMahon was one of the first to really recognize that he wasn't just selling people on getting out to the live events, but also selling the *products* of his product. One of the most ingenious and somewhat cruel tactics that was a favorite of the WWF was to show children at ringside on all the syndicated shows, decked out in WWF gear, playing with an LJN WWF figure or eating a WWF ice-cream bar or holding some other foam or plastic souvenir or branded gewgaw. More often than not, the child had just been handed those toys or trinkets, then was filmed happily playing with them. After the shot was obtained, a producer or assistant would collect the tchotchkes, and then on to the next fan. They probably didn't take the half-eaten ice-cream bars back, although I can't verify that.

Interestingly, even at the earliest onset of rampant Hulkamania, the WWF was still hedging their bets slightly when it came to shoving every last egg into the engorged Hulk Hogan basket. Bruno Sammartino had retired in 1981, but came back off and on during the early years of Hulkamania to give the Northeast ticket sales a good goose whenever they felt it was necessary.

Sammartino was infuriated by the rampant steroid and drug abuse backstage, and finally ditched the company before retiring for good in 1987. He spent the next few years loudly proclaiming his distaste for the current product and eventually spent a quarter century on the outs with the McMahons and their company. But while Sammartino's day was now officially past, business continued to merrily roll along for the Hogan-led Federation.

While the first WrestleMania reached the largest portion of its audience via screenings at closed-circuit television theaters and locations around the country, Vince McMahon and the WWF dipped their toe into a fledgling enterprise on November 7, 1985, when they aired a special one-night singles tournament dubbed The Wrestling Classic on pay-per-view.

The sixteen-man tournament (plus a Hogan vs. Piper world title match) was the bulk of a whopping fifteen-match card, eventually won by the Junkyard Dog (who defeated Randy Savage by countout in the finals). The event was derided by wrestling purists, naturally, and (thankfully for those who had to sit through a fifteen-match show) there wasn't a bout that lasted longer than nine minutes—with three of the tournament matches finishing in under one minute, and two of those lasting less than twenty seconds. The Wrestling Classic never returned, but it was a valuable entrée for the company working out the kinks of PPV prior to WrestleMania 2 (which also aired on closed circuit television).

By the end of the 1980s, PPV would become an invaluable and indispensable part of the professional wrestling business, not just for the WWF but for any company that aimed to be a major player in the national wrestling scene. To this day, PPV remains an important signifier for alternative wrestling companies, as independent promotions build to large events on iPPV and traditional PPV and consider being carried by major PPV providers to be a major feather in their cap.

Perhaps inevitably, WWF ratings and attendance began to sag a bit in 1986. George Scott was the man booking WWF events at the time, as McMahon was more focused on announcing and perpetuating the company's hype machine. It took much longer than you might expect for the WWF to realize that they shouldn't run several Hogan-topped shows in markets very close together, as he would hit large markets like San Francisco every single month and gates would drop precipitously on each subsequent run through town. Eventually, the WWF figured out that Hogan should (rightfully) be used as a special attraction to goose attendance whenever necessary and avoid the risk of killing a town. By June 1986, Hogan was only averaging three matches a month, in startling contrast to many talents working seven days a week, and as many as nine matches a week when the company would do "double shots" in close-together cities on Saturdays and Sundays. By the end of the 1980s, the WWF would have two concurrent rosters of house shows on loops in different areas of the country, with the "A" crew featuring a top draw like Hogan, while the "B" crew featured someone of nearly equal popularity on top, like Randy Savage. By June 1986, George Scott was relieved of his duties as WWF booker, and McMahon took full control of programming his cards, with Hogan in a right-hand-man position, at least as far as the events that he was headlining.

Business would hit a further lull in 1986 with Wrestle-Mania 2. There wasn't a truly compelling main event, as a cage match between Hogan and the massive King Kong Bundy for the world title wasn't quite the crossover appeal that Hogan and T vs. Piper and Orndorff had been. But the largest problem was McMahon choosing to lean a bit too hard into being gimmicky. Yes, even for pro wrestling. His big idea was to hold WrestleMania 2 at three separate locations, each with its own "main event," celebrities, and announce team, but presented as a whole event to the audience watching at home (or via closed circuit). With three different production crews, the product felt disjointed, and live audiences were understandably not coming out in droves to watch one third of a wrestling spectacular. PPV numbers were much lower than the WWF had hoped, and the total attendance across the three venues ended up being just a hair over 40,000. Critics feared the wrestling bubble had already popped, but Hogan was about to be the focal point of the two biggest money-making angles of all time, back to back.

For those angles to really come together, Hogan would need to cement himself into Vince's good graces. In the weeks immediately prior to WrestleMania 2, Hogan proved his loyalty to McMahon and his devotion to his own check-book above all else. Announcer and former wrestler Jesse "The Body" Ventura knew that all eyes would be on the company heading into the second WrestleMania and gave an impassioned speech to the WWF locker room (with-out McMahon present) about the need for a union for the boys. He suggested the roster threaten to sit out the event unless they were able to negotiate a wrestlers' union. The next evening, Ventura claims he received a phone call from a livid McMahon, who threatened to fire Ventura if he ever breathed another word about unionization. Ventura left to film *Predator* shortly thereafter, and proudly joined the Screen Actors Guild, receiving union benefits that precious few other workers have managed to obtain before or since.* But Ventura was determined to find out who ratted him out to Vince, and years later, during a deposition of McMahon when Ventura sued the WWF for unpaid royalties due to his commentary appearing on home video releases (a case Ventura ultimately won, and received healthy compensation for), Ventura says he instructed his lawyers to ask McMa-hon about who informed on him, and without a moment's

* In one of the ultimate examples of McMahon's vision of sports enter-tainment allowing him to have his cake and eat it, too, WWE Superstars are unable to join SAG or AFTRA based on their weekly WWE television appearances alone. SAG-AFTRA considers pro wrestlers to be athletes, not actors, and to date no one has challenged this classification en masse. Over the years, many wrestlers have taken film and television acting roles in part to gain SAG benefits, but the bulk of the roster remains unable to join the actors' union, despite, you know, acting on television for several hours a week, fifty-two weeks a year.

hesitation, McMahon said, "Hulk Hogan told me." At the time, Hogan was literally making more money than the rest of the WWF roster put together, so it's no surprise he had zero interest in anything that could potentially level the playing field. Or paying field, in this case.

McMahon had a dream match he was building toward in Hogan vs. André but ended up stumbling into one more white-hot program in the summer of 1986. Hogan's brief friendship and alliance with his WrestleMania foe "Mr. Wonderful" Paul Orndorff ended in Orndorff's sudden but inevitable betrayal. Fans wanted Hogan to rip the head off Orndorff, and the sellout rivalry (including a 74,000-fan "Big Event" in Toronto) carried the WWF throughout the year. Hogan and Orndorff turned the company's buzz around and positioned them incredibly well for the next major supercard.

Which brings us to Hogan vs. André at WrestleMania III. Perhaps the most written-about pro wrestling match of all time, it's an indelible part of wrestling history, as well as a watershed moment for WWE. One of the most interesting things about the Hogan vs. André match is that the true facts of the event are a completely awe-inspiring accomplishment for Hogan, McMahon, and the company. There's no reason for anyone involved to lie about so many of the details, but lie they do, to inflate the numbers and increase the legend. It's just that deep-down carny wrestling nonsense in the blood, and god bless them for having a story and sticking to it. (Or in the case of Hogan, having a story and inflating and changing it constantly.)

The event was set in motion with a spectacularly well-executed heel turn for André, who had been billed as a smiling and conquering easygoing babyface for the previous fifteen or so years. André's mobility was rapidly declining due to his acromegaly and a recent back surgery, but he still agreed to return to action and work WrestleMania III as a favor to McMahon.

The feud began when, on WWF television, Hogan was awarded a huge trophy for holding the WWF Heavyweight Championship for three years and was congratulated by his good friend André. The next week, André was presented a much smaller trophy for being undefeated for a spectacular fifteen years. (Of course, he was far from undefeated over that stretch, but the kayfabed record was an important part of the story leading into the match.) Hogan came out to congratulate André and just took over the interview,* not letting the Giant get a word in, leading to André leaving in disgust. A couple of weeks later, André arrived with new manager Bobby Heenan to request—and then demand—a title shot against Hogan. If he was such a good friend, why wouldn't Hogan let him challenge for his world title? Hogan began to hedge and plead with André not to let Heenan corrupt him, until André finally grabbed Hulk, tearing his shirt and breaking the chain holding Hogan's crucifix. André and Heenan stormed off as Hogan wept for his former friend, before accepting André's challenge by bugging his eyes out and caterwauling "*Yaaaaaahhhhhhhh*" at the top of his lungs.

On March 29, 1987, the WWF held WrestleMania III at the

---

* In retrospect, much of Hogan's babyface work comes across as staunchly dishonest, condescending, and self-serving. As people got increasingly tired of his shtick in the 1990s, it became a lot less subtext and a lot more text. His off-the-charts charisma covered for a lot in the eighties, but viewed through contemporary eyes, a lot of what "good guy" Hogan did looks like the spiraling ranting of an unhinged sociopath.

Pontiac Silverdome in Michigan. The crowd inside the dome was so gargantuan, and so apeshit throughout the twelve-match card, that it remains a sight you have to see to believe. The WWF, chasing the indoor attendance record, claimed the now-iconic number of 93,173, although various reports of the actual crowd in attendance place it somewhere closer to the 78,000 range, which is still phenomenal. The worked attendance number, however, was accepted by nearly everyone in the media, because the public was only beginning to recognize the publicity machinations of Vincent Kennedy McMahon.

When the main event rolled around, André was clad in his new ring gear, which is now his most iconic look: the one-strap black singlet. The new look served a purpose beyond putting the heel in all black: it helped to obscure a back brace that was alleviating some of the pain the Giant felt following his surgery, which he was probably coming back from sooner than he would have liked. André the Giant rode to the ring in a cart that was a miniaturized version of a WWF ring. Nearly all the wrestlers on the card rode to the ring in one of the carts, and it was an amazing little touch that fans still look back on fondly as an iconic moment of this singularly huge show. In actuality, the carts were mostly added for André, so he wouldn't have to make the extremely long walk from the backstage area to the ring and back.

Backstage, leading up to the show, André and McMahon both ribbed Hogan, suggesting that neither of them was quite sure whether André would allow himself to be pinned, as was the plan. André loved to fuck with wrestlers, and this served as one of the last times in his active career that Hogan was forced to be humble, as he knew that on the off chance

André decided to go into business for himself, there wasn't a whole lot that he or McMahon could do about it. In Hogan's most recent telling of the story on record (in the 2018 HBO documentary *André the Giant*), he claims that he wrote out his vision of how the match would go by hand on loose-leaf paper and had McMahon deliver the pages to André in the weeks before WrestleMania. McMahon would hem and haw during Hogan's repeated attempts to ask whether André was on board, but when they got in the ring that night, André began calling the match, and it was nearly note-for-note the match that Hogan had envisioned.

Two of the key aspects of the story of the match—that André was coming into the match with a fifteen-year winning streak, and that he had never been slammed—were both bald-faced lies that weren't easily disproven in that pre-internet era, but longtime fans probably knew of plenty of times André had taken a loss or had been slammed. The losses were certainly infrequent, and usually of the countout or disqualification or fuck finish nature, but they did happen. In fact, less than a year before WrestleMania III, Antonio Inoki became the only person on record to defeat André via submission, in the 1986 IWGP Tournament in Japan. Luckily for the WWF, few fans had access to or knowledge of the Japanese wrestling scene at that time.

As for being slammed, it was a bit of a rite of passage for longtime André opponents. If he allowed himself to be slammed in a match (often decided by André calling it in the ring), it was seen as a sign of respect. Sometimes, André just let himself be slammed for the hell of it. Any fans who had seen Showdown at Shea II or caught a house show in New York, Hamburg, or Philadelphia certainly saw with their own eyes Hogan slam André.

Nevertheless, the crowd went wild for the match, which was built entirely around André's lack of mobility. The match lasted a total of twelve minutes and one second from bell to bell, and much of that time was spent with Hogan in a bear-hug. When it was finally time for André to be slammed, he got light and went up with ease—despite Hogan's onetime claims that he tore his back to pieces from the effort of hefting the 600-pound Giant. Hogan went right on working after Wres-tleMania, not missing any time, and while André was prob-ably legitimately close to 500 pounds at the time (although nowhere near his billed 7 feet 4, as he was nearly eye-to-eye with Hogan—himself billed at between 6 feet 7 and 6 feet 8, although probably around 6 feet 5 in real life—in their pre-match stare down), he went up with ease . . . in part because he'd been slammed many times before. A leg drop and a three-count later, and Hogan's immortality was sealed. It was the largest and most spectacular professional wrestling event the world had ever seen, even without all the inflated myths and statistics.

As for Hogan's sliding scale regarding André's death soon after the match, André not only stuck around for a few years afterward (although in increasingly rapidly failing health, he was eventually relegated to tag team matches and had to continually hold onto the ropes in order to keep his balance), but he and Hogan actually continued their feud in the ring for over a year afterward. On the first episode of *The Main Event* (a prime-time Friday night spinoff of SNME), Ho-gan once again defended his WWF Championship against

André, who by this time had befriended "The Million Dollar Man" Ted DiBiase and his henchman,* Virgil. DiBiase had set his sights on the world title but was convinced he was rich enough to buy his way to the championship, rather than earn it via fisticuffsmanship. (Or wrestlecuffsmanship?) André had promised to give the title to DiBiase when he won it, because his beef with Hogan went beyond world titles, and even a Giant can use a big sack full of cold, hard cash.

In one of the most wonderfully ridiculous moments of 1980s pro wrestling, with McMahon's vision of fighting-as-entertainment-cum–soap opera, a distracted referee missed a Hogan pinfall on André, allowing André to recover and hit Hogan with two headbutts and a double-underhook suplex. André went for the pin, and despite Hogan very clearly and deliberately raising his shoulder at the count of one, the referee, Dave Hebner, counted to three and awarded the match and the title to André. André was interviewed in the ring by Okerlund, and in a famous gaffe, the Giant twice referred to the world championship as the "world tag team title" before

---

* "Henchman" is probably a charitable read on the Virgil character. Ostensibly he was DiBiase's combination butler, valet, and bodyguard, but fans even at the time recognized that the role was actually somewhere between indentured servitude and outright slavery, especially considering the racial distinction between employer and employee. Virgil finally turning on the Million Dollar Man years later was one of the most bulletproof angles the WWF ever put together, and was pretty definitive proof that you can make a star out of pretty much anyone, at any ability level, if the pieces are in place and the roles are played effectively. Virgil would eventually become a cult favorite of internet fans due in part to sad photos of him alone at fan conventions and his singular focus on being a weirdo huckster, focused on his love of Olive Garden and earning "fuck money." It's also long been rumored that he got the WWF gig as Virgil by displaying his monster hog. So there's that, too.

gifting the title to DiBiase. DiBiase, André, and Virgil departed from ringside with the championship around DiBiase's waist, when a second referee appeared in the ring to confront the first. The two referees looked nearly identical, and Hogan confronted them both before referee-on-referee violence led to Hogan-on-referee violence. As the story line went, DiBiase and his associates had locked the *real* Dave Hebner in a closet backstage, and inserted their own bought man, Hebner's real-life twin brother, Earl Hebner (you'll hear that name again in a few chapters), thus guaranteeing a win for André.

The full story line of the two identical referees, told in the official WWF magazine and across the syndicated weekly shows, didn't necessarily translate to the entire viewing audience, as some fans inferred (perhaps from too many soap operas themselves) that DiBiase had paid an unrelated man to get plastic surgery to resemble Dave Hebner. (That would *truly* have been a long con.) Regardless, the DiBiase-André plot was designed to get the belt off Hogan for a time, and the end result was figurehead president Jack Tunney making the landmark decision that no, you can't just give the world title to someone else, regardless of how much money they gave you. André was stripped of the title, and it was determined that the most direct route out of this brouhaha was a fourteen-man tournament to be held entirely on the evening of WrestleMania IV and comprising the bulk of what would end up being a sixteen-match event and one of the absolute least-liked Manias of all time.

Despite most histories ending André's WWF story at WrestleMania III, he actually appeared at the next four annual events. At WrestleMania IV, he and Hogan brawled to a double disqualification in the quarterfinals, giving DiBiase a bye into the finals, and appeared in the Million Dollar Man's corner in the main event. (Yes, hijinks were involved.) He lost a match via disqualification to Jake "The Snake" Roberts at WrestleMania V when he opted to attack special guest referee Big John Studd, and he defended the tag team titles alongside Haku at WrestleMania VI.

Shortly after WrestleMania VI, André would turn babyface for the last time, and wrestled sporadically all the way into 1991. He made an appearance at WrestleMania VII to assist Big Boss Man in a nonwrestling capacity, and his final appearances in the WWF were on crutches following knee surgery in 1991. He actually wrestled one last match in Japan in 1992 before retiring.

In January 1993, André traveled home to France for his father's funeral. On January 27, 1993, he died in his sleep in a hotel room in Paris. The pinnacle of his long and storied career will always be considered to be the main event of WrestleMania III, when he was many years past the absolute peak of his wrestling ability. But the importance of that match to wrestling history cannot be overstated: the previous biggest draw in the history of the business (who had held that position for over a decade) passed the torch to the new biggest draw in the history of the business, in front of the largest wrestling crowd ever.

Post–WrestleMania III, with André fading from the limelight, Hogan and the WWF would continue, and Hulkamania would dwarf the popularity once enjoyed by André the Giant, the Eighth Wonder of the World.

Besides being one of the most iconic scenes in wrestling history, WrestleMania III was an enormous personal triumph for the McMahon-Hogan machine—a representation of their consolidation of the power in the wrestling world. And the Hulkamania craze made wrestling something it had never before been: mainstream. Finally, Vince's hopes of legitimacy appeared to be coming to fruition.

7

THE WWF'S RELATIONSHIP WITH WOMEN STARTS OUT WEIRD

While women's professional wrestling has been around for approximately as long as its more publicized male counterpart, it has almost never been given equal attention, gravitas, or notoriety—particularly in the United States.

Women's wrestling arose from the same carnival and fair scene as did men's wrestling, but concerns about propriety and patriarchal hegemony meant the women were quickly pushed to the periphery. While the male champions and bigger names fell in with the various trusts and began wrestling in arenas and stadiums, women's wrestling found a home in burlesque venues, saloons, and sideshows.

Arguably the first national women's wrestling superstar was Mildred Burke, a tanned brunette who had better muscles—particularly her shoulders and biceps—than most male wrestlers of the era. Burke broke into the business in 1935 and captured the women's world title by 1937. In the mid-1950s, a group of black women wrestlers began drawing sellout shows coast-to-coast. Ethel Johnson, Babs Wingo, Kathleen Wimbley, and Marva Scott were the first black women wrestlers and were immediate sensations. By 1954, they were performing in main events in front of crowds of 9,000 and were top attractions on the same cards as Gorgeous George. Johnson and Wingo both received title shots against Burke for the NWA Women's Championship, and each of the quartet were among the highest-paid black athletes in the country.

Burke and June Byers faced off for the world title in 1954, which by that point was recognized by most promoters as the NWA Women's Championship. In 1956, the Fabulous Moolah (Mary Lillian Ellison) won a tournament crowning her a *different* women's world champion, mostly recognized in the Northeast. Moolah owned this belt and traveled with it, becoming an attraction as a heel champion. When Byers retired in 1964, Moolah's proprietary title became the de facto NWA Women's Championship. When the WWF withdrew from the NWA in 1983, Moolah joined with the McMahons. With the generally accepted women's wrestling champion in the fold, the WWF was able to create its own title, which was touted as being from the lineage of the same NWA championship held by Byers. They then decided to continue telling tall tales about their women's division.

The WWF chose to recognize Moolah as never having lost the championship since her initial win in 1956, giving her and the title a propped-up prestige and importance that no other women's title in the country could touch.

We must pause here and address Fabulous Moolah and her alleged history of horrible business practices. Originally breaking in with Burke's camp in the 1950s, Moolah and her first husband began training women wrestlers. By the late 1950s, Moolah and her second husband, Buddy Lee, began a very lucrative wrestling factory that was a combination training facility (out of her home) and national women's wrestling promotion called Girl Wrestling Enterprises. Moolah was able to quickly train up a bunch of eager young women in the business and then ship them out all over the country for wrestling shows and promoters of all stripes, while she and Lee took the lion's share of the girls' booking fees.

There have been numerous allegations made about Moolah over the years, ranging from her farming out the training of the girls itself (to less-than-fully-trained lieutenants) to her essentially acting as a pimp for the women who originally came to her to become wrestlers. Several women who worked with and trained under Moolah insisted there was no impropriety beyond hand-waving "that's just how the business worked" excuses about harsh training or exorbitant promoter fees. One thing seems abundantly clear: Moolah was taking an extreme cut from anyone she had under "contract" to her and did so for decades.

Wrestler Kevin Sullivan worked with Winona Littleheart, a valet who was one of "Miss Lillian's girls" in Championship Wrestling from Florida in the 1980s. Sullivan recalled that much of that woman's paycheck would go to Moolah—who had nothing to do with the promotion other than getting her into the territory. "It was a big slice she was giving up," he said. "Like 45 percent—and she was still paying [Moolah] rent [on top of the percentage]."

With Moolah in the fold for Vince McMahon Jr.'s rapidly expanding WWF, the company had access to a pipeline of Moolah's girls if they chose to utilize it, not to mention the WWF's connections to other territories and promotions all over the world. As Hulkamania began to ramp up, the WWF introduced Moolah trainees Leilani Kai, Judy Martin, and Wendi Richter.

Richter, who had the big hair, screaming-loud makeup, and new wave look of the early 1980s, was primed and intended to be a massive part of McMahon's worldwide takeover— literally, she was the "connection" in the Rock 'N' Wrestling Connection that set the world on fire, being managed and seconded by Cyndi Lauper in those massive MTV live specials and at the first WrestleMania in Richter's feud with Moolah for the title. Richter was all over marketing and merchandise in 1985, right alongside Hulk Hogan as one of the faces of the company. An animated version of Richter was the sole heroic WWF Superstar to appear in the *Hulk Hogan's Rock 'n' Wrestling* Saturday morning cartoon.

Shortly after being pushed to main-event-attraction status for the WWF, she and McMahon began regularly butting heads over her pay—the disparity between her paydays and her male counterparts', as you might imagine, was enormous. While she was a draw, she wasn't Hulk Hogan, and thus was expendable.

On November 25, 1985, Richter was set to defend her

women's title against The Spider, a masked opponent who when she appeared was quite clearly the Fabulous Moolah. (There was a real Spider Lady, a woman named Penny Mitchell, against whom Richter had previously thought she would be wrestling that evening. Mitchell also happened to be a good six inches taller than Moolah.) In a screwjob twelve years before Bret Hart had his phantom submission, about seven minutes into the match, the Spider caught Richter in a tight small package and got her shoulders to the mat. With Moolah definitely trying to hold her down but overpowered by the younger woman, Richter kicked out at one, but referee Jack Lotz, the only other person in on the ruse, administered a fast three-count and a befuddled Howard Finkel declared The Spider the new champion.

During the post-match confusion and announcement of the match decision, Richter, furious, attacked Moolah repeatedly and ripped her mask off. After attempting to wrestle the title belt away from both Lotz and Moolah, she whipped Moolah with the championship strap while Moolah paraded around inside and outside the ring with her arms raised in victory. Richter left the building, got on a plane, and never wrestled again for the World Wrestling Federation. She also never spoke to Moolah again.

After Richter's departure, the WWF stopped paying close attention to the women's division for the most part, with spotlights bubbling up here and there—such as in 1987, when the company brought in the Jumping Bomb Angels tag team of Itsuki Yamazaki and Noriyo Tateno. In the ring, the duo (from the world-class All Japan Women's Pro-Wrestling promotion), were light-years ahead of not just the rest of the WWF's women's division but outclassed the ability of nearly every wrestler in the entire company at the time, save perhaps Dynamite Kid and Bret Hart. The team made fans' jaws drop at the 1987 Survivor Series and again at the 1988 Royal Rumble PPV, when they defeated the Glamour Girls of Kai and Martin to win the even-shorter-lived and even-less-paid-attention-to WWF Women's Tag Team Championship. The Glamour Girls won the titles back later in the year before they were deactivated in 1989. The WWF Women's Championship managed to last until 1990, when it too was retired.

While we're discussing the women's division in the 1980s, we must pause and address one of the most serious allegations ever leveled against Vince McMahon. In April 1992, former WWF employee Rita Chatterton appeared on the Geraldo Rivera–hosted show *Now It Can Be Told*. Chatterton, who was the first woman referee in WWF history in the '80s (and possibly the first woman to ever appear as a referee for a national promotion), alleged that Vince McMahon forced her to perform oral sex on him in his limo before raping her.

In the September 1992 edition of *Penthouse* magazine, Chatterton elaborated further, saying the incident took place on July 16, 1986. Chatterton left the company shortly after the alleged assault and waited to come forward with the allegations until both of her parents had passed away. The other allegations about impropriety within the company in 1992 helped make it easier for her to come forward at that time. As she told *Penthouse*, "Now that so many people are speaking up, I feel safer. And I also think people will believe me now." In a chilling summation of the alleged assault in the *Penthouse* interview, Chatterton recalled that she had been explicitly told by McMahon when he hired her in 1985 that she was not to engage in sexual activity with anyone in the WWF. "After he finished raping me, he looks at me and I'm crying and he says, 'Remember how I told you never to have sex with someone from the company? Well, you just did.' And then he starts laughing hysterically. What a sick man he is."

In response, McMahon and his legal team filed a "civil conspiracy" lawsuit against Rivera, Chatterton, and others involved with the production of the episode and have vehemently denied these allegations every time they have come up over the years. The case eventually fell by the wayside when the WWF turned its full legal attention to McMahon's federal charges in the steroid trial.

Chatterton's historical contributions to the WWF and professional wrestling have been erased from WWE's official history books. When former indie wrestler Jessika Carr was hired by WWE as a referee for the Mae Young Classic tournament in 2017 (and later in NXT and WWE), she was widely hailed and publicized by the company as being the first "full-time" female referee to work for a major promotion.

Following the Richter screwjob, the most prominent woman in the WWF in the 1980s was Miss Elizabeth— almost invariably referred to as "the lovely Miss Elizabeth." Dubbed "the first lady of the WWF," Elizabeth was the real-life wife of Randy Savage and was famously introduced as his WWF manager shortly after he made his debut in the company, as every other ultracolorful manager in the WWF (and there were many, from the turban-wearing and unfortunately named Grand Wizard to Bobby Heenan, Lou Albano, and Jimmy Hart). Elizabeth rarely spoke, but always remained poised and elegant. It was one of the most nuanced and unique dynamics in pro wrestling: a thoroughly virtuous and upstanding babyface manager accompanying an unrepentant blowhard and conniving heel to the ring every night. Elizabeth became the wedge between Savage and Hogan's Mega Powers team and ultimately split from Savage, allowing him to partner with the anti-Elizabeth, Sensational Sherri: a garish, caterwauling snake in the grass. Elizabeth was portrayed as the purest character in the company, despite her real-life marriage to Savage being plagued (by nearly all accounts) by abuse, jealousy, anger, and terror. Outside the ring, Savage maintained a worrying obsession that everyone else in the company was trying to get their hands on her, to the point that he reportedly kept her locked in a backstage closet when he was unable to personally keep tabs on her.

Moolah continued to be around the periphery of the WWF in the 1980s and 1990s, but for the time being, the company had soured on featuring women's wrestling prominently after the Richter debacle. It would return in a few years, but that ended up being a strange story as well.

8

NEXT MAN UP

Experiments and Controversies

Vince McMahon learned two things when he took control of the WWF—if he wasn't already aware of them before he bought out his father's portion of the company. The first is that you can never be certain of another Bruno (let alone another Hogan), so you have to be ready to plan for a future without your top star. The second is that pro wrestlers are going to get themselves into trouble, so it's important to keep your head on a swivel and get ready to work the press, the public, and sometimes the authorities in order to maintain your status as family entertainment. The 1980s and early 1990s tested McMahon in both areas, sometimes scarcely affording him a breath in between.

The 1980s were a particularly tumultuous time for WWF. While McMahon and Hogan created the largest wrestling boom to date and shifted the paradigm of the sport within the popular consciousness, McMahon's first scandal happened less than a year after he purchased the company, and before he managed to bring Hogan into the WWF to usher in the Hulkamania era.

On May 10, 1983, an ambulance was called to an Allentown, Pennsylvania, motel, where Nancy Argentino was struggling to breathe, with a yellow fluid seeping from her mouth and nose. She was rushed to a nearby hospital, where she passed away a few hours later. The official autopsy and the first responders would mention more than two dozen cuts and bruises, and her official cause of death was listed as severe brain trauma, likely caused by her falling and striking her head on something during the fall.

At the time of her death, Argentino was the girlfriend of WWF star Jimmy "Superfly" Snuka, whose character was originally introduced as a simple Fijian savage. He resembled a real-life Tarzan, wrestling in bare feet and animal-print outfits, with a deep tan, flowing curly locks, and an almost hilariously jacked physique. Beginning his first WWF run in 1982, he entered with over a decade of in-ring experience and as a villain. His finishing move—the "Superfly Splash" off the top rope, one of the original high-flying maneuvers that caused audiences' jaws to drop from its sheer majesty and athleticism—later aided his rapid rise in popularity, and he turned babyface that same year, after being convinced in a story line that his nefarious manager, Lou Albano, had been taking advantage of his simple nature and had been exploiting and stealing from him. He was one of the biggest stars in the company, if not the most popular, prior to Hogan's return as a conquering hero.

Bob Backlund once told the *Two Man Power Trip of Wrestling* podcast that the only thing keeping Snuka from being the biggest star in the company was his personal conduct. "In the ring, he was a genius," Backlund said. "But out of the ring, he was an embarrassment to society. If he would have been a decent person, then he would have been the WWF Champion, but he didn't have the qualifications and didn't meet the standards, or else he would have been. Vince McMahon Sr. would have made him the WWF Champion if he would have been an honorable person."

It was Snuka who called for an ambulance on the night Argentino died, and his story changed several times over the next twelve hours or so. He initially told as many as five different people that he had shoved Argentino during an argument and she hit her head. After Argentino was pronounced dead, Snuka claimed he had misunderstood the question or had misspoken. Snuka's new version of events was that she had lost her balance and slipped, hitting her head when the two stopped to go to the bathroom on the shoulder of the highway. He claimed she began behaving strangely and was unresponsive when he returned to their motel following a WWF television taping in Allentown, at which point he called for paramedics.

Snuka was questioned by police, but never detained. On June 1, 1983, prosecutors and officials met with Snuka and McMahon at the library of the district attorney. It has never been revealed by any party—including the investigating detective's report on the meeting—what the content of that meeting may have included, but Snuka was never questioned further regarding the situation. There was little, if any, progress or forward movement on the case following that meeting, and Argentino's death would remain a cold case until 2013, when the acting district attorney announced that the case would be reviewed. It would not be until September 1, 2015—a full thirty-two years after Argentino's death—that Snuka would be officially charged in relation to the case. Snuka faced charges of third-degree murder and involuntary manslaughter and pleaded not guilty, but the judge assigned to the case would eventually declare Snuka not mentally competent to stand trial, as his lawyers claimed he was diagnosed with brain damage and was in the throes of dementia. Snuka died on January 15, 2017, from stomach cancer (less than two weeks after all charges against him were formally dropped).

The next two major scandals for the WWF in the 1980s (other than intermittent run-ins with athletic commissions and a marketing-related kerfuffle, none of which ever permeated the national news much, in part due to the relatively slow speed of the news cycle or media reach at the time) both happened at a very inopportune time: during the run-up to the first WrestleMania. Both involved a wrestler trying to protect the business, with awful results from a PR standpoint.

The first incident involved "Dr. D" David Schultz, a towering hick from Tennessee with a moplike shock of curly blond hair and a Southern-fried accent. Schultz had the gift of gab and took particular delight in causing interviewers like Gene

Okerlund to crack up during promos. He had been a top heel in Stampede, the AWA, and Memphis before McMahon poached him in 1984, with the idea that he could eventually be a tremendous foil for Hogan as a title challenger. He probably wasn't wrong. But as it turned out, Schultz ended up being in the WWF for less than a year.

In December 1984, ABC had a camera crew backstage at a WWF show in Madison Square Garden, filming footage and interviews for a segment about professional wrestling that was to appear on *20/20*, which at that time was already an established newsmagazine show with clout. It's easy to understand why McMahon granted access, as he likely envisioned that positive buzz would come out of his exciting product being featured on a national program with a large viewership. John Stossel, the journalist gathering on-camera interviews for the segment, had the misfortune of asking Schultz about the legitimacy of pro wrestling—especially since Schultz claims McMahon approached him earlier that day and instructed him to play his bad guy character to the hilt while talking to Stossel. After getting a very confrontational (but very much in-character) answer from Schultz about whether wrestling is a "good business" ("It's a tough business," replied Schultz. "Which is why you ain't in it."), Stossel offered up a question he assumed (likely correctly) that Dr. D had heard countless times. "I'll ask you the standard question," began Stossel, at which point Schultz instantly bristled. Stossel pressed on: "I think this is fake," he said. (Which, admittedly, is not a question.)

Schultz immediately fired back, "You think it's fake?" Then, snarling, he delivered a full-force right-handed slap across Stossel's face, knocking the journalist to the ground. "How about that? Is that fake?" asked Schultz. Stossel, holding his head, staggered to his feet, stunned, as Schultz continued: "What the hell's wrong with you? That's an open-hand slap." To drive his point home, Schultz stepped forward and hit him with the left this time, swinging the length of his arm and striking Stossel with another open palm, once again knocking him to the ground. In the footage that aired on *20/20*, a full hallway of people watch this transpire. Stossel leaped to his feet and began speeding away from Schultz, who started after him. Unfortunately for Schultz—well, all of it was unfortunate, really—a deputy New York State athletic commissioner was present at the show and witnessed the assault and took it upon himself to suspend Schultz's wrestling license on the spot.[*]

The good news for the WWF is that the *20/20* segment and the televised assault of Stossel did indeed generate a good deal of buzz, but the bad news was it didn't really paint the Federation in a very glowing light. And given that McMahon was trying hard to brand his wrestling as family-friendly and larger than life, he couldn't publicly appear to be pleased with the footage of one of his wrestlers slapping a reporter silly in a dingy hallway. (And if you've never seen the footage, make no mistake: Schultz really did slap the absolute piss out of that poor guy.)

Schultz later sent a written apology to Stossel and to the NYSAC, and Stossel later filed a lawsuit against the World

---

[*] This is likely the most ironic twist in all this: at the moment when David Schultz slapped John Stossel to defend the legitimacy of his profession, his profession was still legitimate enough to be subject to the jurisdiction of a state athletic commission in the WWF's biggest market.

Wrestling Federation for the assault, settling out of court for nearly half a million dollars. Schultz stuck around on the house show loop for a while but had wrestled his last WWF match by March 1985, the same month as WrestleMania. Even though the WWF was derided by die-hard wrestling fans as making a mockery of the business, there wasn't a wrestler alive in 1984 (particularly the old-timers who would have been backstage at that time) who didn't believe kay fabe needed to be defended at all costs, and that outsiders deserved to be slapped to the ground if they used the most insulting f-word of all. Schultz was fired from the company backstage at Madison Square Garden, with the lame excuse that he was "bothering" Mr. T by striking up a conversation with the TV star, but according to Schultz, the true tipping point in his firing was the fact that Dr. D had met privately with Stossel's legal team and informed them that he hit Stossel on McMahon's orders, thus sparing him from the lawsuit.

The other incident happened mere days before Wrestle-Mania, as Hogan and Mr. T appeared on *Hot Properties*, a talk show hosted by Richard Belzer. Belzer, a wiry comedian who is likely best known as Detective John Munch from *Homicide* and *Law and Order*, interviewed Hogan and T about their upcoming main event. Hogan was his usual charismatic self, while Mr. T was surly and busied himself with the flex-bar that was ever-present in his WWF escapades. Belzer joked with Hogan about stepping outside to fight and invited him over to a wide area of the stage to have Hogan demonstrate some moves on him. Hogan and Belzer engaged in some very good-natured repartee about not wanting to hurt each other, while Mr. T barked from the couch, his rancor at odds with the air of cool and calm that Hogan was trying to project.* "Give him a body slam!" T yelled repeatedly as Belzer and Hogan tried to ignore him.

After asking for a "camel crusher" or Hulk's finishing move, Hogan explained that he'd need to stick to the basics. Hogan reached toward Belzer, and as he lightly touched his shoulders, Belzer let out a comical yell and dropped to the ground on his back, taking a pratfall for the virtue of the studio audience and the viewers at home. It's possible this was the moment that Hogan and Mr. T decided he was being a bit too flippant about the whole ordeal, but regardless, when Belzer got to his feet, Hogan explained that he would apply a simple hold. As he bowed Belzer's head and began applying the hold, Hogan and Mr. T joked with one another, in the guise of macho posturing. (Or maybe it was the other way around.)

"You just tell me, brother, when you want him to quit squealing, alright?" Hogan asked, pointing at Mr. T. With Belzer facing him and his head down, Hogan placed his left hand on Belzer's right shoulder and snaked his massive right arm underneath Belzer's chin. Hogan, who already towered over Belzer by at least a foot, looks truly massive at this point, Belzer's head entirely disappearing as Hogan grasps his left forearm with his right hand, cinching in the hold. To MMA aficionados, this move is more commonly known today as a guillotine choke. And it, like most building-block basic moves in professional wrestling, is entirely legit. "This is called a front chinlock," says Hogan, as Belzer splays his arms out to

---

* Before stepping over to show Belzer some moves, Hogan leans over and places a hand on Mr. T's chest and says some gentle words to him, basically doing everything short of yelling "Shut up and calm the fuck down" as T was doing anything but helping the situation.

his sides, clearly mugging to sell his peril. Hogan again looks to the couch for approval. "How 'bout it, T?" he asks.

"Keep it right there for a little while," Mr. T responds, in an understated but unfriendly tone. It's at this point, just a second or two after cinching in the hold, that Belzer puts his hands to Hogan's sides, the move seeming desperate and in contrast to his pantomime distress a moment earlier. Hogan appears to pull back just a bit, sinking the hold in even deeper, but even if he didn't, he didn't need to. About six seconds after Hogan applies the move, Belzer's arms and legs go completely limp. Hogan is now holding the entire dead weight of the co-median under his gargantuan arm. This limpness occurs in conjunction with a huge laugh from the studio audience. The next moment, Hogan releases the hold slightly, and Belzer slips out of his arms, flopping to the ground bonelessly, the back of his head smacking directly on the studio floor with a deep, sharp thud. Hogan steps around Belzer's legs and looks down at the host's face. The audience gasps. "He's alright," says Mr. T, not kindly. "He's just sleepin'. He's sleepin'. That was a sleeper hold. He'll be all right."

As Mr. T continues to say the host is fine, there is a snort, and Belzer raises his head, looking around in confusion. Hogan bends down, asking if Belzer is all right, and offers a hand up. Hogan gently pats each side of Belzer's face twice and says to the audience, "See? It works!" Hogan begins pull-ing him up, and Belzer leaps to his feet, cheerily tossing to a commercial, returning to his bravado to cover for how shaken he is, remaining professional.

When *Hot Properties* returned from that commercial, Bel-zer had been replaced as host by a producer of the program, and Mr. T and Hogan sit on the couch again, looking cowed (especially Hogan). "Richard was hurt," explains the producer. "Hulk didn't mean to do it. These things happen in television, it is live television, and now I think Hulk and T should just talk about this kind of thing, how it can happen, and how to avoid it."

Hogan, now sheepish and nowhere near his earlier bombast, sighs and says, "You know, I feel really bad about the situation. Richard asked me to demonstrate a professional wrestling hold, and that's exactly what I did." The audience, privy to the strange scene and everything that may have occurred during the commercial break, has begun to turn on the wrestlers. Although clearly put off and trying to save face, Hulk is unable to stop trying to sell himself and his company and his profession at every waking moment. He continues, "I put what is called a front chinlock on the man, and when I released him, he fell and hit his head on the floor. It's a situation where you need to be a professional at all times. And the type of hold, when I would put that on a professional wrestler, I would apply probably 10 times as much pressure. I didn't realize that Richard—apparently he doesn't do any kind of physical training at all." There are a couple of laughs, but more groans and jeers from the audience at that.

"I'm not saying that in a smart way," Hogan insists, turning to the audience. "I really apologize." He continues to try and explain away the difference between wrestlers and civilians as the interview goes on for another minute or so, but the PR disaster had already been sealed. Belzer needed nine stitches in the back of his head, and the good guys had choked out a television host on live TV and then joked about it, coming across as arrogant, callow, petty bullies just four days before they expected fans to cheer for them in the main event of the first WrestleMania. Ultimately, of course, the show was a success, but you probably couldn't ask for a worse showing from your heroes before your biggest event ever.

Belzer eventually sued Hogan for $5 million. The two parties settled out of court, and although the case would end up setting New York precedent for attorney's contingency fees due to a squabble between Belzer and his lawyers over how much of the settlement they were owed, nothing further came of it, and what could have been an absolute land mine for the WWF became another footnote in the midst of the company's meteoric rise in cultural relevancy. (Belzer ended up buying a farm in Nice, France, with his settlement money, which he lovingly christened "Chez Hogan." So this incident can also potentially be used as precedent for what one might do when Hulkamania runs wild on them.)

A more straightforward incident that ended up making national news and helped shift the world ever so slightly toward the collapse of kayfabe happened on May 26, 1987. While driving through Middletown, New Jersey, WWF wrestlers "Hacksaw" Jim Duggan and the Iron Sheik were pulled over when a state trooper spotted Duggan drinking beer while behind the wheel. The two men were arrested and were caught with marijuana in the car and three grams of cocaine in the Iron Sheik's shaving kit. Amazingly, when the story hit the Associated Press newswire, the lede was not the drinking while driving or the drugs, but the fact that the two men, currently engaged on television and on the house show circuit in a blood feud, were driving and partying together.

In fact, they were driving to the next town together after

having just faced one another in a heated match. It was one of the largest-scale cracks in the façade of kayfabe to that time but would be far from the last. Both men were fired, although Duggan was rehired in short order, just to keep him away from the competition. It helped Duggan that the coke was in Sheik's bag, because cocaine was pretty much the only thing the WWF really cared about PR-wise at that time. (At least insofar as failing a drug test specifically for cocaine, or cocaine-related arrests. There was plenty of booger sugar flying around backstage.) In retrospect, the WWF probably should have been concerned about more than just cocaine-related bad press. Not coincidentally, it was shortly after this arrest that the company settled with Stossel, because the last thing they wanted was for the *20/20* assault to come up while people were talking about fakery and debauchery in the company, and while Hulk Hogan's cartoon was still airing in reruns on Saturday morning television.

In the midst of all these scandals of varying infamy, Hulkamania and the WWF machine were still barreling happily forward. And while McMahon was reaping all the benefits of having glommed onto the Hulkster when he did, he recognized that his already-quite-bald golden child would not be around forever, and as Hogan was already beginning to eye a potential career as a movie actor, it would behoove him to try and find the next big thing while he was already all-in on the *current* big thing.

McMahon cast about for the next Hogan, and if he had been able to find one, it's possible Hogan's run on top would have been far shorter than the decade or so he enjoyed from the 1980s to the mid-1990s. During this period, McMahon's discerning eye for top talent (in addition to the ever-pressing need to fill out the undercard with non–"main event guys") boiled down to: could this guy draw money against Hogan, or could he potentially be the next Hogan? If the answer through *any* lens was "maybe," he eagerly gobbled him up.

Among McMahon's most notable pet projects as the potential successor to Hulkamania were "The Natural" Butch Reed and "Megaman" Tom Magee, but neither panned out.

Hulkamania Era Wrestlers

Speaking of other McMahon projects, by the late 1980s the WWF was beginning to stretch the bounds of even pro wrestling believability with increasingly outlandish and gimmicky characters. Among the characters who appeared in the WWF by the year 1990:

HILLBILLY JIM, a wrestling hillbilly (which was nothing new to pro wrestling, as "country bumpkin" was a well-worn tradition dating back even before the alpha and omega of the genre, Haystacks Calhoun), whose initial story line was "friend of Hulk Hogan." The seven-foot hayseed appeared in the front row of shows cheering for Hulk Hogan at several tapings, before he ran afoul of some heels and Hogan took it upon himself to train the poor simpleton to be a wrestler. Jim would eventually get his own extended hillbilly universe, being paired with Uncle Elmer, Cousin Luke, and Cousin Junior. His kayfabe family members wouldn't stick around long, but Jim was a beloved, cheerful character, even though he was nearly perpetually sidelined by injuries. He remains a testament to the power of a compelling look combined with an absolute banger of a theme song: in Jim's case, the shit-kicking "Don't Go Messin' with a Country Boy."

THE BUSHWHACKERS, two New Zealanders who were formerly a bloodthirsty team of butchers known as the Sheepherders who traveled the world bleeding buckets and horrifying fans by their brutality. In the WWF, however, they were two cousins who were a strict comedy act, marching to the ring with a trademark arm-swinging motion and pausing to lick fans and each other. They downed sardines, terrorized Mean Gene in skits, and were presented as buffoons with borderline mental deficiencies. It cannot be denied how inconceivably popular they were, but then again, don't discount how fun it is to just swing your arms back and forth over your head like a huge nerd.

CORPORAL KIRCHNER, a bland military type brought in to replace Sgt. Slaughter, whose entire gimmick was "is a soldier."

"LEAPING" LANNY POFFO, who wore a suit of armor to the ring, did cartwheels, and threw frisbees to fans.

AX AND SMASH, THE TEAM OF DEMOLITION, was created as McMahon's own version of the Road Warriors, who he was unable to sign but were the hottest tag team in the world at the time. Ax and Smash appeared to have been concocted by a game of telephone played between someone who had seen the Road Warriors and someone who had seen *The Road Warrior*, and then relayed it to McMahon fourth-hand. They wore face paint, like the actual Road Warriors, but that's pretty much where the similarities ended. Ax and Smash came to the ring wearing studded bondage gear and gimp masks and wrestled in S&M harnesses. Thankfully, since most fans weren't well versed in the intricacies of kink in the late 1980s, they became beloved successes within the WWF.

THE KILLER BEES, B. BRIAN BLAIR AND "JUMPIN'" JIM BRUNZELL, two wrestling bees. Luckily, the Bees existed in the 1980s and 1990s, so they weren't *actually* supposed to be bees. If they had come around a decade later, they likely would have been cutting promos that would have had them buzzing, covering their opponents in honey after matches, and getting distracted by heel managers holding up enticing flowers.

OUTBACK JACK, who appeared in endless vignettes as a hard-scrabble and ill-mannered Australian brawler. He appeared only a handful of times on WWF television before disappearing, because he turned out to be bad even by the standards of the WWF roster at the time.

"KING" HARLEY RACE. By the time he made it to the World Wrestling Federation in 1986, Race had been an eight-time NWA Heavyweight Champion, which was a record at the time. He was regarded as one of the finest and most legitimate tough-guy wrestlers to ever live. He was nearing the tail end of his career, however, and so he was willing to switch up his character to become the cowardly "King of Wrestling"—a literal king, with a cape and crown. Die-hard and purist fans were incensed. Many interpreted the new character as a rib on Race's own reputation and didn't approve of the former take-on-all-comers bruiser suddenly being a foppish king. This would be the first time McMahon was accused of signing a wrestler just to mock him outright. Whether that's true is certainly debatable, but it would be far from the last time that the accusation would be made regarding a wrestler. Race's kingship ended up being a title that could be won and lost via wrestling, eventually passing to King Haku, King Hacksaw Jim Duggan, and finally to the Macho King Randy Savage until the latter "retired" for the first time. To be honest, monarchical lineage via combat sports is something that other countries might want to look into. McMahon might be on to something here.

THE HONKY TONK MAN. For whatever misguided reason, McMahon believed that an Elvis impersonator could be a massive fan favorite, based on his assumption that hip people in 1986 still thought 1970s-era Elvis was the epitome of cool. After a disastrous series of tapings with Honky getting booed out of the building as a good guy, the command decision was made to turn him heel. Suddenly, his complete inability to sing or play the guitar became an asset in generating heat, and he eventually (through no small amount of backstage politicking and strong-arming) became the longest-reigning Intercontinental Champion of all time. It's not likely his 454-day reign will ever be topped.

THE RED ROOSTER. Terry Taylor, a journeyman wrestler and "good hand" in the NWA and throughout the South since 1979, was rebranded "The Red Rooster" shortly after he landed in the WWF in 1988. Styling the middle of his blond hair into a firetruck-red cockscomb, he preened and crowed in the ring and may or may not have been meant to be an actual human-rooster hybrid.

THE BROOKLYN BRAWLER, a brawler from Brooklyn. The Brawler was one of two quintessential WWF jobbers in the 1980s, the other being Barry Horowitz, who had the far less refined gimmick of "arrogant nerdy Jew."* The Brawler is more notable for the person who portrayed him: Steve Lombardi, who parlayed his reliability as an enhancement talent into a longtime behind-the-scenes figure and road agent—essentially, he was a lifer for the WWF. His other claim to "bad gimmick" fame came in 1994, when he played baseball-faced Abe "Knuckleball" Schwartz, a heel MLB player designed to attempt to get heat off that year's major league strike. You'll be stunned to hear that didn't work out.

AKEEM, THE AFRICAN DREAM. One of the most infamous gimmicks of all time, Akeem started life in the WWF as the 400-pound behemoth the One Man Gang (which is an all-time-great name, if you ask me). Gang's manager, Slick (himself a regrettable character: a jive-talking heel pimp introduced via a vignette where he gleefully devours a bucket of fried chicken), revealed to the big man his secret roots, which traced back to Africa. In a vignette, Gene Okerlund met Slick in a graffiti-covered alley. Slick held a boombox as a group of African warriors in loincloths, holding shields and spears, danced around a barrel fire. Out of the barrel fire emerged Gang, wearing a tall hat and a dashiki, and dancing incessantly. Slick introduced him as Akeem, the African Dream, and then they danced out of the segment with Akeem toting the boombox on his shoulder. Reportedly (and not so subtly), this character was envisioned as a rib on NWA star and booker Dusty Rhodes, who throughout his career was both praised and scoffed at for "acting

---

*   When Horowitz was finally given entrance music during a minipush in 1995, it was a MIDI version of "Hava Nagila," and when he was given the opportunity to cut a backstage interview, they dressed him in everything short of a pocket protector to really drive home the point: this guy, emphatically, does not fuck.

black" in promos and in his mannerisms. Akeem began to be billed as hailing from "deepest, darkest Africa" (which I'm choosing to interpret as a Paddington reference) and teamed with corrupt prison guard the Big Boss Man as the Twin Towers. While this character is reviled today for many justifiable reasons, through a contemporary read, it may accidentally be one of the WWF's most woke creations of all time: a heel who deserves to be booed because of egregious, privileged cultural appropriation. He was the Rachel Dolezal of his time, only he didn't really believe it.

There were many others, of course, although they were nothing compared to what was coming down the pike in the next decade. And in addition to these bizarre gimmicks were other cartoonish characters who were instant home runs and genuinely solid ideas: Jake "The Snake" Roberts,* "The Million Dollar Man" Ted DiBiase, and a supernova who caught fire right when McMahon was searching for his next surefire star. He was the Ultimate Warrior.

---

* According to Roberts himself (who was a karate pants–wearing, no-nonsense shitkicker prior to moving to the WWF), in his first meeting with McMahon, he was silently bristling at demands for wearing green spandex and snakeskin boots and carrying a snake with him everywhere he went—until Vince slid a salary figure across the desk. Jake "The Snake" was eagerly born there on the spot.

9

WARS AND WARRIORS

The Torch Doesn't Get Passed

In 1990, Vince McMahon attempted to transition the balance of power—both in kayfabe and behind the scenes—away from Hulk Hogan. There was a runaway star already in the fold who was drawing sellout crowds and garnering reactions that sometimes blew away the cheers that the Hulkster received. By 1989, it was clear that this man was both positioned and groomed to be the next star on top, the superstar who would carry the company into the 1990s and beyond. The Ultimate Warrior's time seemed to be now, but his ascension proved both the difficulty of replicating a worldwide pro wrestling sensation and the discerning nature of a fan base that can put a halt to the magic show once all the smoke and mirrors in the building have been exhausted. The grand Ultimate Warrior experiment very nearly worked just like McMahon hoped it would, but in the end the man playing the role proved to be as volatile as his unhinged in-ring persona, and Vince ended up having to return to the devil he knew: Hulk Hogan.

The 1990s also kicked off a new level of fans gaining knowledge of the inner workings of wrestlers' lives—and all the unsavory details that came with that knowledge. Fans started to distrust the heroes they'd previously been looking up to and cheering for, which continued to further erode the increasingly tenuous world of kayfabe.

As the bodies on camera in the WWF (and most other promotions) became more swollen by steroids and growth hormone, the only ways to stand out from the pack in 1987 were to have a body that was ridiculous even in comparison to your coworkers, to have charisma that bled right through the television screen, or to have a character that truly captivated. In the Ultimate Warrior, Vince McMahon was delighted to find all three components.

Jim Hellwig, a former bodybuilder originally from Indiana, was one of the most jacked freaks anyone had ever seen when he broke into the business alongside Steve Borden—now best known as Sting—in 1985. He was notable for his physique, but also for his complete lack of ability in the ring. At the time, he was in a team with a man who got beat up for being so bad at wrestling, and yet he was considered the *less* talented of the two. As Hellwig broke from the team and moved to World Class Championship Wrestling (WCCW) in

Texas in 1986, he took on the new name Dingo Warrior, and began wearing tassels around his arms—further enhancing his already distressing biceps—and honed his "mask" face paint. He also began cutting maniacal, ranting promos that were nonsensical but inarguably fascinating. Promoters soon learned that, much like Hogan before him, he benefited from shorter matches to best hide his limitations as a worker. Working as a babyface, he got fans on his side with his unbridled energy and natural charisma, which of course drew comparisons to Hogan, because there was really no one else to compare him to. He was jacked and shredded and making a big buzz, so McMahon brought aboard the Dingo Warrior in 1987.

After doing some loops in the WWF as the Dingo Warrior, McMahon told him at a taping that he didn't know what a dingo was, so he should find a new name. In one of his trademark rambling, free-association promos, Hellwig proclaimed himself to be the Ultimate Warrior, and one can only imagine that the sound inside McMahon's brain at that instant was the *cha-ching* of a cash register opening. The final formula fell into place with the addition of the entrance theme penned for the Warrior by Jim Johnston, a four-chord blast of pure adrenaline, blaring over arena sound systems in staccato bursts, followed by a thudding and chugging locomotive of energy. Warrior would sprint to the ring, shake the top rope as though it was electrocuting him, and then plow through opponents in under two minutes before sprinting away to the back again as his music played once more. In longer matches against tougher opponents (although still not very long at all), Warrior would take another page from Hogan's playbook: the superhuman comeback. He would feed off the energy from his fans (whom he also called Warriors or Little Warriors; totally distinct from Hulkamaniacs) and would shake the ropes until he was able to get to his feet, where his rope-shaking would have rendered him temporarily impervious and allowed him to muscle up his foe for the gorilla press slam and big splash before getting the pin. It was a whole lot like the Hogan act, but more visually tactile. He was an instant hit.

Warrior's body set him apart from everyone else in the company: he not only had a body full of steroid-swollen muscles, but was shredded to pieces, looking like he was from a different planet from the 1980s roid-gut strongmen who populated the company, like Dino Bravo or Hercules—or even Hulk Hogan. He combined Hogan's size with Rick Rude's striation, definition, and vascularity. He looked like a Rob Liefeld comic book character come to life (only he had feet and pretty much no pouches to speak of). Side by side, the visual was striking: Hulk Hogan was your steroid-enhanced meathead from the 1980s, and Ultimate Warrior was the steroid-enhanced ultrameathead for the burgeoning 1990s. (Insert GIF here of floppy-haired kid in a backward baseball cap surfing on a Nacho Cheese Dorito and chugging a Mountain Dew.)

Meanwhile, down in the South, Jim Crockett was finding it difficult to overcome the WWF's perpetual hype machine and glitzy production values that drew in viewers—not to mention McMahon's ruthless and continued counterprogramming tactics, which had WCW and the NWA on the losing side again and again in terms of sheer viewers and attendance. By the summer of 1988, Jim Crockett Promotions and WCW were sold to Ted Turner, who had long had a soft spot for professional wrestling. According to Vince, Turner rang McMahon immediately after closing a $9 million deal for Crockett's roster, shows, and assets, and gleefully exclaimed, "Hey Vince, guess what? I'm in the rasslin' business now!" Without missing a beat, McMahon allegedly responded, "That's great, Ted. I'm in the entertainment business." Perhaps the incident has endured in lore because, even if apocryphal, it perfectly encapsulated the differences in philosophy between the WWF and traditional pro wrestling and foretold the outside ventures upon which McMahon would immediately embark.

Vince's philosophy would lead to another legendary kayfabe break. In 1989, the McMahons found a whole new way to piss off lifelong, die-hard wrestling fans, when the *New York Times* reported that both Vince and Linda McMahon testified under oath before the New Jersey State Senate what many had suspected (or known) for years: that pro wrestling is staged. Linda had testified in Pennsylvania about wrestling being a work a full two years earlier, and McMahon admitted this in interviews as far back as 1985 and 1986, but for whatever reason, the story in the *New York Times* (and another in the next day's *New York Post*) spread like wildfire. As we've covered before, the media or whistleblowers pulling the veil down regarding kayfabe was nothing new, happening every few years since the turn of the twentieth century. This was different, however. First of all, this was the wrestling company itself willingly going on the record to expose the business. And second, the reason it was being done was in the company's own self-interest: The WWF, at the time, was desperate to get away from the influence and oversight of—and fees owed to—state athletic commissions. The civil lawsuits were part of extensive lobbying by the WWF in New Jersey to get themselves free of the New Jersey State Athletic Control Board. And yet, in spite of months of national news coverage and investigative reporting on the pro wrestling industry and other companies as a result of Vince and Linda's testimony—Lou Albano hilariously suggested on *Nightline* that maybe the WWF was rigged, but the *rest* of pro wrestling was on the level, brother—the heart-staking of kayfabe by the McMahons was all for naught. The bill failed to pass in New Jersey, and the WWF continued to have to pay percentages to the NJSACB until 1997, when Governor Christine Todd Whitman advanced a bill that finally got the WWF away from state regulation. Great job, everyone!

That same year, Hogan and McMahon collaborated on what they hoped would be a legitimate crossover smash hit: the feature film *No Holds Barred*, which McMahon and the WWF bankrolled.* New Line Cinema won the rights to distribute the movie when every other distributor passed, and while the movie somehow opened at No. 2 at the box office in its opening weekend, it was savaged by critics and quickly disappeared from theaters. Insiders considered it a minor miracle that the film grossed $16 million at the box office,

---

* As is the case with all good stories where Vince and Hulk work together, the actual budget and final cost of the movie remain completely unknown. The estimates and stories that have been told by all parties involved range from a few million to $8 million (claimed by Hogan in his autobiography), to occasional mentions of a $19 million budget. There are also long-standing legends that, dissatisfied with the script turned in by screenwriter Dennis Hackin, McMahon and Hogan holed themselves up in a hotel room and rewrote the entire script over a sleepless weekend. If you've ever seen the movie, you'll understand why most wrestling fans believe the story of the script bender to be true.

although McMahon somehow managed to triple-dip with *No Holds Barred*. Never one to leave fiction alone, McMahon came up with the idea to train Hogan's film opponent, Tiny Lister, to be a wrestler, and to come into the WWF to play his character from *No Holds Barred*, Zeus. Zeus faced Hogan at SummerSlam, and then two full months after the movie was released on home video, McMahon put together the brilliantly stupid No Holds Barred: The Match/The Movie, a pay-per-view featuring the full movie (already available on home video), followed by a pretaped match with Hogan and Brutus Beefcake taking on Zeus and Macho King Randy Savage inside a steel cage. The match was under ten minutes long, but somehow the PPV managed to be a success. It's generally believed that McMahon and the WWF made their money back on *No Holds Barred* given all the revenue streams they created around it, no matter what the budget might have been.

Hogan's dreams of being a movie star were now, as far as he was concerned, a reality, and he began preparing for more and more time away from pro wrestling. It wasn't tough for McMahon to decide to whom Hogan needed to pass the torch, and in 1990, the WWF began building to a Hogan vs. Warrior match, with the story line kicking off at the Royal Rumble in January. Almost an hour into the match, Hogan and the Warrior found themselves alone in a WWF ring, on television, for the first time. Once Hogan tossed the Honky Tonk Man and the Warrior dumped Shawn Michaels and Rick Martel, the fans leapt to their feet as one, realizing the import of the situation. Hogan and Warrior circled each other, then shoved one another, then crisscrossed the ropes before connecting with simultaneous clotheslines for a big double-down. The two men were alone in the ring together for just over a minute, but the dream match was already all but destined to happen.

At WrestleMania VI in Toronto just a few months later, Hulk Hogan defended his WWF Championship against the Ultimate Warrior, who was also putting his Intercontinental Championship on the line in a rare babyface vs. babyface and even more rare title vs. title (there were only three men's championships in the company at that time), winner-take-all match. Hogan knew he would be taking time off in the fall of 1990 to film *Suburban Commando*, his second turn as a lead in a wide-release movie, and had hopes that this match could very well be a swan song of sorts. Wanting to make sure their long-awaited dream match in the near 70,000-seat SkyDome lived up to expectations, the two combatants not only meticulously laid out their match ahead of time—as Hogan had done with his script for André at WrestleMania III— but they rehearsed the full match several times. Their main event match went nearly twenty-three minutes and was one of the best matches either man had in their careers, before or after. Warrior came out the winner, and Hogan handed over his championship belt, both figuratively and visually passing the torch.

With the Ultimate Warrior as champion, business began to sag more than anticipated. To make matters worse, Warrior was beginning to prove himself to be more and more of a headache. Deciding to go back to his winning formula, McMahon made the call to put the world title back on Hulk Hogan in 1991. To do this, his booking decision needed to be twofold. First, he needed to get the title off the Warrior, in order to not dilute the specialness of the first Hogan-Warrior match just a year earlier and to save some juice in case they wanted to have them face off again at a later date. Second, McMahon wanted to return to the tried-and-true American patriot act that helped spark Hulkamania back when he defeated the Iron Sheik for his first title in 1985. Why, it had been *years* since Hogan had to overcome a good old-fashioned foreign invader. (And vanquishing the Canadian Earthquake at SummerSlam 1990 didn't count. He was better known as a Big Fat Villain than a Foreign Villain. You can be a big fat villain, or you can be a foreign villain. You can't be both. Unless you're Kamala. Or Yokozuna. Look, just forget I started this parenthetical.)

Luckily for Vince's planning, but unluckily in just about every other sense, especially for what most people considered to be good taste, the United States was in the thick of an all-new foreign tension: the actions of Saddam Hussein regarding Iraq's invasion of Kuwait. Wanting to play into the American public's suspicion and fear of Iraqi aggression, McMahon gambled on a Cold War–type tension rather than all-out war, and reintroduced Sgt. Slaughter to the WWF as a former American soldier turned Iraqi sympathizer. Dressed in an Iraqi military uniform and waving the flag of Iraq, and flanked by a new manager named General Adnan,* Slaughter proclaimed his love for and support of Saddam Hussein and the Iraqi people. He challenged Warrior for the WWF

---

* General Adnan actually was a Baghdad-born Iraqi whose real name was Adnan Bin Abdul Kareem Ahmed Alkaissy El Farthie. Adnan claimed in his autobiography that his family was a big deal in Iraq and that he went to high school with Saddam Hussein. In a truly classic soupçon of wrestling irony, this Iraqi-born pro wrestler spent the 1960s and 1970s pretending to be Native American, working under the name Billy White Wolf.

Championship at the 1991 Royal Rumble, and with the help of the Macho King's interference, he won the title.

The Iraqi-sympathizer story line, already an iffy idea when it was conceived, suffered from two final, poorly timed real-life events. Two days before Slaughter won the title at the Rumble, the United States and coalition forces began Operation Desert Storm, an actual war with Iraq. No longer was the WWF playing off racial and international tensions; they were now officially exploiting and attempting to profit off an active conflict in which American soldiers were losing their lives. And even worse for business (which is the only thing the company has historically cared about), the war lasted only five weeks. It was over completely by the end of February, which meant that WrestleMania VII on March 24, 1991, would give the WWF an entire month to try and play out the string of a conquering American hero fighting valiantly against the forces of Saddam Hussein to bring the championship "back" to the good old U.S. of A.—but given that the war had already been fought and won in unprecedented time, with a historically lopsided victory, it all came across as not only gauche, but redundant. Even for pro wrestling!

To compound disasters, even though the WWF had announced the Los Angeles Memorial Coliseum would host WrestleMania VII an entire year ahead of time—with hopes of filling the 106,000-seat stadium and breaking their own attendance record set by WrestleMania III—they had only managed to sell somewhere between 14,000 and 17,000 tickets before they cut off sales on February 5. Less than two months before the event, the WWF announced that they would be moving to the nearby Memorial Sports Arena, which was a tenth of the size of the original venue, but where they could claim a legitimate sellout. With arena employees working hard in the run-up, the WWF managed to rearrange everyone who had already bought seats. And while the 16,158 who made it into the Memorial Arena provided a legitimate sellout, it was a stinging embarrassment for McMahon, who had spent the past year assuming he was going to preside over the spectacle of 100,000 rabid Hulkamaniacs at what would have been the first outdoor WrestleMania.

In a great ironic twist, the most fondly remembered match from WrestleMania VII involved the Ultimate Warrior, who put his career up against Savage's career and came out the winner.

The summer of 1991 was spent with Hogan feuding with Slaughter in bloody "Desert Storm matches" (always gotta triple down on exploitation, even when it's biting you in the ass), culminating with Hogan teaming with Warrior to take on the allied Iraqi forces of Slaughter, Adnan, and Colonel Mustafa (the Iron Sheik with an Iraq palette-swap) at SummerSlam. But a backstage argument and demands by the Warrior ended up leading to a sudden and drastic falling-out between the company and one of its top stars.

Not feeling like he was getting his due, Warrior tried to strongarm McMahon into a bigger payday, threatening to no-show SummerSlam, the second biggest show of the year. "Ultimate Warrior basically came up to me and figuratively held a gun to my head and said, 'Hey, I'm not going to perform unless you pay me X number of dollars," McMahon said in the WWE-produced hatchet-job documentary *The Self-Destruction of the Ultimate Warrior*. "My responsibility is to present what I advertised," he continued. "My responsibility is to the audience. So I agreed to Warrior's demand, knowing what I was going to do as soon as he came out of the ring."

The match ended with Warrior chasing Adnan and Mustafa to the back while Hogan pinned Slaughter. Warrior wound up running all the way out of the company, and he wouldn't return until the following year's WrestleMania. "It gave me great pleasure to fire him and to let him know why I was doing it," McMahon said in the documentary. But of course, that isn't the whole truth.

Correspondence unearthed in 2014 revealed that Warrior had indeed made demands for a $550,000 payday and a reduced schedule a full six weeks before SummerSlam, stating that he wouldn't appear at WWF shows until he got his money. McMahon acquiesced, not only giving him his money, but stating in writing that "no other WWF athlete will be paid at a higher pay rate than you on pay-per-view events" and expressing his regret over the perceived slights, signing off with apologies and noting his respect for Warrior "as a man and as my friend."

On Warrior's own self-produced documentary, *Always Believe*, he revealed that he was pulled into McMahon's office immediately after making his way backstage after chasing the heels away from the ring in the SummerSlam main event. There, he was served with a suspension letter—mere moments after fulfilling his SummerSlam obligations. All the lip service, it seems, had been just that: a way to soothe Warrior long enough to get him to SummerSlam, and not a moment longer. The suspension letter was as scathing as McMahon's previous correspondence had been kind. "Your principal complaint apparently is that you are not being compensated at the same rate as Hulk Hogan," the letter read, "although 'Hulk' is a living legend, [Hulk] is a bigger star and draw at WWF events, is more dependable and is far more revered and respected by WWF fans and by the public at large.

"You have become a legend in your own mind; you are certainly entitled to your opinion."

Warrior attempted to refuse the suspension and resign on the spot, but the WWF instead refused to release him from his contract until it expired the following month.

The reality of the Ultimate Warrior assuming the top spot from Hogan just hadn't been as exciting as expected, and Warrior's charisma lacked even the puddle-deep nuance and variance of Hogan's character. But reinstalling Hogan wasn't a balm either, partly because fans were tiring of his antics and began turning on him, finally sick of seeing the same formula and routine after nearly eight years with Hogan on top, but also largely because of a brand-new scandal, one that threatened to tank the whole enterprise. Here's a hint: it rhymes with "steroids." Because it's steroids.

In January 1991, McMahon officially unveiled the World Bodybuilding Federation (WBF) with the introduction of the thirteen juiced bodybuilding monsters who he had poached from the IFBB (which then promptly blackballed them and promised outright war against McMahon as a bodybuilding interloper). Borrowing from his WWF branding, McMahon declared these men were not bodybuilders, but "WBF BodyStars." He announced plans for a weekly television show, a glossy WBF magazine, and the company's first pay-per-view championship, to be held on June 15. The PPV was an all-time-great train wreck: McMahon had worked to craft a gimmick or character for each of the BodyStars, all of which boiled down to "is jacked and also fucks." McMahon's gushing commentary on the various competitors' musculatures is a gift that continues to deliver to this very day.

Fans had already begun booing Hogan by mid-1991. The Hogan act was stale and getting staler, he refused to switch up his match formula, his look, or his shtick, and yet he remained the focal point of attention on WWF shows and as world champion. The longer Hogan remained on television, the clearer it became to the rapidly maturing young viewers that the character of Hulk Hogan smacked of disingenuousness. To naive children, Hogan looked like a confident superhero. To the more jaded and cynical eyes of preteens and teenagers, he just sort of acted like a jerk all the time. To older viewers, his attitude was even more jarring. Hulk Hogan was the guy who acted like your most over-the-top ardent supporter to your face, fucked your girlfriend behind your back, and then thought *you* were the asshole for not being able to figure it out. (And sometimes, like in the Hogan vs. Savage story line, that wasn't even the subtext—it was right out on front street.)

To make matters worse, there was a new star who had just arrived in the WWF who instantly captivated fans: Sid Justice. The former Sid Vicious in WCW was even bigger than Hogan, and while he lacked Hogan's in-ring skills, he was always infused with an ability to hold people's interest and attention. Even though the Ultimate Warrior experiment had failed, fans were still very eager to find a new hero to rally behind after eight long years of little else except Hulk Hogan at the center of the pro wrestling universe. Fans began going ballistic for Sid, especially when he was in the ring with Hogan.

By the January 1992 Royal Rumble, fans were chanting for Sid in opposition to Hogan. The WWF's response was to turn Sid against Hogan, retaining Hogan's positioning as their main-event babyface, and to edit replays so that chants for Sid were turned into cheers for Hogan. This video manipulation to achieve a desired fan reaction would remain part of WWE's repertoire to this very day. The Sid/Hogan backlash and the WWF's insistence on sticking with a wrestler and a story despite vehement crowd objection was the first modern example of the WWF refusing to let new stars be created organically. It's possible McMahon was gun-shy after his most recent groundswell star, the Ultimate Warrior, flamed out on top and developed an ego that he could never get a handle on how to properly manage—unlike Hogan's. Whatever the case, the WWF's bullheaded need to control fan emotion and reaction would not go away.

As for Hellwig, he dabbled in various ventures for a few years before returning to the WWF for less than four months in 1996 before being terminated for missing house shows in July. This was the final straw for McMahon, who washed his hands of him entirely. Warrior took part in three matches in WCW in 1998, and then only wrestled one more match over the course of the rest of his life, in 2008. The split with the WWF and his presence as a headache for McMahon for so much of his run led to him being persona non grata with the company for nearly twenty years. The rift between Warrior and McMahon culminated in the release of the aforementioned DVD, *The Self-Destruction of the Ultimate Warrior*. The quasi-documentary portrayed Hellwig as a delusional buffoon who believed too much in his own gimmick and developed an unchecked ego that outpaced his limited ability as a wrestler. The documentary caused Warrior to go scorched earth on WWE for years, until the two parties finally made peace in 2013. In 2014, Warrior (who legally changed his name to "Warrior" in 1993 for trademark purposes) was inducted into the WWE Hall of Fame during WrestleMania weekend, then appeared on *Raw* on the Monday after WrestleMania to give an impassioned speech in his Ultimate Warrior character. He died of a heart attack the very next day.

Posthumously, the company leaned into the Ultimate Warrior as an inspirational figure, hero, and role model. It was a surprising choice to many fans and critics, as Warrior had spent nearly all his time away from WWE being an outspoken bigot, one who would nowadays be recognized as a far-right pundit. He lambasted homosexuals and non-Americans, shamed Hurricane Katrina victims, celebrated a cancer diagnosis for Bobby Heenan, and cried about reverse racism on Martin Luther King Day (after suggesting King was a trumped-up blowhard who exaggerated his own accomplishments to gain notoriety). In light of his extensive history of being a deeply hateful human, it was jarring to see his name and likeness attached to endless breast cancer awareness campaigns* with the slogan "Be a Warrior." His widow, Dana Warrior, became a public relations and community ambassador for the company and eventually moved into a role in weekly WWE Creative in 2019.

When news outlets contacted WWE to inquire as to why

---

* WWE's long partnership with the Susan G. Komen Foundation is another sticking point for many fans, as this nonprofit is under constant fire for its shady business dealings, its focus on litigating the pink ribbon as its intellectual property, and the tiny amount of money it donates to cancer research compared to how much it rakes in from donors annually.

someone who once celebrated celebrities getting cancer as proof that "Karma is just a beautiful thing to behold" would be the face of a cancer awareness campaign, WWE issued a press release clarifying that the *spirit* of the *character* of the Ultimate Warrior was the focus of the campaign, not the actual person who *portrayed* that character. (You know, the only person who ever played the character and was so personally invested and linked to it that he legally changed his name to close the gap between the two.) So, much like Hulk Hogan's ten-inch penis, the *character* of the Ultimate Warrior is something pretty impressive that almost no one got to see—because it never existed.*

The Ultimate Warrior experiment had failed spectacularly, and the WWF found itself in a spectacularly unsavory position. With no other star big enough or trusted enough to carry the company, they were forced once again to let everything ride on Hogan—someone for whom fan sentiment and public opinion was at an all-time low.

---

* Two of the most incredibly tone-deaf moments regarding the posthumous Ultimate Warrior legacy occurred within a recent eight-month window: for GLAAD Spirit Day in 2018 and then again for Pride Month in 2019, Dana Warrior posted on social media a message of solidarity with and empathy for the LGBT community—accompanied by a studio photo of her in full Ultimate Warrior face paint. You'd think that in 2019, it would be understood that you shouldn't tell the gay community how much you love and respect them while literally cosplaying as the most notoriously homophobic pro wrestler of the modern era, but some wrestling personalities just seem determined to wade through a river of shit and tell you it's a great day for fishing.

10

HULK WHO?

The Gamble of the New Generation

Ninety seconds into the main event of SummerSlam 1992, a gasping Davey Boy Smith whispered to his brother-in-law, Bret Hart, as a raucous, sold-out Wembley Stadium crowd screamed hard enough to shake the hard camera of the PPV broadcast. "Bret, I'm fooked. I can't re-member anything," Smith panted.

According to Hart's autobiography, Smith, formerly one-half of the British Bulldogs, had been spending the weeks leading up to his first PPV main event smoking crack nightly with their other brother-in-law, Jim Neidhart. The Bulldog was given a chance to be the conquering hero by capturing his first singles title in the WWF—Hart's Intercontinental Championship—on his home soil. It was the World Wrestling Federation's first (and to date, only) domestic pay-per-view to emanate from the United Kingdom, but Smith had arrived strung out and bloated. Less than two minutes into a twenty-five-minute main event, he was completely gassed and couldn't recall a single spot of the match Hart had meticulously tried to put together as a showcase. "Davey, just listen to me," Hart replied. "I'll carry you." And carry he did, lifting the dead weight of his opponent for the next twenty-three minutes.

As it turned out, the replacement for Hogan (at least in the short term) ended up being under McMahon's nose the entire time, already in his employ and never having caused a problem before. It took that emotional, instant classic main event in England for Vince to finally realize that he'd found his next world champion.

The departures of Hogan, Warrior, and Justice in short order, combined with a growing desperation to find top draws and faces of the company who weren't likely to get busted for drug or steroid abuse (mostly the latter), opened the door—for the first time since Vince Jr. took over the company—for the smaller wrestler to have his day in the sun. Keep in mind, of course, that the "smaller guy" epithet was all relative. Most of the performers in question were still over six feet tall and somewhere in the neighborhood of 230 to 250 pounds.

This was going on between 1992 and 1995, at the same time as the WWF was hit with a series of major scandals that turned parents, interest groups, and advertisers solidly against the company and hurt the bottom line of every aspect of the WWF's business. By 1994, with the CEO of the

WWF staring down the barrel of serious federal charges, the company was facing the twin dangers of bankruptcy (or going out of business altogether) and figuring out how to keep the company running if Vince McMahon found himself serving prison time.

In the midst of the attempted transition away from Hulk Hogan as the company's foremost (and at times only) drawing card, McMahon threw himself into multimedia ventures, making his one and only foray into promoting a boxing PPV in 1988. (It was a disaster.) He moved on to the other love in his life, bodybuilding, founding the World Bodybuilding Federation. Long a devoted muscle freak (if the chemically enhanced bodies he snatched up to feature on his television programs weren't already loving exhibits of his passion every week), McMahon was an amateur bodybuilder himself, spending hours in the gym every day starting in the 1980s until he was well into his seventies. Wrestling fans wouldn't find out for nearly another decade, but the Lego-haired announcer who appeared on WWF television each week had an assortment of engorged and jostling muscles under his pastel-colored suits that put to shame many of the wrestlers he employed. Though it's likely the WBF was never going to catch on like McMahon hoped, he literally could not have picked a worse year to launch a company almost entirely based around performance-enhancing drugs.

While McMahon was presenting steroid-engorged monsters on weekly WWF television and tumescent, anthropomorphic steroids in the WBF, the United States government was nearing the end of its three-year-long pursuit of the doctor who had been the dedicated source of steroids and growth hormone for many of McMahon's wrestlers since

1981. The sports world had been given a more-or-less free ride up to the 1980s regarding steroids. They weren't criminalized, and while it seems strange to imagine today, the negative side effects of long-term steroid abuse were not at all well known and were actively downplayed among athletes and weightlifters. As the 1980s bowed, this is when the freakish physiques adorning the covers of *Flex* and *Muscle & Fitness* became the norm. Bodybuilders saw what Arnold Schwarzenegger and Lou Ferrigno looked like in the 1970s and said, "Well, shit, we can get on WAY more gas than those guys." So they did!

In 1988, the federal government really began cracking down on illegal steroid use and steroid trafficking. One of the first whales it landed was a urologist named George Zahorian, a lifelong wrestling fan who had ingratiated himself with the WWF to such an extent that he was known as "the good Doctor" by the boys in the back. In 1991, a sting operation by the feds led to the arrest and indictment of Zahorian, who was tipped off to heat on him by someone in the WWF front office, but still didn't manage to clean house (or stop dealing in tens of thousands of dollars' worth of steroids at a time to clients) before the hammer came down. Officers found him in his office tearing up FedEx receipts for shipments to WWF clients, including Roddy Piper, as he surreptitiously attempted to "call his lawyer." Remember, kids: if you're going to commit a series of felonies, always invest in a paper shredder.

According to an indictment from the Justice Department, Zahorian "sold steroids to 43 pro wrestlers, 37 of whom were employed by McMahon's WWF when deliveries were made" over the course of nearly the entire span of the original Hulkamania era. Zahorian was about as close as you could get to an official pipeline for steroids to get to WWF wrestlers, and his branching out into supplying steroids to amateurs in the bodybuilding world, as well as to aspiring Olympians, attracted the attention of the feds. He was indicted and went to trial in 1991 following a sting operation where he was caught on tape selling steroids to a powerlifter and boasting that he was giving him a better deal than he gave his wrestler clients.

During Zahorian's trial in June and July 1991 (beginning just after the first WBF PPV, in a chef's kiss of delectable timing), wrestlers Billy Graham, Rick Martel, Dan Spivey, and Roddy Piper were compelled to testify. Zahorian named names on the witness stand regarding his clients—the most notable being the biggest name possible: Hulk Hogan.

Zahorian was convicted of twelve felony counts and sentenced to three years in prison, plus many years of probation. Considering he faced up to forty-four years in prison for selling controlled substances and distributing steroids for nonmedical purposes, he probably considers himself pretty lucky. Almost immediately upon conviction, Zahorian began cooperating with the Justice Department as they began building a much more high-profile case: one against Vince McMahon and the World Wrestling Federation.

The WWF claimed it would soon be implementing an across-the-board and unbeatable steroid-testing policy, with dire consequences for failure. The WWF's first steroid-testing policy would end up not being implemented until November, and it was far from unbeatable. (No such testing policy was ever put in place in the WBF, for obvious reasons, although that endeavor would be shuttered in 1992. In 2020, public relations for WWE is a well-oiled juggernaut, offering expert deflections or mea culpas or minor concessions as the situation dictates. In 1991, however, a company-wide attempt at saving face in the wake of a national scandal was still getting reps in.) Another devastating blow was dealt to the reputation of the company shortly after the Zahorian verdict, and it came from the worst possible source: Hulk Hogan.

Mere weeks after the end of Zahorian's trial, with newspapers across the country running a photograph of the doctor flanked by a beaming Hogan and a disheveled McMahon, the three men arm-in-arm, Hogan appeared on *The Arsenio Hall Show*—a booking that had been scheduled for a good amount of time. The WWF and Hogan had enough advance notice to either pull Hogan from his appearance during this time of increased scrutiny, or to come up with a game plan that would have allowed the company and their biggest star to attempt to get back in the good graces of their fans and the general public. Most observers assumed Hogan was going to come to the show hat in hand, humbling himself and making a full apology—perhaps even asking for forgiveness. None of that happened. Instead, Hogan took the defensive, insisting that he was clean and that he had only used steroids three times in his life, all when he was world champion in 1983, and merely for rehabilitation purposes, dealing with an arm injury that threatened to keep him out of action for an entire year. The lie was palpable to everyone in the studio audience and watching at home, and not just because he was never world champion in 1983 and there is no record of him being injured nor of any injury rumor in 1983 or 1984, or indeed any record of him missing any time at all over that span.

Many in the public eye were well aware of Hogan and the WWF's penchant for exaggeration, but this was the first time most were seeing these talents on display in the service of outright lying to the public about real-life, serious concerns. It did not go over well, and the public outcry was swift. Parents did not like knowing that the role-model face of a family entertainment company was on steroids—they probably long suspected that was the case, but to brazenly deny responsibility made it all seem worse. Hogan began appearing toxic to advertisers and the general public.

To make matters worse, while trying to put out the fire of the steroids taint getting out into the open, they were hit by a slew of allegations all at once. The shit completely hit the fan beginning in January, when *Inside Edition* ran a story on Hogan's rampant steroid use, featuring comments from Billy Graham and David Schultz and complete with FedEx receipts for shipments from Zahorian. As a cherry on top of the dunk-on-Hogan sundae, the program spliced together clips of various Hogan interviews where he explicitly contradicted himself—the first of many times Hogan would be publicly called on the carpet for his constantly shifting personal narrative depending on whatever suited him best at any given moment. According to a 1992 issue of *The Wrestling Observer Newsletter*, WWF lawyer for life Jerry McDevitt (who began representing the company in 1987, helping to get charges against Jim Neidhart dropped after Neidhart was accused of assaulting an airline attendant) attempted to get *Inside Edition* to kill the story, but no dice. Shortly thereafter, Graham went on a radio show to talk about Hogan's cocaine use while the two were back in the AWA, and that story also picked up steam. By February, advertisers and licensing execs across the board were viewing Hogan as a toxic name and face. As such, they began pulling away, and the WWF began featuring him less prominently outside of the weekly television shows.

In mid-February, the St. Louis police staged a major raid on a WWF show in the city. Luckily for the WWF, the boys were tipped off prior to arriving at the arena and ditched their shit, leaving the drug-sniffing dogs with nothing to sniff and the cops with nothing to find.

Not all the scandals were drug-related. Right on the heels of an ill-timed arrest and suspension of the deeply troubled Kerry Von Erich for drug possession, Barry Orton, who was Bob Orton's brother and worked for several years as a WWF enhancement talent under the name Barry O, began speaking to several outlets about sexual harassment he suffered by executives within the WWF. At the end of February, WWF senior vice president of wrestling operations Pat Patterson and his vice president of wrestling operations Terry Garvin (one of two pro wrestlers of the era who went by that name, much to the chagrin of the *other* Terry Garvin) resigned from the company following allegations of sexual misconduct against company employees made by two former members of the ring crew, both of whom were underage at the time of the alleged assaults, in addition to the separate accusations coming from Orton. The *New York Post* picked up the story, as *Post* columnist Phil Mushnick rolled the steroid and sexual assault allegations into a series of spectacular scorched-earth columns—kicking off a bitter vendetta between McMahon and Mushnick that continues to this day.

Later in March, national outlets like *People*, *Entertainment Tonight*, *SportsCenter*, and *The Phil Donahue Show* all ran stories about allegations of steroid abuse, underage sex abuse, and sexual harassment after the *San Diego Union-Tribune* ran a front-page story detailing what sounded like a bacchanal of illicit activity behind the scenes in the supposedly family-friendly company. Even McMahon himself admitted in an interview that Hogan wasn't exactly telling the truth during his appearance on *Arsenio* but insisted that the WWF's steroid-testing policy—which was finally implemented in November 1991 after months of delays, keep in mind—was more rigid than that of the International Olympic Committee.

Patterson, the first-ever WWF Intercontinental Champion and Vince's right-hand man at the time, was known as a booking savant, having come up with the concept of the Royal Rumble match and other innovations. It was no secret among the boys that in his personal life, he had been openly gay since the 1970s, and in kayfabe it was one of the most open secrets in all of professional wrestling. Thanks to the spectacularly abysmal social mores of the time, his being a gay man was occasionally a running joke of blunt double entendres on WWE commentary throughout the nineties. After finally coming out on WWE television and in WWE canon in 2014, Patterson claimed to have been with the same partner for over forty years until his partner's death in 1998, but the rumors and stories of his sexual appetite are plentiful.

Of course, given the prevailing culture, such workplace harassment may have been dismissed as harmless grab-assery had it manifested itself as heterosexual groping in a corporate environment. Given that it was alleged to have happened backstage in the 1980s and 1990s at a pro wrestling show, few batted an eye. Graham alleged to have seen Patterson and Garvin groping the genitals and bottoms of ring boys—Orton claimed Garvin and Patterson groped him during a car ride between towns years earlier—and heard promises to wrestlers of increased television time and pushes in exchange for blowjobs and other sexual favors. Graham eventually recanted, and there is no concrete evidence to back up any of his allegations. (Years later, wrestler Paul Roma would also claim to have been offered "career advancement" within the company in exchange for sexual favors for Patterson. According to Roma, this offer was given in the home of Patterson and his partner, with both men sitting beside him.)

Just before all this news broke, former WBF announcer Murray Hodgson sued McMahon for wrongful termination, and initially was planning to sue for sexual harassment, claiming he was fired for turning down advances from Patterson—although he quickly dropped that count from the legal proceedings. Around the same time, ring announcer Mel Phillips was suspended, and then later quietly released after being connected to a number of child molestation allegations, including reportedly performing oral sex on a ten-year-old in a car in 1982.

Two of the ring boys accusing executives of sexual harassment went on the record, including Tom Cole, who was twenty at the time the piece ran, but was just thirteen when he first allegedly got pressured into sexual favors while working on the ring crew. He claimed that at age thirteen, a WWF employee (believed to be Phillips) would film the boys rubbing their feet on his crotch. Cole claimed that he was driven to a WWF official's house and offered drugs and sex with a man there. After refusing, he was fired by the WWF the next day. However, just days after going public with his story, Cole's harassment lawsuit was settled out of court. Cole received in the neighborhood of $70,000, plus a multiyear contract working behind the scenes for the WWF.

In the most lasting and memorable document of the sexual harassment allegations, McMahon inexplicably agreed to be part of a panel of guests on *The Phil Donahue Show*—a panel that also included Billy Graham and Bruno Sammartino (long at odds with McMahon), Hodgson, Orton, Dave Meltzer, and others. Viewed today, the show is a stunning example of closed-mindedness and insensitivity, as the crowd continually bursts into full-throated laughter nearly every time there is a mention of gay sex or sexual favors between men. McMahon, for one of the first times, played the public role of the villain (albeit not intentionally), continually booed by the crowd and coming across as callous in his remarks to Hodgson and Orton, in particular. He repeatedly stressed that all men accused of misconduct were no longer with the company, and that he was completely unaware of any impropriety in the WWF at any time during his position as owner. Although, as Phil Mushnick reported, McMahon had told both him and Dave Meltzer weeks prior that Phillips had been fired in 1988 because "Phillips' relationship with kids seemed peculiar and unnatural." In fact, Phillips was rehired just two weeks after his 1988 firing under the proviso that he stay away from kids.

Thanks in large part to getting Tom Cole into the fold, the scandal blew over within months and all remaining lawsuits were dropped, after which Patterson was immediately rehired. Patterson remained full-time with the company until

2004, including a prominent on-air role during the Attitude Era as one of McMahon's "Stooges," not a reference to the slapstick legends the Three Stooges, but to the long-standing pro wrestling epithet for front-office lackeys who inform on the boys to a promoter in exchange for staying in a company's good graces. Patterson remains with WWE in various capacities to this day, occasionally working as an ambassador, appearing on WWE television or WWE Network, and sometimes called in to assist with booking. He was inducted into the WWE Hall of Fame in 1996—a class that also included Jimmy Snuka and Vince McMahon Sr.

The sexual assault scandal dovetailed with the continuing conversation about steroids in the public eye—in sports in general, and in the WWF in particular. Hogan's blatant lies on national television about his past and current steroid use continued to rankle fans and nonfans alike, and with the WWF's first actual steroid policy in place, Hogan and everyone else up and down the card began slimming down and looking less impressive. (In hindsight, the less-bloated and more defined physiques of people who were cycling off steroids but worked out constantly are still hugely impressive, but the roster moving from "freak show superhumans" to "very in-shape guys" was at odds with the aesthetic McMahon had been cultivating since taking over the company.) When the Ultimate Warrior returned at WrestleMania VIII to save Hogan from a postmatch beatdown in the main event, he was so much smaller than when he first left the company (combined with a new haircut, notoriously confusing to pre-internet sports fans) that an instant and pervasive rumor (which lasted nearly the rest of Hellwig's life) popped

up insisting this was an all-new performer using the Ultimate Warrior gimmick.

With the heat on the steroids scandal only beginning to
pick up steam, the convicted Dr. Zahorian continued to
work with federal prosecutors to build a case against Mc-
Mahon and the WWF. As such, Hogan took an extended
leave of absence from the company, leaving a vacuum at the
top of the card that one would imagine McMahon hoped
to fill with Sid Justice, but Justice quit the company in the
same month that Hogan left, largely due to issues working opposite the notoriously difficult Warrior (whose professional demeanor hadn't improved much during his time
away). Any hope of Warrior taking Hogan's spot as top dog
in the company dissolved completely in September when he
decided to get braggy about steroids. Given all the heat on
the company for steroid use, the internal policy at the time
was that steroid levels should be *decreasing* from the base-
line levels present at the time of the public scrutiny. Not a
terrific policy, but what are you going to do, ban steroids in
wrestling? Perish the thought. Warrior opted to volunteer
on a phone call to McMahon (later recalled in depositions
and court testimony) that he had just attempted to order a
shipment of HGH, but it had been seized at customs. He also
happily divulged that Davey Boy Smith had hooked him up
with the growth hormone supplier in question. Since that
casual phone conversation arrived at possibly the least opportune time for the WWF, both Warrior and Smith were
fired and finished with the company by November 1992.

There were three main performers who were given a look
as focal points of the new, smaller WWF. The first was Ric

Flair, who was at that point a multitime world champion and a pro wrestling icon on the same level as Hulk Hogan—but, in contrast to Hogan, was known as the very best in-ring pro wrestler in the world. To fans of the NWA, WCW, and Southern wrestling, Flair was the end-all and be-all, and could both wrestle and talk rings around McMahon's top draws—including (and especially) Hulk Hogan. Whether as a good guy or a bad guy, Flair's flamboyant "Nature Boy"— following in the tradition of Buddy Rogers before him—was a jet-flying, limousine-riding, kiss-stealing, wheeling-dealing son of a gun—and fans of both the WWF and its competitors had dreamed of a Flair vs. Hogan match throughout the 1980s to settle the question of who was the biggest and best in the sport.

In an unbelievable stroke of good luck for McMahon, Flair jumped ship from WCW to the WWF in late 1991 while being the active WCW and NWA World Heavyweight Champion. When Flair first popped up on WWF television in August 1991, he carried the iconic "big gold belt" of the NWA with him and proclaimed himself the "real world champion." WCW filed suit in short order to block their intellectual property from being paraded around on WWF television, but the impact had been made.

When Flair first came aboard, the plan was to build to a series of Hogan vs. Flair matches, with the idea that the longtime face of WWF would take on the longtime face of pretty much all non-WWF wrestling to determine who was the biggest and best star in the entire world. The two did face off at a number of house shows early on, but the dream match failed to provide a significant boost to ticket sales, and the two wrestlers' egos clashed. So, Flair captured the vacant

WWF Championship by winning the 1992 Royal Rumble. (Thanks in part to an all-time dick move by Hogan, who, as a supposed babyface, grabbed onto his supposed "friend" Sid Justice's arm after being eliminated *in a there-are-no-friends, anything-goes match* and allowed Flair to eliminate Justice and win the match. Fans rightfully and lustily booed Hogan for his treachery, but the WWF continued on with a heel Justice vs. babyface Hogan as the main event of Wrestle-Mania that year, undaunted. Hogan stepped away from the company after that match, much to everyone's relief.)

The second major, "smaller" star at the time was Shawn Michaels, who in late 1991 turned on his Rockers teammate Marty Jannetty by throwing him through a fake barber shop window. Rechristening himself "The Heartbreak Kid," Michaels quickly became the most notable heel in the midcard and became a legitimate World Championship contender by the end of 1992, not least because of the increasingly close friendship he was cultivating behind the scenes with Vince McMahon. In time, McMahon would come to view Michaels as a surrogate son—or at the very least, someone he watched out for—which is surely the only reason Michaels got away with as much bad behavior as he did. But Michaels's singles run began a long run of kissing ass, politicking, and throwing other wrestlers under the bus to suit his own aspirations.

And the third major new "little guy" star, coincidentally enough, was the man who had once made greener-than-goose-shit "Megaman" Tom Magee look so good that McMahon thought he had found his next world champion. It took some circuitous travels, but eventually Bret "The Hitman" Hart parlayed his loyalty and his reputation as the best wrestler in McMahon's employ (or at least the best wrestler who wasn't a perceived outsider, like Flair) into the main event. After gaining legions of fans over the course of a couple of Intercontinental Championship reigns beginning in 1991, he captured his first world title from Flair in October 1992, two months after helping to sell out the 80,000-seat Wembley Stadium in London at SummerSlam 1992. The event and its success were made possible almost entirely on the strength of the feud between Hart and his real-life brother-in-law, the British Bulldog Davey Boy Smith. Intrigue was ramped up leading into the match with the idea that Hart's sister and Smith's wife, the conveniently named Diana, was torn as to whom to support in the match. Smith was enormously popular, especially in England, where he was the most prominent star on WWF television to hail from the United Kingdom. The WWF, while still airing on Sky, had taken over ITV's Saturday morning wrestling spot in 1987, eventually giving *World of Sport* the boot altogether, and by 1992 was the foremost wrestling promotion in the minds of U.K. fans.

As a bowl-cut-and-windbreaker-clad child noted in Hart vs. Smith's opening fan atmosphere pretape, "The British Bulldog's gonna win . . . whether he wants to or not." While Smith did emerge the victor—the hometown boy making good in front of his home crowd as fireworks went off over London—he was carrying far more muscle than his body was built for, and was woefully unprepared for the conditioning required for the match that Hart had plotted out for them. He was completely gassed less than a minute into the bout and whispered that Hart would have to carry him from there. Hart did, as he was determined to make both of them live up to the main event spot they'd been given. At times literally carrying Smith and more or less wrestling dead weight for nearly twenty-six minutes, Hart pulled off a miracle, willing himself to an instant classic. McMahon took note of all of it: the professionalism, the pride, the work ethic, and the rapturous attention and ear-shattering reaction of the sold-out throng at Wembley. Hart was the only logical choice to elevate to world champion and unseat Flair, whose contract would be up sooner than not.

After a brief world title feud with Michaels, Hart moved on to his biggest opponent—literally. Rodney Anoa'i, a 6-foot-4, 600-pound Samoan whom McMahon was able to pass off as a Japanese sumo wrestler named Yokozuna, merged two of McMahon's favorite tropes: evil foreigner and literally larger-than-life human. And yet, even as Yokozuna was being groomed to become champion, McMahon couldn't resist one more dalliance with his favorite son, the Hulkster. WrestleMania IX, still the consensus pick as the worst WrestleMania of all time nearly thirty years later, was an afternoon show in a chintzy venue, with a lackluster card being presented in front of a lackluster crowd of 16,000 people or so at Caesars Palace in Las Vegas. Bret Hart lost the WWF Championship to Yokozuna, but Hogan appeared at ringside after the match and "valiantly" challenged Yoko for the title in an impromptu main event, defeating him for the title in a paltry twenty-two seconds.

Via a combination of steroid scrutiny, Hogan's ego, and a number of other, lesser factors, Hogan and his manager and consigliere Jimmy Hart laid the groundwork to make their official break with the company. As such, Yokozuna regained the title in June 1993 at the first King of the Ring pay-per-view. In typical Hogan fashion, the original plan was for him to drop the title to Hart at SummerSlam, but he refused on the grounds that Hart was "too small" to believably defeat him. Hart had to instead settle for being crowned the first recognized King of the Ring, and Yokozuna continued to feud with Hogan on the house show circuit until August, when Hogan took his ball and went home.

In 1994, Hogan signed an absolutely massive contract with Ted Turner to become the new face of WCW, where he instantly began a lengthy "greatest of all time" feud against Ric Flair (who had himself returned to WCW in early 1993). WCW had McMahon's biggest-ever star and the potential money feud that McMahon had passed on, and McMahon now had an undersized (in his mind) roster and a looming federal steroid trial. McMahon tried to create one more muscleman in the Hogan vein with a freshly patriotic Lex Luger, but WWF fans preferred Hart as their world champion.

New Generation Wrestlers

While McMahon's focus on "sports entertainment" above both "sports" and "wrestling" had always yielded some strange results (as we touched on when we ran down some of his more baffling character creations in the late eighties and early nineties), he seemed to go into overdrive with goofy, over-the-top cartoon characters as gimmicks in the mid-1990s, possibly to compensate for or distract from the fact that the roster was no longer juiced to the gills. Between 1991 and 1998, when the New Generation was finally supplanted by the Attitude Era, McMahon's WWF introduced the following characters. (And this is just a small sampling of the gimmicks we were treated to.)

IRWIN R. SCHYSTER. The wrestling accountant was possibly meant to be viewed as a literal manifestation of the Internal Revenue Service. Journeyman wrestler Mike Rotunda was turned into IRS, who wrestled in suspenders, a dress shirt, dress pants, and a tie, and carried a briefcase that probably contained important, confidential tax documents and almost certainly shouldn't have been left at ringside. IRS was joined (although not as one unit or stable, which would have been incredible) by similar "wrestling occupation" characters such as wrestling garbage man **Duke "The Dumpster" Droese**, wrestling monk **Friar Ferguson**, wrestling plumber **T.L. Hopper**, wrestling hockey player **the Goon**, wrestling baseball player **MVP, aka Abe "Knuckleball" Schwartz**, wrestling dentist **Isaac Yankem, DDS**, wrestling pig farmers **Phineas I. Godwinn** and **Henry O. Godwinn** (look at the subtle coding of their initials), wrestling NASCAR driver **Bob "Spark Plug" Holly**, wrestling personal trainers **the Bodydonnas**, wrestling roadie **the Roadie**, and wrestling Mountie **the Mountie**. They don't all have to have a clever name, people.

GIANT GONZALEZ. Poached from WCW, the former El Gigante was an Argentinian former basketball player who stood at a legitimate 7 feet 7 inches tall and was the tallest wrestler in history at the time. As such, he was billed as being eight feet tall by any promoter who booked him, and McMahon adorned him in a nude body suit with conveniently placed tufts of fur and called him Giant González, insinuating he was either some sort of missing link or an actual Sasquatch (or perhaps a fucked-up wendigo). His most notable WWF appearance was at the aforementioned WrestleMania IX, where he was such a fearsome, savage beast that he *attempted to murder the Undertaker in the ring by chloroforming him*. He lost the match by disqualification, and the Undertaker was a forgiving enough man to not press charges for attempted murder.

THE BERZERKER. John Nord, who aped many of the mannerisms of the far more beloved Bruiser Brody, was brought into the WWF as a living, breathing Viking giant, complete with sword, shield, furry boots, and horned helmet. He picked up the lion's share of his victories by countout, as his character was too addle-brained to know how to pin opponents, but he was cognizant enough to once *attempt to murder the Undertaker by stabbing at him with his actual, real sword*. The Undertaker has been attempted-murdered by so many opponents over the course of his career that he has an extremely good case for an unsafe working environment lawsuit against the WWF. In kayfabe, I mean. And also in real life.

DOINK THE CLOWN. The original concept of Doink the Clown (and the gimmick's original performer, Matt Borne) is far more inspired than it ended up being. Doink debuted as a twisted, evil clown who wanted to make children cry through malicious pranks. It was basically Pennywise crossed with the Joker. After a series of less-than-inspired goofs, Doink just became a straight-up, pie-throwing circus clown who wanted to make people laugh, accompanied by his diminutive doppelganger, Dink. Dink the Clown.

REPO MAN. It is a relief, many years after the fact, to learn that there is an actual reason why the Repo Man character made not a lick of sense. Played by Barry Darsow, who was Smash in Demolition and fake Russian Krusher Kruschev prior to that, the Repo Man wore a Hamburglar domino mask, a trench coat, and a singlet with tire tracks on it, and carried a rope and hook to the ring. He would "repossess" the cherished items of babyface wrestlers (like Randy Savage's urn, which he really shouldn't be making payments on anyway) and would cackle and scurry like a Hanna-Barbera villain. According to the *Wrestling Observer*, there was a wrestler in Florida working under a Repo Man gimmick (which was much closer to an actual repo man and not a Riddler knockoff), and that Repo Man's friend called *his* friend at the WWF, J.J. Dillon, to tell him about the cool gimmick. After the tip, the WWF cut out the middleman and trademarked the "Repo Man" name in 1991, then started suing the poor guy in Florida for gimmick infringement. By the time Darsow needed repackaging, the company already had the Repo Man trademark in-house. Waste not, want not. Don't feel bad for Darsow, because he eventually made his way to WCW, where he became an evil golfer named "Mr. Hole-In-One" in 1997.

MANTAUR. It's a wrestling minotaur, only the half-bull guy would remove his bull head before wrestling, revealing a chubby guy with horns painted on his face. If you think this gimmick sounds like it actually kind of rules, I don't think you're wrong.

CRUSH, AKA KONA CRUSH. Formerly the third member of Demolition, the Hawaii native was repackaged as a Fanta-colored do-gooder with one of the most resplendent mullets the wrestling world has ever seen (which is no small feat). His gimmick was that his whole life, he's been so strong that he's just been *crushing* things. So now he wants to crush—for good! For the *children*. His finishing move was squeezing a guy's head, and in kayfabe you were supposed to believe that if the guy didn't give up in time, this crush-happy noodlehead would just make pulp out of someone's brains. For the children.

BASTION BOOGER. Mike Shaw actually started his New Generation WWF career in 1993 under the name **Friar Ferguson**, a wrestling monk. Shockingly, this gimmick wasn't dropped because he was a *wrestling monk*, but because of complaints by the Catholic Church, which has always definitely had its priorities in order. Shaw was repackaged as Bastion Booger, a gross fat guy in a stained singlet who would eat during matches. His gimmick was that he was fat and gross, because fat people are gross, and you should boo them when you're not being horrified by their mere presence.

ETHNIC WRESTLER LIGHTNING ROUND! Saba Simba was played by 1970s wrestling star Tony Atlas, who now became a spear-toting noble African warrior. **Tatanka** cashed in on the popularity of *Dances with Wolves*, but was at least played by actual Lumbee tribe member Chris Chavis. I hesitate to lump in **Papa Shango** with bad gimmicks, but he was a black voodoo doctor who made the Ultimate Warrior barf and bleed green oil from his forehead and caused jobbers' feet to burst into flame via incantations, so I have to retain my journalistic objectivity somehow. **The Headshrinkers** were the 1990s' entry into the not-very-proud tradition of Samoan savages, although team member Fatu would get a positive makeover in 1995 as a former gang member who wanted to "make a difference" in the lives of the youth. But whoops! The only difference he made was being whisked off television and reintroduced as **The Sultan**, an evil, masked mute who was evil in part because he was vaguely from the "Middle East," and in part because his tongue had been cut out. Don't worry—Fatu eventually found lasting fame and success as dancing, ass-based wrestler Rikishi, whose love of putting his enormous derriere in opponents' faces was several steps up from his previous gimmicks. Speaking of repackaging, longtime midcard babyface stalwart and two-time Intercontinental and Tag Team Champion Tito Santana was reintroduced in 1991, as the storied Mexican hero inexplicably became Spanish bull-fighter **El Matador.** The masked, martial-arts-practicing "evil Oriental" wrestler **Kwang** didn't stick around long, instead opting to retool the actual Puerto Rican wrestler portraying Kwang into the proud Puerto Rican **Savio Vega**, originally introduced as a close childhood friend of fake Cuban Razor Ramon. **"The Portuguese Man O' War" Aldo Montoya** put eventual ECW World Champion Justin Credible under a bright yellow mask that everyone agreed looked exactly like a jock strap. Last (not actually anywhere close to last, but for the sake of brevity, last in this rundown), there was the extremely black-pimp-coded **Flash Funk**. Apparently, the problem with Flash Funk was that his being a pimp was mostly subtext: onetime Papa Shango Charles Wright would eventually find himself in the WWE Hall of Fame on the strength of being Literal Pimp with Agency **The Godfather**. The lesson here is that ethnic characters are definitely the pits, but you never know what might happen for your career if you really lean in.

XANTA CLAUS. Late ECW legend Balls Mahoney got his WWF start by playing an evil relative of Santa Claus. That's it. That's the gimmick.

ADAM BOMB. One of the rare "really jacked guy" performers of the New Generation, Adam Bomb wore radiation goggles that revealed glowing green eyes and sported a bright red tongue and claimed to be the result of a mutation resulting from his surviving the Three Mile Island nuclear disaster. The wrestler playing Adam Bomb, Bryan Clark, in reality grew up not far from Three Mile Island, which leads me to believe that McMahon came up with the Adam Bomb character via Clark telling him about his background while McMahon was opening a pack of Garbage Pail Kids.

SKINNER. Future WWE trainer Steve Keirn's run in the WWF was as a tobacco-drenched alligator hunter named Skinner. We couldn't even have the pleasure of a meme, as Skinner had come and gone well before Superintendent Chalmers's signature wail made its debut on *The Simpsons*.

NAILZ was a plodding 6-foot-5, 300-pound wrestler of very little wrestling ability beyond a worked chokehold. He was brought into the WWF to play a convicted felon who was abused in prison by Big Boss Man, and presumably McMahon hated the way performer Kevin Wacholz's naturally high-pitched voice sounded, because his promos were pitch-shifted to a comically low register. After an altercation with McMahon that by some accounts got physical, Nailz departed from the company. He'll reappear in our story later as a notable witness in the WWF steroid trial.

PHANTASIO. Painted like a mime, Phantasio was a wrestling magician who did tricks before his matches. "Wrestling magician" is a great gimmick if you're a good magician, as current independent wrestlers Zicky Dice and Jarek 1:20 have proven. A mediocre wrestler who learned three tricks on the fly and looks like Paul Stanley got ready in the dark is *not* a good gimmick, no matter how many scarves he barfs up.

MAX MOON. This gimmick was originally earmarked for massive Mexican lucha star Konnan, who wisely bailed after he got a look at the final costume. Max Moon was a wrestler *from the future and/or from space*, who shot fireworks out of his gauntlets, somersaulted a lot (apparently due to the difference in gravity between his galactic residence and our oppressive Earth), and looked like a guy in a particularly low-budget porn parody of *Battlefield Earth*. A cult favorite for the ages.

THE RINGMASTER. When future one-of-the-biggest-stars-of-all-time Steve Austin got to the WWF, he wasn't the Stone Cold bad-ass with whom we're familiar. He was introduced as a lackey of the Million Dollar Man who went by the moniker The Ringmaster, because he was a good wrestler. This marks the one time in modern history that Vince McMahon's instinct was to toss out character and have someone attempt to get over based purely on their in-ring ability, rather than tap into the *There Will Be Blood*–sized ocean of personality residing within the performer in question.

HUNTER HEARST HELMSLEY. I include the once and future Triple H's original character only because he ended up being a key part of the New Generation (and every generation thereafter) and because Hunter Hearst Helmsley is such a complex look into the psyche of Vince McMahon. Introduced as a snobby, elitist, entitled Connecticut blueblood, Helmsley was mincing, preening, underhanded, boorish, and stuck his nose up at everyone and everything around him. The character was McMahon's critique of his snobby Greenwich neighbors, but that hatred contains multitudes. McMahon grew up with a massive chip on his shoulder due to his impoverished upbringing in a trailer park, and he constantly strove to make more of himself and prove people wrong who chose to look down on him. He is (at least in his own mind) the ultimate example of the promise of the American Dream and views himself as the ultimate common man. At the same time, he adores being rich, is a legitimate billionaire, and his wife is now part of the GOP elite as a former member of Trump's presidential cabinet. While he has famously looked deathly uncomfortable at fundraisers and political functions, there's no denying that Vince McMahon and his family are firmly—and have been for the past twenty years or so, if not longer—part of the absolute elite and pals with the innermost of inner-circle movers, shakers, and modern barons of America. The Helmsley character also calls to mind McMahon's ambivalence about the very industry that made him a billionaire: he hated the stereotype of mouth-breathing, illiterate backwoods hick as wrestling fan, but has also long insisted that his company *isn't* wrestling; it's entertainment. Perhaps it's for the best that Triple H stopped being an aristocrat and just became a guy who rides a Harley, loves Motörhead, and tells everyone to suck his dick all the time. The Aristocrats!

GOLDUST. Last, I have to include a character that would have been absolute death and one of the most infamous and least-loved pro wrestling gimmicks of all time if *literally anyone else* had played the character. With Goldust, McMahon created a double-whammy of a persona: a gay panic character for the nineties who also took those stuck-up Hollywood weirdos down a peg. Covered in gold face paint and a gold, full-body rubber suit, Dustin Runnels (son of Dusty Rhodes) was transformed into the creepy cinephile sociopath Goldust, a man who loved the movies so much that he turned himself into a living Academy Award. Constantly stroking himself and getting turned on by all the men he faced, he was accompanied by his cigar-smoking real-life wife, Terri, who really drove home the Freudian overtones. Taking cues from *Silence of the Lambs* androgyne killer Buffalo Bill, Goldust stalked his rivals, filmed them, flirted with them, and occasionally planted one on their lips, much to the babyface's inevitable rage. The character raised many eyebrows at the time and ran afoul of a good many parent groups, but only through the sheer ability, passion, and love of Runnels did the character not only become slightly worthwhile, but transcended and persevered. Goldust became a beloved, indispensable part of wrestling lore, and Runnels's portrayal of the character in its various forms over the years belongs in the pro wrestling pantheon—even though it started out as a gay panic character, with a brief stopover as a fake Tourette's sufferer in the early 2000s.

As McMahon was attempting to breathe new life into his company via the cartoon-character-heavy New Generation, he was indicted on federal charges of steroid trafficking and conspiracy to distribute illegal drugs, and the entire WWF was turned upside down when that case went to trial in 1994.

Confusion reigned within the industry as jury selection took place in July, as no one was quite sure whether the government was attempting to take down McMahon, the WWF, or pro wrestling in general. Eventually, it became clear that the most serious charges alleged that McMahon was in cahoots with Zahorian in a conspiracy to obtain and traffic drugs, disseminating them to wrestlers in order to increase gates with their juiced monsters.

Zahorian testified to everything that he had already been convicted of and explained how he would send package after package of steroids, painkillers, and Valium (and occasionally Rogaine, for use by Gene Okerlund).* While several

---

* God bless Gene for trying to reverse nature, as he'd sported his trademark cue-ball horseshoe hairdo since the moment he entered the WWF.

wrestlers testified, the media focused on Hulk Hogan, who had been compelled to take the stand. Hogan (who if you recall was now wrestling for the competition, WCW) testified that he was never forced or asked or told by McMahon to use steroids, and that he took them of his own volition. He admitted that Zahorian had provided him with an entire prescription pad, with every single page filled out. Hogan testified that he generally used Zahorian to obtain HCG, which is used during and in between steroid cycles to restore testosterone and fertility. For the majority of his anabolic steroids, he used a different doctor—Dr. Bob Panovich from Colorado. Also of note: Hogan admitted that he lied during his appearance on *Arsenio* and that Vince had told him it wasn't a good idea to go on the talk show. Sometimes you just gotta listen to the boss, Hulkster.

Former WWF wrestler Nailz (he of the alleged shoving match with McMahon) was meant to be one of the prosecution's star witnesses, as he testified that he remembered McMahon telling Rick Rude, "I suggest you get on the gas." He also claimed that during a meeting with McMahon in 1992, Vince said Nailz "should be" on steroids. During cross examination, WWF lawyer Jerry McDevitt brought up a number of salient points that seemed to run counter to Nailz's recollections. Among those points: Nailz's current lawsuit against McMahon and Nailz's character wearing a head-to-toe orange convict's jumpsuit, thus making the need for being on the gas extraneous at best. Nailz testified that the jumpsuit showed off his musculature—but it didn't. It really didn't. Unless you think "slender forearms" is a big signifier of what it takes to be a body guy. As a coup de grâce, McDevitt got Nailz to admit that he hated Vince McMahon.

Contemporary analysts point to Nailz as the witness who put forward such a disingenuous showing that it turned the jury in McMahon's favor.

Among a couple of other WWF employees, there were two key front office women who testified at the trial and offered up seriously damaging statements. WWF director of compliance and regulations Anita Scales recalled the rumors and heat surrounding Zahorian years prior, at which point she tried to book other doctors on the Philadelphia-area shows. When Zahorian found out he was in danger of being left off the shows, he bristled and went over her head. Scales was told by Pat Patterson and then Linda McMahon to keep Zahorian on the shows so that he could deliver the boys their "candy" in person.

The other major witness for the prosecution was Emily Feinberg (née Arth), who was Vince's personal secretary and the person who had been in charge of the original drug-testing policy prior to their steroid testing after the increased public scrutiny in the early 1990s. She testified that although the tests would come back positive for any number of drugs (notably barbiturates and opiates), the official policy was only to penalize those who tested positive for cocaine. Feinberg also testified that McMahon, Pat Patterson, and others would talk openly about steroids and steroid use in the office, and that when the steroid shipments from Zahorian came to Titan Towers, McMahon would keep half the shipments for himself and have her pack up the rest and ship them directly to Hogan. She claimed that McMahon had told her that he got on the gas after Hogan showed him how to inject himself with steroids on the set of *No Holds Barred*, and that the WWF honcho stopped using steroids himself in 1990 after contracting hepatitis. Her last bombshell was that, in January 1991, McMahon ordered her to destroy all records linking the WWF to Zahorian and then gave her the leftover steroids that were in the office and told her to keep them at her home until the heat died down. Feinberg ended up dumping all the steroids but one vial, which she eventually gave to prosecutors as evidence. WWF lawyers went after Feinberg hard on cross examination, insinuating that she was angling for a big payday with a tell-all book about the WWF, suggesting she was out for revenge following her termination from the company in 1991, and attacking her personal character, painting her as an actress, meticulously coached by the prosecution.

After all the witnesses had testified, the judge in the case threw out the two steroid distribution charges against McMahon due to lack of evidence, leaving only the conspiracy charge. In the end, there just wasn't enough to go on, as McMahon had kept himself mostly out of the fray and with no credible wrestlers going on the record as having been ordered by him to use steroids. There ended up being stronger ties to Linda McMahon and Pat Patterson as being in league with Zahorian, but unfortunately for the prosecution, they had singled out Vince.

The verdict came in as not guilty, after which McMahon spoke to the media about his unfair treatment during the case. He wore a shit-eating grin as well as a neck brace, as he had coincidentally scheduled an overdue neck surgery that would require him to wear a corrective and nasty-looking brace for the duration of his trial. Vince stood outside the courthouse beaming ear to ear, with the customarily stoic Linda by his side. "I'm elated," McMahon told the press. "Just like in wrestling, in the end the good guys always win." Why this isn't a more widely quoted McMahonism, or why the quote and a reproduction of Vince's courthouse steps photo isn't the content of the hottest bootleg shirt around, I'll never know.

The legal proceedings allegedly cost the WWF $3 million, which was no small amount considering that up to that point, the company's best year ever had yielded a profit of $6 million.

Regardless of all the nastiness that came out over the course of the trial and the disastrous PR hit from rampant admissions of steroid abuse and other improprieties, the worst was over for McMahon and the WWF. The steroid scandal was now in the rearview mirror, and it was time to turn the company's attention back to pro wrestling, and the impending war with Ted Turner. McMahon was now going head-to-head against the full power of Hulkamania—and Turner's coffers hadn't just been depleted by a tremendously costly trial.

11
WCW TAKES COMMAND

Lex Luger, his all-time unrivaled blond mullet blow-dried and flowing like the mane of a hockey-playing lion, strode into the Mall of America in Minneapolis on September 4, 1995, wearing a papal-white dress shirt with a mandarin collar (buttoned all the way up, of course). With signs behind his head blaring the names of intriguing businesses like "The Great Train Store," he stood in the middle of the aisle, hands on his hips, staring at the ring set up in the middle of the country's largest mall. The combatants in the ring were Ric Flair and his archrival Sting—but this was the debut episode of WCW's *Monday Nitro*, the live weekly show going head-to-head with WWF's *Monday Night Raw*. Luger had wrestled on WCW PPV eight days prior at SummerSlam, and had in fact wrestled at a WWF house show the night before waltzing into the Mall of America, live on TNT. Luger's contract had quietly lapsed during the summer, and he had reached out to his friend Sting to let him know he was interested in heading back to his former promotion.

The *Nitro* commentators were beside themselves, wondering what the hell Luger was doing here and playing it up like some sort of minor invasion—an interloper had arrived. "Wait a minute," Bobby "The Brain" Heenan noted on color commentary. "He's got a right to be here. This is a public mall."

He had a right to be there, and WCW took it as their right to take the fight directly to Vince McMahon. They'd taken the WWF's all-time biggest star in Hulk Hogan; now the new regime wanted to take a page out of Vince's own playbook and become the biggest game in town. WCW kicked off the first chapter of what would become known as the Monday Night Wars with innovation, blurring the lines of kayfabe— and kicking the absolute shit out of the WWF week in and week out.

McMahon had always had a desire to be the only game in town, and although his tactics counterprogramming NWA and Jim Crockett throughout the eighties had always been part of the game plan, his obsession with crushing the competition ratcheted up to a new level after Ted Turner got involved. There was now someone opposite McMahon with unlimited money to pour into the rasslin' business, and the first order of business had been to poach McMahon's biggest star. Even before the dueling Monday night programs sparked a war, it had started out personal. While one of the most unfortunate side effects of the Monday Night Wars is the insistence upon wrestling fans to stare at television ratings as if they mean something in the year 2020, it always meant much more than ratings. (Although both companies were indeed racking up the eyeballs at an all-time rate.)

The defining difference between Ted and Vince was that for Ted it was a lark; something else to do while he was busy being a billionaire and world-famous powerful businessman as his day job. He was a wrestling fan, sure, but he wrote the checks and let someone else worry about day-to-day operations of WCW. For McMahon, it was his sweat and blood being poured out every day, on every television show and in every booking meeting. Vince signed off on merchandise, brokered partnerships, and had final say over every single aspect of his company. With all that in mind, one could easily imagine Vince thinking, "Ted Turner wants to put his company up against mine? *How fucking dare he.*"

From the time that Vince took control of the WWF, his plans for national expansion relied heavily upon syndicated television. As his Black Saturday hostile takeover showed McMahon in the 1980s, not all time slots in all markets were successful for the WWF, but starting in 1983, the company developed a strong working relationship with the cable company USA Network—one that has continued off and on to this day. Beginning with weekly weekend syndicated shows, the most successful prime-time WWF show to air on the USA Network was *WWF Prime Time Wrestling*.

On January 11, 1993, the *Prime Time Wrestling* time slot would morph into *WWF Monday Night Raw*, a weekly one-hour pro wrestling show that aired live, adding an unpredictable edge (this continued until 1993, when budgetary reasons forced them to pretape it). Vince McMahon wanted to set *Raw*, which originated from the Grand Ballroom in the

Manhattan Center, apart from traditional pro wrestling television, as well as add an edge to what had always been viewed as kid stuff. Other innovations added to make *Raw* seem like a more adult product and bring the show in line with its title were ring card girls (one of whom was overweight, to the immense amusement of McMahon's proxies serving as color commentators) who paraded around before and after commercial breaks with cards bearing absolute nonjokes such as I LIKE SUSHI BECAUSE IT'S RAW. The ring card girls lasted less than a year, likely to the chagrin of Jerry "The King" Lawler, who joined *Raw* as permanent color commentator in 1995, bringing to the show his trademark blend of bathroom reader–level abysmal dad jokes and full-throated horniness.

Luckily for the WWF, *Raw* had no television equal or competition throughout its first two years and through the steroid trial of 1994, but Turner's WCW (now boasting not only Hogan, but Flair, Savage, and a number of Hogan's former WWF midcard buddies) entered into direct competition with the debut of *Nitro* on Turner-owned TNT. Unlike *Raw*, Turner had the budget to run *Nitro* live every week, and WCW announcers were soon given directives to spoil pretaped *Raw* results on the air.

On that first episode of *Nitro*, the debut of Luger (who everyone—including the WWF—thought was still under WWF contract) landed as intended: a spectacular bombshell that could not be ignored. But Luger's ship-jumping was never a sure thing. Sting had urged WCW vice president Eric Bischoff to meet with Luger and see if they could strike a deal, but Bischoff wasn't very interested in bringing Luger back, since he never cared for the Total Package's ring work or attitude. During the meeting, Bischoff deliberately lowballed his offer to Luger, and was stunned to find Luger accepted without hesitation. Not having given McMahon warning or notice, Luger appeared live on national television on the first episode of *Nitro*, shocking nearly everyone who worked at the WWF.

While both companies had freely poached from each other for years, this was a whole new paradigm. Bischoff, an almost impossibly good-looking business executive with a resplendent dyed-black mullet, and a man who your mother would probably have a crush on if she watched wrestling, had been put in charge of all of WCW in 1994. Bischoff cut his teeth in the AWA in the late 1980s (long after Hogan and Gagne split) and was now heading up the second-biggest wrestling company in the world. His first orders of business included bringing aboard Hogan, increasing WCW production values and amount of annual PPVs, and being the brainchild behind *Nitro*. He had impressed Turner executives by explaining that the key to WCW's future success was to fight the WWF juggernaut head-on. Turner gave Bischoff virtual free rein with the company's deep pocketbook, and WCW had its new marching orders: all-out war.

Another WCW-orchestrated statement of "You know what? Fuck the WWF" took place in December 1995. Debrah Miceli—the cornerstone of the WWF's resurgent 1990s New Generation women's division from 1993 to 1995, when she was known as Madusa (not only a play on "Medusa," but also short for "MADe in the USA," which McMahon almost certainly loved)—signed with WCW without ever giving the title belt back to the WWF, and on the December 18, 1995, episode of *Nitro*, Madusa appeared, stared into the camera, and angrily threw the WWF Women's Championship into a garbage can.

The women's division had stopped being a going concern for several years as Hulkamania and WrestleMania continued to rake in money for the WWF. In 1993, McMahon signed a trio of All Japan Women stars around which to reinvigorate women's wrestling. Bull Nakano, Rhonda Sing, and Miceli were brought aboard, in addition to a few other Stateside and in-house wrestlers. Madusa was rechristened Alundra Blayze and became the fighting babyface center of the division.

For longtime viewers, this new women's division focused on Blayze and Nakano was an eye-opener. For the first time, women in a major American wrestling promotion were presented as world-class athletes with abilities on par with the men—and they were having the best matches on the show every night, to boot. Blayze, Nakano, and Sing—now going by the name Bertha Faye—traded the title for a couple of years, with Blayze's initial reign lasting a whopping 342 days.

In December 1995, the WWF axed their entire women's division as part of their year-end cost-cutting measures. They released Blayze from her contract but neglected to recover the WWF Women's Championship belt from her prior to letting her go. Next thing you know, she's throwing it in the garbage on the competition's live television show. WCW's quickly established women's division never quite lived up to the promise of that moment, but it was a large enough "fuck you" to Vince McMahon's company that she was completely blackballed from the company for the next twenty years.

Bischoff's "fight fire with fire" plan was not without its stumbling blocks, of course. WCW's core fan base of Southern and traditional pro wrestling, which had long prided itself on WCW's virtue of *not* being the WWF, was thrilled to have Flair back in the fold (especially given the bad blood swirling around that led to his departure in the first place back in 1991), but was equally dismayed when so much of the company's weekly programming was turned over to Hulk Hogan and his cronies. Hogan, long synonymous with the WWF and all the excesses of the Rock 'N' Wrestling era, was not only the literal face of the enemy, but was now also carrying into WCW the additional baggage of his steroid scandal lies and his year-plus of being a toxic public relations nightmare. Shortly after coming aboard, Hogan beat Flair for the WCW Heavyweight Championship, and then held that title for 469 days—his first reign with that title finally ending an entire month into the advent of *Nitro* and the nascent Monday Night Wars. Even after losing the title, the exploits of Hulk Hogan became the dominant focus and the main event of any WCW programming, while Flair and Savage traded the world title on the undercard.

Despite longtime WCW and NWA fans loudly grumbling about their beloved promotion being turned into WWF Jr. after railing against the competition for so long, the addition of Hogan and whatever lingering remnants of Hulkamania paid off for casual fans, as attendance and viewership increased and led to WCW's first-ever profitable year in 1995.

Meanwhile, in the WWF, the New Generation had created new stars, complete with new egos to go with them. While Bret Hart remained the consensus locker room leader and consummate professional—an upstanding and loyal employee any promoter would be thrilled to have representing its company—a second camp was cordoning off its own corner of the locker room, and politicking to keep their key placement on television or in the main-event scene, as the respective case may be.

The appropriately named Kliq (a debated spelling, originally introduced in the WWF as a Vince Russo–created term to refer to Shawn Michaels's fans, although it never caught on in the same way as "Hulkamaniac") consisted of world champions Shawn Michaels and Diesel (real name Kevin Nash), along with sometime main eventer Razor Ramon (real name Scott Hall) and midcard mainstays Hunter Hearst Helmsley (years before popularizing the Triple H shorthand) and the 1–2–3 Kid (real name Sean Waltman). Many performers on the WWF's undercard were rankled as the Kliq continued to gain and flex its power behind the scenes, choosing who they would work with (usually one another) and who they would put over (usually no one).

As many—including Nash, Jim Cornette, and Bruce Prichard—have said in interviews over the years, McMahon viewed Michaels as a type of surrogate son in many ways. As such, he recognized Michaels's immense popularity, talent, and marketability while also knowing that the prima donna "Showstopper" that Michaels acted out both in front of the cameras and backstage was a headache to put up with. Still, he would be more valuable kept in the fold than left to the competition. By keeping Michaels close and coddling him, McMahon felt he could let him get away with politicking murder no one else could, if it meant he could stop Michaels from self-destructing in other, more tragic ways, given The Heartbreak Kid's penchant for booze, partying, and painkillers, and his inability to keep his dick in his pants.

The Kliq understood the power and value in Michaels's quasi-father/son relationship with Vince. The long leash granted to Michaels would not be the same length afforded to Nash, Hall, Helmsley, or Kid, but *through* Michaels, the group was able to expand their influence backstage and get away with whatever they wanted—so long as it mostly went through Shawn. They knew they were untouchable, and it was with this power in mind that Scott Hall and Kevin Nash began secretly negotiating close to million-dollar contracts with WCW—while still remaining a huge focus of WWF television.

As the interpromotional war continued to heat up and WCW began flashing huge dollar amounts at prospective signees, Kevin Nash and Scott Hall opted to sign with the competition after their contracts expired in May 1996. WWF couldn't match the guaranteed-money deals provided by Turner, so Diesel and Razor Ramon finished up their dates with the company and prepared to head to WCW. Unfortunately for the WWF, in addition to losing two of their top stars to their rivals, the Kliq embarrassed the entire company on Nash and Hall's way out, thanks to an event that lives on in infamy to this day: the Madison Square Garden "Curtain Call."

On May 19, 1996, Hall and Nash wrestled their final contractual obligation for the WWF at a house show in Madison Square Garden. The Kliq spontaneously decided that they wanted to have a final farewell to all of them being in the WWF, and they knew that with Nash and Hall already being out the door and Michaels being completely untouchable as the top draw, they could essentially do whatever they wanted. Their spur-of-the-moment show of friendship manifested in a show-ending and kayfabe-breaking act of solidarity, love, and respect for one another. It just so happened that their acting out of turn also served as a huge "fuck you" to the WWF. In keeping with how the Kliq operated, they didn't give a shit either way: they wanted to have their moment. What was Vince going to do, fire them?

The main event saw Michaels defeat Nash in a steel cage match, after which Hall came to the ring and hugged Shawn Michaels. While that was all well and good, as both Michaels and Razor Ramon were squeaky-clean babyfaces at the time, they were soon joined in their emotional embrace by Diesel and Helmsley, two of the company's most notorious villains. Waltman was not present at the event, but the four remaining members of the Kliq proceeded to celebrate in the steel cage and pose for the MSG crowd, raising each other's arms and hugging one another. Kayfabe was still in strict effect at the time, and while the fans in attendance reacted positively—albeit confusedly—this impromptu curtain call flew in the face of company policy, not to mention the way that business had always been done in the pro wrestling industry. The curtain call was also caught on bootleg video, leaking to wrestling newsletters and the burgeoning online wrestling community.

McMahon was livid, but he was in a tough spot. He knew this had been a bridge too far for the Kliq's backstage muscle and that an example had to be made, but Michaels was the current world champion and top remaining star, and Nash and Hall didn't work there anymore. Thus, Helmsley ended up taking the fall for the curtain call, going on an extended losing streak for months. He had allegedly been earmarked to win the upcoming 1996 King of the Ring tournament, but that was off the table now. Helmsley took his punishment without complaint, which led to two remarkable things coming out of the embarrassing mess caused by the Kliq.

The first is that, according to no less an authority than the Undertaker, Helmsley's head-down, humble acceptance and cooperation with his punishment earned him the widespread acceptance of the WWF locker room, whom he had long rubbed the wrong way. Second, Helmsley's removal from the 1996 King of the Ring tournament resulted in Steve Austin getting that spot, and cementing himself as the iconic "Stone Cold" Steve Austin with his legendary "Austin 3:16" promo.

On May 27—the same night that TNT expanded *Nitro* to two hours, thus giving them an uncontested hour in addition to the head-to-head hour against *Raw*—Hall appeared in the crowd during a match on *WCW Monday Nitro* and cut a promo in his Razor Ramon Cuban accent. Borrowing from the endlessly quotable 1993 capoeira movie *Only the Strong*, Hall finished his cryptic comments by saying, "You want a war? You're gonna get one." Later in the episode, Hall grabbed lead announcer Eric Bischoff and told him to get three of his best wrestlers together. Fans immediately began buzzing about what this could all mean, as Hall's appearance (including not being properly introduced, appearing in the middle of a match that then ground to a halt with no resolution, and perplexed announcers unable to clue viewers in on what was happening) was unlike anything wrestling fans had seen at that time. Hall appeared again the following week and was then joined by Nash on the next episode, the two men continuing to make threats and referencing a "war" that they were bringing to WCW. The two quickly became known as the Outsiders and appeared in street clothes, causing trouble and picking fights outside the context of pro wrestling matches and continually needing to be escorted out of buildings by WCW security.

This **"worked shoot"** angle—a complete work presented as if it is legitimate and breaking kayfabe—worked like gangbusters, leading fans to believe that a pair of WWF-contracted talents were showing up on WCW television and looking to pick legitimate fights. This fake invasion was the talk of the pro wrestling world during the summer of 1996. The WWF was less than pleased, especially since Hall appeared to still be using his Razor Ramon character. A lawsuit by the WWF resulted in Hall dropping his bad accent for good. Bischoff (having been outed by Hall and Nash as the man pulling the strings at WCW, rather than simply an announcer) finally acquiesced to the Outsiders' demands for a three-on-three war at the Bash at the Beach pay-per-view on July 7, selecting Sting, Lex Luger, and Randy Savage to be WCW's representatives. Nash and Hall, in return, declined to name their third man prior to the match, and in fact began the match by themselves. Fan speculation was at an all-time high leading up to the event about who could be the third man in this pack of wolves. After Luger was taken away on a stretcher, evening the playing field, WCW looked like they were on the verge of scoring a big victory and sending these interlopers packing.

And that's when Hulk Hogan appeared.

Hogan, who had been away from WCW television since this whole Outsiders ordeal began, headed to the ring, causing Nash and Hall to flee in terror as the Hulkster entered the ring and tore off his shirt, seemingly permanently tipping the scales in favor of WCW.* An instant later, Hogan turned and delivered his big leg drop to Randy Savage. He then hit his finisher twice more as Nash and Hall joined him in the ring to celebrate. An incredulous Gene Okerlund entered the ring to ask Hogan just what gives, and the freshly heel Hogan gloated that WCW fans are now looking at "the future of wrestling." In his trademark full-chested voice, he proclaimed, "You can call this the New World Order of wrestling, brother!" For the first time in fifteen years, Hulk Hogan was a villain.

In the weeks that followed, Hogan rechristened himself Hollywood Hogan, leaning into the better-than-wrestling attitude he'd always cultivated just below the surface and finally making it okay for fans to boo him in good conscience. He dressed in all black, began using every dastardly trick in the book, dyed the beard around his bleached-blond horseshoe mustache black, and stopped leaning on the Hulk-up routine that had defined his matches for the past decade and a half. On its own, the Hollywood Hogan character could be viewed as one of the first metatextual and postmodern takes in wrestling on a large scale, but in Hogan's hands, it didn't come across as nuanced or innovative—it seemed more that he was merely leaning into the only way he understood he

---

* While the other members of the broadcast team gleefully celebrated the appearance of the Hulkster, color commentator Bobby Heenan hoarsely shouted, *"But whose side is he on*?!" While now viewed as a classic call, fans in the arena at the Bash at the Beach went wild, completely unaware that Heenan had foreshadowed what was to come. It was completely true to Heenan's long-established character to be mistrustful of Hogan at all turns, but the idea of a heel Hulk Hogan probably wouldn't have been in most people's minds had not Heenan hollered that moments before the big reveal.

could remain the focal point of the company for another handful of years. After recapturing the WCW World Heavyweight Championship at the Hog Wild PPV, he spray-painted the surface of the beloved and iconic "Big Gold Belt" with the initials "nWo." The New World Order was officially the hottest thing in wrestling, and starting in June 1996 (even before Hogan revealed himself as the third man), *Nitro* pulled in more viewers than *Raw*. WCW then continued to defeat the WWF in the head-to-head Monday night ratings every single week *for 83 consecutive weeks*. Thanks to the nWo, the WWF was fighting from underneath for the first time since Vince Jr. took over the company.

If Hogan's tactics as a good guy rankled the traditionalists, his antics as a heel drove them completely up the wall. Taking the Four Horsemen "powerful heel stable" playbook and, well, putting it on steroids, the nWo continued to balloon week after week. The "outsider group" positioned itself as not being employed by WCW at all; they were an independent faction, hell-bent on obliterating all the WCW wrestlers and driving them out of business. It was a unique story line, to be certain, but one that instantly brought up issues of how this story could possibly come to an end—especially once it was revealed that WCW honcho Eric Bischoff was the man responsible for the formation of the New World Order.

The ranks of the nWo swelled as a torrent of former WWF employees and friends of Hogan came aboard: Ted DiBiase, Sean Waltman (now rechristened Syxx), Miss Elizabeth, Vincent (the former Virgil, his name a not-veiled-at-all shot at McMahon by giving his first name to one of the least effective pro wrestlers of all time), Bubba Rogers (the former Big Boss Man), Michael Wallstreet (the former Irwin R. Schyster),

Randy Savage, The Disciple (the former Brutus Beefcake), Curt Hennig, Rick Rude, Brian Adams (the former Crush), and on and on. Even Hogan's nephew Horace Hogan got a paycheck and a featured spot as a member of the sprawling nWo. Members joined and left and joined again, and eventually over sixty people were part of the group in its various incarnations. If you think that's excessive, even for pro wrestling, you're right. For a good stretch of those eighty-three weeks that WCW won in the ratings, most episodes of *Nitro* ended with the entire nWo in the ring, beating down WCW babyfaces, as fans hurled trash into the ring and announcer Tony Schiavone yelled/apologized that the broadcast was out of time.

Regardless, throughout 1996 and into 1997, the war between the nWo and WCW was the hottest thing in wrestling, and the cool factor of the nWo and their signature ubiquitous black and white shirts allowed the Monday night wars to cross over into pop culture at large, earning write-ups in *TV Guide* and other major publications as the hip and cool thing to watch over the summer while everything else was in reruns. WCW even got major mainstream celebrities to join in the fun. Right when future NBA Hall of Famer Dennis Rodman was the most talked-about athlete on the planet, he buddied up with Hogan as a full-fledged member of the New World Order and wrestled his first (although not his last) WCW match at the 1997 Bash at the Beach PPV. The following year, WCW would book a tag team match featuring Jay Leno.

Despite the messiness and endlessness of the story line, nWo vs. WCW remained the central story line of *Nitro* and of the company. As the New World Order continued to run roughshod over poor, helpless WCW, the good guys' savior appeared to be the superhero who was positioned against Hulkamania for so long while Hogan was leading the WWF to unprecedented heights: Sting. Previously a neon-face-painted and bleached-blond surfer with a rat-tail hairdo (and a man who once teamed up with RoboCop), in the last great long-term storytelling WCW employed, Sting grew tired of his WCW comrades not believing he wasn't in cahoots with the nWo (including some of his closest friends continually being fooled by a fake nWo Sting played by Jeff Farmer) and chose to excise himself from the fray altogether. When he finally reappeared on WCW television, Sting had ditched his screaming bright multicolored look for all-black attire and face paint lifted from the graphic novel and hit film *The Crow*. Silent and acting as a combination Phantom of the *Nitro* and nWo-seeking vigilante, Sting would appear in the rafters of arenas, gazing down at the nWo in stark and ominous judgment. Often, Sting would appear in the ring or rappel down from the rafters to even the odds or mete out justice against the nWo with his black baseball bat but continued to operate on his own and not participate in actual wrestling matches for over a year. The company built the story all the way out to the end of 1997, when Sting would finally, at long last, get his hands on Hogan and end the war once and for all, dealing a killing blow to the cancerous nWo. But—it didn't quite work out that way.

Throughout 1996, *Raw* scrambled to find ways to catch up to *Nitro* in the ratings. Not surprisingly, the WWF's tactics often resorted to pettiness and playing the victim. Beginning in January, WWF television began airing satirical vignettes titled "Billionaire Ted's Rasslin' Warroom," which featured a theatrically villainous Ted Turner character referred to only as "Billionaire Ted" who prided himself on dishonesty, deceit, and theft. The skits also featured parodies of former WWF talent like the Nacho Man and the shriveled and geriatric Huckster, who in the skits was thrilled about WCW's lack of steroid testing.

More than anything, the skits painted WCW as thieves, who stole all of the WWF's good ideas and talent and lied to the faces of the fans. The vignettes slowly morphed from satirical shots at WCW's wrestling content to personal attacks against Ted Turner. Not coincidentally, it was around this time that the WWF's lawyers sent files to the FTC suggesting that Time Warner's proposed merger with AOL (at that time the biggest corporate merger in history and one of the biggest news stories of the year) was fueled primarily by a personal vendetta against McMahon and a desire to put the WWF out of business. The WWF took out large ads in newspapers addressed to Time Warner stockholders, suggesting the very same thing. In March 1996, the final Billionaire Ted sketch focused on the impending AOL/Time Warner merger with a parody of *A Few Good Men*, where Billionaire Ted was grilled by senators about whether he'd created a monopoly by driving all his competitors out of business, and accused him of targeting the WWF next. If you're wondering how no one at the WWF saw the hypocrisy and irony in these statements about monopolization and personal vendettas, maybe I haven't told you quite enough about how the wrestling business works just yet. The USA Network finally put the kibosh on the Billionaire Ted segments following the *A Few Good Men* parody, but McMahon still managed to finish up his pet project with a pretaped match between the Nacho

Man and the Huckster (with Billionaire Ted as referee) that aired before WrestleMania XII.

While a myriad of WWF wrestlers jumped ship to the guaranteed contracts and cushier schedule in WCW in the *Nitro* era, the WWF was able to snare a handful of key players who were disgruntled at WCW from 1995 to 1997. These included Steve Austin, Dustin Rhodes, Mick Foley (who had been working for WCW as Cactus Jack), Brian Pillman, Vader, Marc Mero, the returning "Sycho" Sid Justice, and Ron Simmons, a former WCW world champion who was renamed Faarooq Asad and given an African gladiator gimmick when he arrived in the World Wrestling Federation. All these men would contribute to the WWF's next boom period, but it would be a long and slow process.

In addition to making their roster younger and more versatile, another key component of the WWF's reinvigoration was a working relationship with a fledgling indie promotion based out of Philadelphia: ECW.

Eastern Championship Wrestling had existed since 1989 and had reentered the NWA in 1994—much to the NWA's eventual chagrin. Since ECW television ran late at night (or early in the morning, depending upon your perspective), head booker and promotional mastermind Paul Heyman was able to push the envelope with sex, violence, innuendo, and mature subject matter to an extent that no other televised wrestling product had ever done at that point. Heyman had a singular eye for talent, but an even greater ability to showcase wrestlers' strengths while never putting them in situations to be undone by their weaknesses. He allowed WCW castoffs Steve Austin and Mick Foley to come in for short runs and cut loose, letting their creative juices run rampant and putting them at the forefront of hot angles before both men moved on to the WWF.

Heyman was also the first to give a major English-language platform (and on the East Coast, which was even more invaluable for exposure) to up-and-coming luchadores. The breakneck pace and high-flying cruiserweight style were completely new to those who hadn't watched lucha libre before (which was most English-speaking U.S. wrestling fans), and word of mouth quickly spread about the luchadores who Heyman was bringing in from Mexico. WCW took Heyman's innovation of showcasing cruiserweights and ran with it: soon, the first hour of *Nitro* was chock-full of top Mexican lucha prospects like Misterio, Psicosis, Juventud Guerrera, La Parka, Super Caló, Silver King, Eddie Guerrero, Ciclope, and El Dandy (whom one should never doubt).

By the middle of 1995, ECW was already a phenomenon in Pennsylvania, and by September 1996, the WWF and ECW began a working relationship, with ECW wrestlers appearing on episodes of *Raw* and even a pay-per-view. McMahon and Heyman kept in close contact regarding talent, with Heyman tipping the WWF off to several players to keep an eye on. At various times, McMahon even kept Heyman on an unofficial payroll and assisted in keeping ECW afloat—unbeknown to anyone who was working for ECW at the time. ECW wrestlers would steadily trickle onto both *Raw* and *Nitro* as full-time WWF and WCW wrestlers over the next several years, while Heyman reaped the benefits of being an unofficial feeder for both major promotions while retaining ECW's street cred as the hip, edgy counterculture alternative to the nationally televised "big leagues."

McMahon continued to view himself as the scrappy

underdog in this fight and to play the role of victim until his next batch of stars popped up to take over for the New Generation. In one of the most ill-advised and least-loved moves of all time, the WWF attempted to counterpunch the white-hot nWo story line and Hall and Nash's invasion by sending a villainous commentator, Jim Ross, on television to run down the company he was employed by and to promise the fans that he was going to bring Razor Ramon and Diesel back to the World Wrestling Federation. In short order, Ross produced "Razor Ramon" and "Diesel," two wrestlers who were emphatically *not* Scott Hall and Kevin Nash but were dressed in their character outfits and portraying the gimmicks trademarked by the WWF. It was maybe the ultimate "weird flex but okay" in response to their taking umbrage that Hall appeared on WCW television portraying what they felt was a version of the Razor Ramon character, which was *their* intellectual property, dammit! Fake Razor and Fake Diesel died on the vine and were gone by early 1997.

It went like this in fits and starts for the World Wrestling Federation as WCW continued to eat their lunch in the ratings and poach their talent with aplomb. The WWF would not turn things around and overtake WCW, however, until after one of the most embarrassing, controversial, and scandalous acts to ever take place inside a wrestling ring: the Montreal Screwjob.

12

SCREWJOBS, LOOSE CANNONS, AND DIRT SHEETS

It's nearly impossible to tell the story of contemporary popular culture without discussing the effect of the internet, but there are few businesses—to say nothing of art forms—that have been as fundamentally altered by the emergence of the internet as professional wrestling.

I vividly remember my first encounter with what today is often derisively referred to as the Internet Wrestling Community (or even more derisively by its shorthand, IWC). By sheer accident, I managed to wade into the waters of extreme online wrestling fans in the immediate aftermath of the most transformative moment in modern pro wrestling: the Montreal Screwjob.

On November 9, 1997, the World Wrestling Federation presented the eleventh annual Survivor Series, then still viewed as a cornerstone of the annual "Big Four" pay-per-view events for the WWF, with lots of hoopla surrounding the main event, which pitted WWF Champion Bret Hart against his bitter archrival, Shawn Michaels. It was a simmering summer that led up to the Screwjob, which would end up being Hart's final appearance in WWE for nearly a decade.

Shawn Michaels began his career as a blond babyface in a tag team called the Midnight Rockers, which was eventually shortened to just "The Rockers" when he and his partner Marty Jannetty landed in the WWF. Originally just a rip-off of the tried and true Southern tag team the Rock 'n' Roll Express, the Rockers were energetic and high-flying, and young. Kids and women loved them and were thus all the more betrayed when Michaels threw his partner through a barbershop window (long story) and turned heel. Now calling himself the Heartbreak Kid, Michaels patterned himself after a male stripper—chaps, leather cap, and all—and went through various stages of being a good male stripper and a bad male stripper before clashing with Hart both in front of the cameras and behind the scenes.

Michaels, who had formed D-Generation X with Triple H (and Triple H's valet/bodyguard, Chyna) in the wake of the Madison Square Garden Curtain Call and the other half of the Kliq's departure to WCW, was bringing an obnoxiousness and edge to WWF television that hadn't really ever been seen before. He and Triple H were ostensibly heels, but their constant showing-up of stick-in-the-mud traditionalist authority figures like Sgt. Slaughter—and their incessant dick jokes and exhortations for those in opposition to them to suck their dicks—led to more and more fans loving them and their attitude. Remember, this was only a few months after the first episode of *South Park* landed on Comedy Central, leading to a spectacular wave of pearl-clutching from authoritarians and traditionalists the world over. It was no longer cool or admirable in the minds of most adolescent-and-older wrestling fans to be concerned about avoiding foul language, fighting fair if no one else was, and priding yourself on being morally upstanding. Telling people to suck it, accompanied by a brief yet emphatic double-handed chop toward your genitals? That was cool.

Someone who wasn't cool with it was Hart, the staunchly Canadian favorite son of a Canadian traditionalist institution of a family, whose edginess was constrained almost entirely to a man wearing pink and a pair of sunglasses that had only one wide lens, rather than the traditional two. But Bret seemed more and more like a remnant of the past, and orders for fellatio as catchphrases were the wave of the future.

In light of this new cultural paradigm, the WWF attempted a seldom-used but always-bulletproof angle for Hart: the character who is a hero to certain parts of the fan base, but an abject villain to everyone else. In this case, the morally upright Canadian native began badmouthing the sliding morals of fans in the United States, who would choose a pair of kielbasa-deepthroating rogues as heroes rather than Bret Hart, who believes in tucking your shirt in and pulling your pants up, and quit having such potty-mouths, Americans.

Hart doubled down on his own legitimate status as a Canadian hero and icon and quadrupled down on calling the American fans cheering for Austin and Michaels a bunch of "degenerates." In fact, Hart's labeling of Michaels, Hunter, Chyna, and their fans led to Michaels claiming the term as the name of the faction. In other words, Hart is directly responsible as the catalyst for two of WWE's largest acts of all time: Stone Cold Steve Austin and D-Generation X.

As a result of his badmouthing of these two white-hot acts and the fans of the WWF who were slowly getting used to cheering for the "edgier" and "cooler" acts (the support of which involved a plenitude of middle fingers and crotch-chopping), Hart became a babyface to every wrestling fan in the world, except the fans within the United States—the audience to who the entire product was marketed. Hart reformed the Hart Foundation, this time consisting of the returning Jim Neidhart, Owen Hart, brother-in-law the British Bulldog, and close family friend Brian Pillman. When his group toured outside the United States, they were treated as heroes who weren't afraid to say on national television that America needed to have an enema.* And in Canada, that adoration was at a fever pitch. On July 6, 1997, the WWF presented an In Your House pay-per-view called Canadian Stampede from the Harts' hometown of Calgary. The main event was a ten-man tag team match pitting the entire Hart

---

* Hart's emphatic insistence that the administration of a countrywide enema would involve sticking the hose in Pittsburgh is now beloved the world over by pro wrestling fans—perhaps with the exception of the residents of Pittsburgh.

Foundation against the team of Steve Austin, Goldust, Ken Shamrock, and the Legion of Doom. Canadian Stampede has been considered a classic pretty much ever since it aired, almost entirely due to the nearly unmatched energy of the crowd, which roared to the point of shaking the hard camera in support of anyone even moderately in line with Hart's ideologies, and was so loud during the main event that even a contemporary viewing leaves you wondering how 12,151 people could ever possibly get that loud.

Tragically, Brian Pillman would be found dead in his hotel room in Minnesota on October 5, 1997, the day he was set to wrestle Dude Love at the Badd Blood: In Your House pay-per-view in St. Louis. Austin's autobiography, *The Stone Cold Truth*, explains that Pillman's death at thirty-five was the result of a heart attack due to hereditary heart disease, which had also caused the early death of Pillman's father.

Badd Blood saw Bret Hart and the British Bulldog defeat The Patriot (an actual personification of the United States of America, portrayed by Southern rasslin' fixture Del Wilkes) and Vader in a Flag Match, a contest where you have to be the first to retrieve your country's flag to win. (Of course, due to all four men in the match dealing with injuries, the Flag Match rules in this instance were amended to allow for pinfall or submission, and it actually ended with Hart rolling up The Patriot for the pin and the victory, thus making this a Regular Match, but with Flags!) In the main event, Shawn Michaels faced the Undertaker in the first-ever Hell in a Cell match to determine the No. 1 contender for the WWF Championship at Survivor Series. Hell in a Cell, a first of its kind for the WWF, was a traditional chain-link-fencing steel cage with a roof on top that surrounded the ring and the entire ringside area, thus ensuring no outside interference. Naturally, the match ended with outside interference, when the Undertaker's not-dead-at-all brother, Kane, made his debut by tearing off the door of the cage, attacking the Undertaker, and allowing Michaels to get the pin* and set up the title match at Survivor Series.

Michaels and Hart legitimately despised one another, going back years. Hart disliked Michaels's attitude and politicking, and was resentful of what he perceived as preferential treatment due to having the unilateral support of Vince McMahon. Hart bristled at the new look of foulmouthed ne'er-do-wells who would be heels in any other era of wrestling to that point, and felt that he might be getting left behind by the shifting social mores of the era. And he may have been justified in feeling that way.

Things had seemed to be going swimmingly for the Hart-McMahon team-up the year before. In October 1996, WCW had offered Hart a multiyear, $8.4 million contract, but Hart instead signed a twenty-year deal with the WWF—essentially a lifetime contract, and something that had never before, and would never again, be offered to anyone in professional wrestling. The deal pleased both Hart and McMahon, as they had great mutual respect, demonstrated in part

---

* Despite the goofy finish, the match was an instant classic due to its brutality and Michaels's virtuoso selling throughout. It ended up being just the fourth WWF match to receive a five-star rating from Dave Meltzer of the *Wrestling Observer Newsletter* and would be the last five-star match in WWE for fourteen years.

by Hart's loyalty—by the time Survivor Series 1997 rolled around, Hart had been with the WWF for fourteen years. But in the year after Hart signed that twenty-year deal, just about everything changed. The first major bump in the road between Hart and Michaels was surrounding WrestleMania XII in 1996. McMahon was eager to anoint Michaels as a new face of the company and wanted Hart to drop the world title to Michaels in the main event of the biggest show of the year as a means of passing the torch. Hart, who already didn't like how Michaels conducted business backstage, balked, and McMahon gave him assurances that Michaels would repay the favor and give him his win back at Wrestle-Mania 13. Things never went as Hart wanted them to, starting with the match itself. The main event of WrestleMania XII was a babyface vs. babyface Iron Man match between Hart and Michaels, which went to sudden-death overtime after neither man scored a pinfall on the other within the allotted sixty minutes.

This was also the first real onscreen screwing of Bret by an authority figure—completely in agreed-upon kayfabe, of course. (Ironically, Hart's long-term story line that turned him heel was a series of on-screen and worked injustices.) When the time limit expired in a draw, Hart collected his belt and made as if to leave, as was his right, because that's literally how the match should work. Then—on-screen commissioner Gorilla Monsoon appeared to declare the match would go to sudden death overtime, and Hart complained, as he should have, because that almost certainly wasn't in the make-believe contract for this fake fight, and Hart would have a hell of a complaint to make to the California State

Athletic Commission if this thing weren't rigged. After Michaels won the title, he told referee Earl Hebner to get Hart out of the ring, because the presence of the former champion was "ruining the moment." Obviously, that didn't sit well with Hart, but what sat even less well came in February 1997, when Shawn Michaels lost his smile.

After signing that twenty-year contract, and continuing to operate under the assumption that he'd get his win back against Michaels at WrestleMania 13, Hart was instead angered all over again when Michaels went on *Thursday RAW Thursday* (a special two-hour presentation after *Monday Night Raw* was preempted in favor of a dog show—a regular occurrence in those days) on February 13, 1997, and forfeited the WWF Championship, saying that he was stepping away from wrestling for a while to try and fix some injuries and rediscover his passion for the business. In actuality (according to most people involved), Michaels knew he was in the thick of the lead-up to WrestleMania 13, and thought of a way to avoid having to lose the title back to Bret. Eventually, Hart would face Austin in one of the greatest WrestleMania matches ever, turning himself heel and Austin face in the process and helping to strap the rocket to Austin's ass. (While most fans [and official WWE history] remember the Austin 3:16 promo directly leading to Stone Cold Steve Austin being the hottest thing in wrestling history, the truth is that Austin languished for months afterward, never really lining up with WWE's plans until that perfect feud with Hart cemented his face turn.) The main event of WrestleMania 13 would be a WWF Championship match between Sycho Sid and the Undertaker, where Shawn Michaels sat in on commentary.* Hart came out during the main event to badmouth Michaels, try to insert himself in the match, and really drive home that he was a bad guy now. Undertaker would win the title, and would lose it to Hart at Summer-Slam when special guest referee Michaels attempted to wallop Hart with a chair but instead brained the Deadman. That gave Hart the title and set up the first-ever Hell in a Cell match between Michaels and Undertaker.

There was just one more piece to the Montreal Screwjob puzzle behind the scenes: Hart's new twenty-year contract, and how it butted up against the newly launched Monday Night Wars. In less than a year since Hart put pen to paper, the WWF found itself with some tighter budgets due to WCW winning the ratings wars in the early days. At the same time, McMahon looked around at the new landscape and saw the money laid in Steve Austin and to a lesser extent D-Generation X. Hart's unicorn of a contract didn't give him a lot of wiggle room in terms of roster-building and operating costs, and it wasn't where the wind was blowing. In the months leading up to Survivor Series, and with Hart holding his company's top title, McMahon went to Bret, hat in hand,

---

* In a shock to no one within the company, Michaels managed to find his smile again almost immediately after WrestleMania 13, and in May 1997 was able to enrage Hart even further by suggesting on live television that Hart was having an affair with WWF interviewer and sometimes-manager Tammy Lynn Sytch, better known as Sunny. Ironically, several years after the fact, it would be common knowledge that Sunny was actually sleeping with Michaels at the time, and that she and Hart were nothing more than friends. If you want to know more about Tammy Lynn Sytch, any wrestling fan will tell you plenty if you ask. And even more if you don't.

to tell him he would have to withdraw from Hart's contract.*
He offered Hart a restructured deal but encouraged him to
take a better offer if WCW was able to extend one—knowing
full well that Ted Turner's pockets were deep, and Eric
Bischoff was regularly writing much larger checks for talent than McMahon was capable of doing. Hart reached out
to WCW and did get that big money he was seeking, signing
a three-year contract while still holding the WWF Championship. All that was left was for him to fulfill his contractual
obligations to the World Wrestling Federation.

Hart, to all who knew him and interacted with him, was a
man of his word, a guy who was concerned about doing business "the right way" to a fault. As it turned out, that would
ultimately be his undoing. Hart was under contractual obligation to the WWF at least up through the *Monday Night
Raw* following Survivor Series, but everyone in the company
knew that he was on his way out the door, and that Survivor
Series would be his last pay-per-view with the WWF. Hart
and Michaels even began making allusions to the fact that

---

* A large part of the reason that fans know so very much about the buildup
to and the execution of the Montreal Screwjob is thanks to the documentary *Hitman Hart: Wrestling with Shadows*. The Paul Jay–directed film provides an unprecedented look behind the scenes of the WWF at the time
and was the perfect storm of a documentary crew being in the right place at
the right time. The film, coproduced by the National Film Board of Canada,
was initially pitched (and all waivers signed) as a look at Hart during the
final year of his contract in 1996, and facing the difficult decision ahead.
That's how the film begins, and then follows Hart through his contract ne-
gotiations, his signing of the twenty-year deal, the withdrawal of that deal,
and then the Montreal Screwjob and its aftermath. If you've never seen it
before, you should probably do that as soon as possible. (Once you finish
this book, of course.)

that Survivor Series might very well be the last anyone would see of Bret. Even though I wasn't online at the time, I was watching every week, and even I picked up on the enormity that this match appeared to be taking on. It was Hart, Canadian hero and American villain, taking on his archrival Michaels one last time in his home country, for the biggest prize in pro wrestling. For those fans who were clued in on the internet at this time, the rumors were already swirling about Hart potentially having signed with WCW.

McMahon and the WWF, despite having pushed Hart out the door and into WCW, were of course desperate to avoid a repeat of the Alundra Blayze incident, and it's likely that WCW offered Hart a whole bunch of extra money to jump ship while still holding the championship, but Upstanding Guy Bret Hart would obviously never do such a thing (legal considerations aside). Knowing that Bret would be a company guy to the end, McMahon began preparing for his desired outcome: Hart losing the title to Michaels, to ensure the lineage of his top title would be uninterrupted. It's likely that McMahon also began preparing contingency plans as soon as Hart began negotiating with WCW. For his part, Hart was willing to play ball, to a point: He was willing to lose the WWF Championship to anyone of McMahon's choosing, at any point, in any situation. He was even willing to appear on *Monday Night Raw* and relinquish the title voluntarily the day after Survivor Series.

But there were only two things he flat-out refused to do, under any circumstances: he would not lose the title to Michaels, and he would especially not lose the title to Michaels in Canada. Given that very broad range of options, you would think McMahon could have come up with a whole host of other possibilities to get the title off Hart. But he was insistent: it had to be Michaels, and it had to be at Survivor Series.

Everyone at the WWF was aware of the rising tensions behind the scenes, but everyone managed to remain as above-board and professional as possible during the lead-up. On the day of Survivor Series, the two sides reached an accord: the main event would have a fuck finish: Michaels would be on the verge of victory, but the Hart Foundation would run in to cause a disqualification. Hart would retain his title, Michaels would win the match, and then Hart would drop the title on television the next day (or shortly thereafter, but before departing for WCW, at any rate). That's what was agreed to;* but of course, that's not what happened.

At about twelve minutes into the match, in front of a raucous Montreal crowd that was solidly in Hart's corner, Michaels and Hart have a double-down along with a ref bump: Hart comes off the top rope with a double axe handle, but Michaels pulls referee Earl Hebner in between them. Hebner, Hart, and Michaels all go down. Michaels takes advantage of the referee being down to rake Hart's eyes, then applies Bret's own trademark finishing submission hold: the Sharpshooter.

Normally when a referee is bumped, they remain down for at least a full minute, to really sell the superhuman might of the combatants, and just how inadequately a normal human

---

* Again, we know this because of *Wrestling with Shadows*. The film depicts a backstage meeting at the Survivor Series prior to the match. Hart, still wearing a microphone, enters a closed-door meeting with McMahon and others, where they put together the match, including the schmoz finish and the plans for the forfeiture of the title on *Monday Night Raw*.

is prepared for the strength of your average professional wrestler. However, in this case, Hebner begins moving right away, and is on his feet and fully cognizant the moment that Michaels locks in the hold. As Bret is moving his arm toward Michaels's leg to counter the Sharpshooter, Hebner calls for the timekeeper to ring the bell. Hebner then instantly leaves the ring and heads up the aisle just as Michaels and Hart collapse onto one another in a heap, both men operating as though Hart has broken the hold. McMahon, who had come to ringside before the end of the match, will later be seen in alternate angles yelling at the timekeeper to "ring the fucking bell" as Hebner gestures for the same.

As Michaels's theme song begins to play, Hart stands up and, from the ring, hocks the greatest and most accurate loogie of all time directly into Vince McMahon's eye. Michaels, joined at ringside by Triple H, looks absolutely livid. McMahon, Slaughter, and McMahon's right-hand men and bookers Gerald Brisco and Pat Patterson instruct Michaels to grab the WWF Championship and depart with it. As trash and thunderous boos begin raining down from the crowd, Michaels and Triple H depart up the aisle, animatedly arguing with Brisco and Patterson the whole way. Just before Michaels reaches the entrance curtain, he lifts the championship title and gifts one half-hearted victory jump before disappearing into the back. Once backstage, he would immediately get in a vehicle and leave the arena, which was probably best for all involved. The pay-per-view broadcast went off the air just then, with beyond-confused commentators Jim Ross and Jerry Lawler trying to puzzle out what happened in real time just as they performed a hasty sign-off to the viewing audience. The crowd was unable to reap the benefit of even that, as there was seemingly no explanation or sense to be made out of what they had just seen.

Back at ringside (and off camera), Hart went nuts, destroying commentary desk monitors, air-writing the letters "W-C-W" with his finger in the air, and venting his frustrations (off mic) to the crowd, which continued to boo the WWF in support of their hero. The other members of the Hart Foundation joined Bret in the ring, stunned. When Hart finally made his way backstage, he was no less livid. He went into the locker room, and shortly thereafter was joined behind closed doors by Vince, Brisco, Patterson, and Shane McMahon. As Hart's wife, Julie, confronted wrestlers backstage to see what they knew about this deceit, Hart supposedly decked McMahon, knocking him out cold.*

Of course, I didn't know any of this at the time. I didn't even know what had happened in the main event of Survivor Series, or anything else on the card. Although I was deeply, personally invested in the story line at the time (and firmly on the side of Bret Hart), I was scheduled to work a late shift at my job at Hollywood Video, and was thus forced to miss out on the pay-per-view entirely. But I was determined to find out what happened, and I knew from the many shout-outs on WWF television that you could learn more about the

---

* Say it with me once more: thanks, *Wrestling with Shadows*! The documentary catches some of the argument through a closed door, and a groggy McMahon is shown being helped out of the locker room by Shane after the alleged knockout punch. It's no surprise that unfettered access to backstage areas would not be given to another outside source again for decades. It's just the company's bad luck that both *Wrestling with Shadows* and another indispensable documentary, *Beyond the Mat*, managed to finagle free rein behind the scenes during the WWF's early Attitude Era boom years.

WWF by logging into America Online and using their keyword. That's how the internet worked back then, and it still doesn't make any sense. My household didn't have a personal computer, let alone the internet. And I had precisely one friend who I knew had AOL, and would be up, and wouldn't mind my coming by to check the results. That was my only option for finding out what happened at a wrestling show until *Monday Night Raw* in another twenty-four hours. We managed to survive before smartphones, but I'm not entirely sure how. And I was there.

I managed to get onto AOL and type in "WWF" as a keyword, and somehow navigated to what I remember as the more-or-less official chatroom, where there was a steady stream of endless conversation I couldn't make heads or tails of, but everyone was very animated. I leapt into this stream of discussion to ask whether anyone knew what happened in the main event. A kind soul curtly informed me that Michaels won with the Sharpshooter. A couple others quickly confirmed the result, and the conversation continued to flow, which I now know was rampant speculation about what went down and what this meant for Bret Hart and the WWF and WCW, but I was so crushed at Hart losing that I turned off the computer and sadly went about my evening. I didn't know that professional wrestling was about to change forever—probably had already changed forever—and that I accidentally ended up being at Internet Wrestling Speculation Ground Zero, despite not even owning a computer.

Meanwhile, back in the real(ish) world, Vince McMahon got what he wanted: Michaels as champion, winning in Montreal like a true heel through the most devious tactics possible, and Hart done being a headache and out of the company.

He wouldn't be showing up on *Nitro* to throw the WWF's top title into a trash can, and in fact would not appear on WWE television again until long after he retired.

Although there had been a few allusions here and there in 1996 and 1997, it had never been public knowledge to the average wrestling fan—and certainly never mentioned on television or through any official WWF publication—that Vince was ever anything more than a host and strangely bombastic play-by-play man who managed to rarely know the names of common moves.* That all changed in the aftermath of the Montreal Screwjob, as eight days after Survivor Series, on November 17, 1997, *Monday Night Raw* featured a sit-down interview with Vince McMahon, conducted by Jim Ross. McMahon, sporting a black eye (generally believed to be enhanced slightly by makeup), sat beneath a large photo of Bret Hart and, speaking from his position (officially, for the first time on WWF television) as chairman of the company, emphatically and famously said that, in his opinion, he didn't screw Bret Hart, because "Bret screwed Bret" by refusing to play ball. (In the last great irony of Hart's WWF career, his evolution into a heel by repeatedly claiming that "everyone

---

* The great irony of Vince McMahon's commentary career: at the time, he was viewed as a *terrible* announcer by most fans, and the knowledge that he tends to feed contemporary announcers a lot of lines and bullet points makes a lot of fans loathe him as well. But the truth of the matter is that in hindsight, Vince was sort of *fantastic* as a play-by-play man, and his style of bombast and befuddlement was a perfect companion to the Hulkamania era and beyond. His constantly lampooned calls of "Oh! What a maneuver!" and "One, two . . . He got him! No he didn't!" are good, gentle nostalgia mocking, but I'll always remember them fondly for being just the right amount of cheesy and excited, and for helping to keep me hooked.

is screwing me" at every turn led to "Bret screwed Bret," the ultimate encapsulation of the death of kayfabe and the birth of Mr. McMahon, the character.)

By purposely coming across as self-important and full of shit in this interview, McMahon officially became An Important Character within the context of WWF television. More than that, he transitioned into being the actual, acknowledged owner of the World Wrestling Federation, a company that previously had only employed on-screen "commissioners" and "presidents" who were really backstage or front office employees under Vince, like Jack Tunney, Monsoon, or Slaughter.* McMahon was now front and center, and within months would transition into being "Mr. McMahon," the evil, underhanded owner of the company, and run afoul of his greatest nemesis, Steve Austin, the living embodiment of Johnny Paycheck's song "Take This Job and Shove It."

The acknowledgment of McMahon as Hart's and Michaels's boss, along with the announcement on WWF television of Hart jumping ship and going to the competition, was a claxon to an entire generation of wrestling fans: there's something weird going on here, and there's a lot more to this story, and I need to figure out how to find out about as much of it as I can. If fans with access to the internet weren't already Extremely Online about pro wrestling, this event spurred them to dive in deep.

The Montreal Screwjob was not the beginning of the

---

* This may surprise current wrestling fans, but for the majority of the WWE's existence, on-screen authority figures were rarely used. Jack Tunney was the supposed president of the WWF for over a decade, but only appeared on television a few times a year.

Internet Wrestling Community and the smart fan, but it was absolutely the turning point not only for the advent of the internet wrestling fan, but for the entire concept of kayfabe. There had been "worked shoots" before, not just with the jumping of Hall and Nash and the formation of the nWo, but going back for many years, like in Memphis with Jerry Lawler and Andy Kaufman bringing their in-ring feud to David Letterman (and beyond). But the Montreal Screwjob really struck a nerve, especially with the groundbreaking sit-down McMahon interview just a week after Survivor Series. While it would eventually become a joking shorthand for worked shoot angles, the WWF said outright for the first time, "Most of what you see is fake, but this specific thing was real."

There have been fans and insiders and critics who have known about the nonlegitimacy of professional wrestling about as long as it has existed, but it was a lot easier to keep a lid on kayfabe until the 1980s. Regional television stations and the lack of mass instant communication made it possible to run eight shows a week in most territories with very similar results from show to show, and for 99 percent of the audience to be unaware of that. There was little concern that the attendees of a show in, say, Austin, on Monday night would know that Dick Murdoch and Dory Funk would be scrapping tooth and nail beat-for-beat the same way they did in Amarillo the night before.

There were mass-market pro wrestling publications during these time periods—lots of them. But all of them were deeply invested in preserving kayfabe, to the point that even the "wrestler interviews" were written by the people who put out the magazines. Bill Apter was the lead writer and photographer (and eventually editor) for a number of magazines published by Stanley Weston beginning in 1970. *Pro Wrestling Illustrated*, *The Wrestler*, and *Inside Wrestling* eventually became known as the "Apter Mags," and *Pro Wrestling Illustrated* is still going strong today, publishing its trademark PWI 500 every year: a ranking of the top 500 wrestlers in the country. Being named in a blurb on the list is considered a badge of honor for independent and up-and-coming wrestlers, even in a completely kayfabe magazine. If *PWI* thinks you're important enough to be mentioned, that means something.

But *PWI* and the Apter Mags, and the other glut of publications during wrestling's various boom periods, were always kayfabe, and it wasn't until 1982 that an alternative emerged. That's when the first official issue of the *Wrestling Observer Newsletter* was published by Dave Meltzer. Meltzer, a divisive yet influential figure in the world of pro wrestling, was a lifelong wrestling fan prior to starting the *Wrestling Observer* and had for years traded tapes and reels and corresponded with fellow fans all over the country. Every few weeks, Meltzer would compile match results and provide recaps and send these off to subscribers. As the years progressed, *WON* evolved and adapted, and Meltzer made the newsletter his full-time job beginning in 1987. Eventually, the newsletters contained show recaps, reviews, and reporting, and as he made more and more friends and contacts within the industry, he began to get exclusive tidbits and break news to subscribers, as well as keep people posted about when a star was leaving a company or going to a new territory. Kayfabe wasn't observed within the *Observer*, as Meltzer had a line into the inner workings and was more interested in keeping fans informed about their passion than entertained by fluff pieces and fake interviews. The other groundbreaking thing that Meltzer brought to pro wrestling fandom was the idea of a star rating for matches. His basic idea was that if you could boil a movie or an album down to a star rating that determines whether that bit of media is worth your time, why not apply it to the medium of the professional wrestling match? Working in conjunction with Jim Cornette, Meltzer devised a rating system on a scale of zero to five stars (occasionally a match is bad enough to earn negative stars, and occasionally a match has Kenny Omega in it, and earns more than five stars). This rating system informed generations of wrestling fans and critics, and every time there is a pay-per-view or large event, fans anxiously await Meltzer's official star ratings. Matches rated 4.5 stars or above are generally considered to be Match of the Year candidates. Occasionally, fans remember that criticism of any medium is subjective by definition, although this tends to be the case less often than you'd think.

Needless to say, the existence of the *Observer* and similar publications that followed, like Wade Keller's *Pro Wrestling Torch*, infuriated many within the industry—none more so than the bookers who ran the major promotions, who took to calling these publications "dirt sheets." By the time the internet arrived, the dirt sheets were already public enemy number one to the boys in the back, who bristled at having kayfabe be flaunted so cavalierly. During WCW's World War 3 pay-per-view in 1995, Hulk Hogan took it upon himself to burn a copy of the *Observer*, calling it a "rag sheet" and crapping all over its report that Randy Savage had suffered an injury and would be pulled from the event. Ironically, immediately upon burning the *Observer*, Hogan declared it "a dinosaur compared to the internet, brother. The internet's got the scoops!" Boy, does it ever! *WON* and the *Torch* would of course soon move to that same internet, to be followed by *Pro Wrestling Insider* and literally the million other pro wrestling sites in existence today (most of which just copy and paste news initially reported by either *WON* or *PWInsider*). All things considered, Dave Meltzer and the *Wrestling Observer Newsletter* are probably the entity most responsible for "smartening fans up" in the pre-internet era, and they probably continue to be the portal through which most fans get their behind-the-scenes news, directly or filtered through other sites, at times accurately and at other times— not so much.

But while *WON* is essential to the proliferation of the smart fan in general, it's only tangential to the rise of the internet wrestling fan. Until the advent of America Online and beyond, most of the internet was made up of enclaves of message boards. There are now incalculable numbers of pro wrestling websites, most of which are clickbaity nonsense or bot-generated SEO gobbledygook aggregated from other, larger sites, which have in turn usually aggregated that content from one of a dozen or so sites that do actual reporting.

But wrestling fans on the internet are pretty much always thinking about wrestling, and they'll pretty much always click on anything about wrestling. They'll never get enough content. The fact that there is a vast, bottomless audience of hungry pro wrestling fans searching for content has even managed to reach the attention of media giants like *Rolling Stone*, CBS, *Sports Illustrated*, ESPN, and FOX over the past several years, and they're starting to try to snatch up some of that free money.

The Montreal Screwjob shined a massive spotlight on something lying beneath the already-a-façade-clearly-labeled-"façade" façade of professional wrestling, and it sparked something in a whole lot of wrestling fans who either had access to or an interest in the internet. For many fans, this was the first tacit acknowledgment the WWF would make about pro wrestling being a work. The toothpaste was out of the tube, and over the next couple of years, kayfabe would slowly dribble out until the renaming of WWE in 2002, when the company would officially state in press releases that they're not a sport, they're entertainment. (The truth of the matter is that it can be both. And thank goodness for that.) As the World Wide Web became ever more ubiquitous in society, it allowed anyone with a passing curiosity in the sport to type "wrestling fake" into a search engine and go down any one of a billion rabbit holes that all lead to the same place: yelling at a stranger on the internet about why your favorite wrestler is better than theirs. And it all began because Bret Hart and Shawn Michaels hated each other's rotten, stinking guts.

As the year 2000 approached, it was time for a tougher type of wrestling. Shawn Michaels's success as an antihero babyface inaugurated the Attitude Era.

PART III

THE ATTITUDE ERA AND THE WWE MONOPOLY

13

GET READY TO SUCK IT

The Rock, Stone Cold, and the Attitude Era

As the late 1990s set in, the WWF began adding tits, ass, weirdos, freaks, sex, fetishes, foul language, car crashes, and threats of genital mutilation. Vince Russo's concept of "crash TV" meant that you couldn't turn the channel to WCW, because who knows *what* the fuck might happen. Everything was screaming or exploding or falling through a table or on fire or bleeding or covered in some other viscous fluid at any given moment. It was a two-hour train wreck of beautiful people trying to beat the shit out of each other, every single week. And it worked. By 1998, there was a term in place for this bold new direction for the WWF: the Attitude Era.

There are many reasons you should pour one out for the poor, departed Big Boss Man, but perhaps the biggest is that in his second WWF run as Mr. McMahon's enforcer, the man who was born Ray Traylor had to suffer through the absolute worst story lines that the Attitude Era had to offer. (And it had plenty.)

The Big Boss Man, between the years 1998 and 2002, did all of the following: he crashed the kayfabe wedding of Big Show's father driving the Bluesmobile before hitting on Big Show's mother and attaching a chain to the casket before driving off, forcing a sobbing Big Show to cling desperately to his not-even-close-to-street-legal daddy's coffin; he was hanged from the neck live on PPV by the Undertaker following a match at WrestleMania XIV, leading to a seeming kayfabe death (he got better); he cooked and fed Al Snow's pet chihuahua, Pepper, to Snow under the auspices of treating his rival to a fancy(?) home-cooked(?) hotel room(??) meal; and perhaps worst of all, he was forced to culminate his dog-based feud with Snow in the first and last Kennel from Hell Match, where the two men wrestled inside a cage inside a cage as nonthreatening guard dogs shat at ringside.

This was all just the material that *one man* in a company of dozens of performers had to work with throughout what is somehow lovingly referred to as the Attitude Era.

The late 1990s were marked by a transition to grown-up story lines (or at least a teenager's view of what a "grown-up story line" would be) and a growing awareness of the death of kayfabe. With the rise of *South Park* and other crass and irreverent cultural touchstones, the kids who watched wrestling were ready to be honest with themselves—and so too, finally, was pro wrestling. The dick and fart jokes ramped up, but another key factor of the next explosion of the WWF's popularity among the masses was more cerebral: for the first time ever, things really got meta.

With Bret Hart off to WCW, Shawn Michaels on top as the world champion, and Vince McMahon established as the owner of the WWF, the company leaned into its strengths and remaining roster and tried everything they could think of to catch up to World Championship Wrestling in the weekly television ratings. And when I say "everything they could think of," I mean that they ran with whatever they thought up at any given moment, no matter how outlandish or ill advised, and embraced chaos.

At the beginning of the year in 1997, WWE promoted Vince Russo to the position of head writer for its television shows and story lines. Russo, a tall Long Island native with a thick and barking New Yawk accent, had gotten his start for the WWF in 1992, writing for the official *WWF Magazine* under the name Vic Venom (a character who would eventually make it all the way onto WWF television in 1998, appearing in black and white ads for the magazine that aped Denis Leary's edgy-for-1993 MTV bumpers*). He joined the television creative team proper in 1996, and in short order he was steering the ship (inasmuch as anyone working under Vince McMahon *can* steer a ship, as all decisions must go through Vince). Russo's emphasis on being the loudest

---

* True to form for the WWF at the time, the Vic Venom Leary send-ups were a pop culture reference that was only about five years late.

and most correct guy in the room rubbed a lot of people the wrong way—including Jim Cornette, who left the creative team shortly after Russo came aboard and has sworn to live long enough to piss on Vince Russo's grave—but McMahon loved his ideas, and Russo's mix of titillation and potty humor was mother's milk to the WWF honcho.

There were a few key components of WWF television in a post–Montreal Screwjob world. On top you had Shawn Michaels and Helmsley's D-Generation X, a feud between "brothers" with perennial main eventer Undertaker and his newly introduced brother Kane,* the increasingly unstable corporate suck-up Mankind (aka Mick Foley), and the slow burn toward making Steve Austin the biggest star in the world.

WWE Hall of Famer Jake "The Snake" Roberts recalled knowing there was money in Austin the very first time he worked with him. "The thing I remember," Roberts said, "is Vince McMahon telling me that Austin would never be more than a third or fourth match on the card. I told him, 'That's your next superstar,' and he just laughed at me."

---

* Kane is perhaps the ultimate example of a wrestling idea that probably shouldn't work, but then ends up working spectacularly well for decades. Introduced by Paul Bearer as the long-presumed-dead brother of the Undertaker, the masked "Big Red Monster," Kane, was a supposed burn victim and mute (although he got better) who had been left for dead when the family funeral home burned down, and terrorized Taker for years afterward, alternately seeking his revenge and teaming up with his kayfabe sibling as the Brothers of Destruction. The former Isaac Yankem and Fake Diesel, Glenn Jacobs, would evolve the Kane character many times over the years, as Kane developed the ability to speak, make friends, and repeatedly beat up Pete Rose. Kane eventually became one of the most beloved and decorated characters of the past quarter-decade, and was elected mayor of Knox County, Tennessee, in 2018. (Jacobs was elected, not Kane. But really, there's no difference.)

As we've already covered, the former Ringmaster (and even more former "Stunning" Steve Austin in WCW) seemed to be on the precipice of something big after winning the 1996 King of the Ring and immediately cutting his legendary Austin 3:16 promo, but he languished near the top of the midcard until his nearly yearlong feud with Bret Hart culminated in the spectacular double-turn at WrestleMania 13. Finally, here was main event player Stone Cold Steve Austin, no longer an anti-Canadian vulgarian, but now an ass-kicking, beer-swilling, middle-finger-aloft take-no-bullshit antiauthority loner. He wore plain black trunks and boots in the ring, pounded "Steveweisers" like they were going out of style, and told everyone who hove into his field of vision to, emphatically, go fuck themselves.

Meanwhile, Vince quickly perfected his own "Mr. McMahon" evil boss character in the wake of the Montreal Screwjob. The moment was lightning in a bottle. Never were a heel and a babyface more perfect foils for each other and never was there a more opportune time for a foulmouthed character to tell his boss to eat shit and die. The WWF audience had grown up and was sick of cartoon heroes. For the first time, the WWF product grew up with them and said, "Hey, yeah! We *should* do cusses and not trust anyone!"

To that end, D-Generation X's signature crotch chops and entreaties to "Suck it," with "it" being their various and/or collective dicks, was in short order the subject of many a principal-office visit in schools nationwide. This was now, officially, if not an adult product, at least a product for kids who cussed in front of their parents or snuck cigarettes and for teens who couldn't believe they ever loved that goofy Hulk Hogan stuff for babies. It was a new era for a new audience and a new moment in the larger culture. This was a wrestling product for a world where *South Park* existed.

WCW was running on a combination of liberal doses of the nWo paired with established big-name stars from the past or from other companies: Hogan, Flair, Savage, Piper, Hall, Nash, Luger, Sting, Hart et al. WCW was innovating with cruiserweights, technical masters, and international stars from Japan and Mexico, but while work-rate connoisseurs thrilled to the great opening matches on *Nitro* and on PPVs, these new and smaller stars were firmly delineated from the talents and story lines that "mattered." Their next big breakout star (arguably their first in the *Nitro* era), Goldberg, wasn't a phenomenon until well into 1998.

WCW ended 1997 with a spectacular wet fart, as they bungled the biggest story line in the company's history and the culmination of an eighteen-month story in stellar fashion. At Starrcade 1997 on December 28, Sting finally got in the ring to challenge Hollywood Hogan for the world title in the main event of the company's biggest show. What's more, WCW now had in the fold the world's most talked-about and hottest free agent in Bret Hart, although he was restricted to "special referee" duties for the evening due to a sixty-day no-compete clause. In a rare case of Bischoff and Hogan not being on the same page, they had different endings in mind for what should have been the final, happy ending of the Sting vs. Hogan, WCW vs. nWo war. And in a not-rare-at-all case of Hogan going into business for himself, Hogan—shockingly!—went into business for himself.

The planned finish of the match would go like this: Hogan would hit Sting with his finisher, the big leg drop, and then corrupt nWo referee Nick Patrick would make a very visibly fast count and award the win to Hogan. Hart, sanctioned as a referee for the event, would order the match to be restarted and would shortly thereafter call for the bell as Hogan submitted to the Scorpion Deathlock—which just so happened to be the same inverted figure-four leglock as Hart's own Sharpshooter and the crux of the Montreal Screwjob. This finish would allow WCW to have Hogan and the nWo cheat one last time, get overruled, spoof the Montreal Screwjob, and give catharsis to Sting, Hart, and legions of die-hard WCW fans frustrated by the endless amok-running of Hogan and the nWo. Guess what: it didn't work out that way.

Prior to the match, after Hogan had agreed to the finish, he approached Patrick and told him, in no uncertain terms, to explicitly not perform a fast count after the leg drop. Patrick, just a cog in a very big machine, acquiesced to the demands of the person who he felt had the most power, and after the fact feigned ignorance in order to keep his job. What actually ended up happening at Starrcade was this: about ten minutes into the main event, Hogan delivered the leg drop and Sting was pinned, 1–2–3, clean as a sheet. As fans booed, Hart stormed the ring, yelling loudly about a crooked referee and a fast count, and ordered the match restarted. The move made both Hart and Sting look like idiots and crybabies, proved that Hogan had no problem beating Sting fair and square, and confused pretty much everyone. To make matters even worse, the title was vacated the next night on *Nitro* on the grounds that everyone involved was a moron, and fans had to wait until SuperBrawl VIII on February 22, 1998, for Sting to beat Hogan fair and square—in the second try, nearly two full months after everyone shit the bed. That's a long time for a bed to remain shitted, and Starrcade 97 was where WCW lost the faith of a good many longtime fans—for good.

But at least WCW remained top-heavy with established stars. In contrast to WCW's name-brand star power, Shawn Michaels was less than two years into his status as a world champion, and the longest-tenured, established main event player on the WWF roster at the time was the Undertaker. By necessity, the WWF was forced to create or elevate new stars up and down the card, which ended up being one of the main strengths of the early Attitude Era. As jobbers and squash matches were mostly phased out, there was an emphasis placed on an abundance of storytelling: if a character appeared on WWF programming, they were involved in a feud or story line. Every character was important on some level, and every character had a motivation or a skit or a blood feud. These weren't interchangeable cartoon characters stomping on "local talent"; they were WWF Superstars embroiled in drama, betrayal, the pursuit of a championship, or maybe just trying to avoid genital mutilation. (And what could be a more relatable pursuit than that last one?) As a result, nearly everyone who appeared on TV ended up getting over, because the WWF insisted their stories were worth the viewers' time. Serialized storytelling had been popularized with shows like *The X-Files* in the early 1990s, and now it had caught up to wrestling entertainment.

In the lead-up to WrestleMania XIV in 1998, the middle of the card was held down by Owen Hart (the only member of the Hart Foundation not to demand out of his contract and follow Bret to WCW, as Jim Neidhart and the British Bulldog did after the Montreal Screwjob), early UFC star "The World's Most Dangerous Man" Ken Shamrock, Jeff Jarrett,

"Wildman" Marc Mero and his valet and real-life wife, Sable, and perhaps most important, the Nation of Domination.

While former WCW world champion Ron Simmons was initially given a cringe-worthy gladiator gimmick when he first landed in the WWF in 1996 (complete with ill-fitting, bright blue helmet), he quickly scrapped everything but his name—Faarooq—and formed a Nation of Islam–inspired stable called the Nation of Domination. By mid-1997, he finally noticed that his black militant stable consisted mostly of nonblack wrestlers. He purged the group, keeping only D'Lo Brown, and rounded out the new Nation of Domination with "The World's Strongest Man" Mark Henry, "The Supreme Fighting Machine" Kama Mustafa (the former Papa Shango), and the newly returned-from-injury and freshly heel Rocky Maivia.

Touted as being the first third-generation pro wrestler in WWF history,* "Blue Chipper" Rocky Maivia debuted in 1996 after cutting his teeth under the name Flex Kavana in the United States Wrestling Association (USWA) that same year. Greener than goose shit on freshly sodded grass, Maivia had an impressive physique and, two years removed from a college football career as a defensive tackle for the Miami Hurricanes, undeniable explosiveness and athleticism. Maivia's pedigree was unimpeachable: he was the son

---

* In fact, Maivia wasn't even the only third-generation wrestler on the WWF roster at the time of his debut. Jeff Jarrett, who had his first run with the WWF in 1992 and joined the roster full-time in 1993, was the son of Jerry Jarrett and the stepgrandson of Eddie Marlin, both Memphis wrestling institutions as wrestlers and promoters. Granted, Marlin never worked for any of the McMahons' incarnations of the WWF in any capacity, so semantics win yet again where history is concerned.

of twenty-five-year veteran and former 1980s WWF Tag Team Champion "Soul Man" Rocky Johnson, who in turn was the son of "High Chief" Peter Maivia, a native Samoan who traveled the globe before eventually becoming the largest promoter of wrestling on the Hawaiian islands, in tandem with his wife, Lia Maivia, who ended up running the couple's promotion for years after Peter's death. If Maivia had entered the company as another face in the crowd, he might have found his footing. Instead, he entered with boatloads of hype, was given a run as Intercontinental Champion soon after his debut, and bounded to the ring with a springy mop of hair and a bright blue costume, beaming ear to ear and just happy to be there.

In any era before, say, 1992, Maivia would have been the blandest possible smiling babyface, a good-looking guy fighting for the love of the game and pleased to drink milk and remind kids to brush their teeth. Unfortunately for Rocky, his boundless enthusiasm, abundance of television time, and goofy appearance made him an anachronistic doofus; the first casualty of the late-nineties mindset of do-gooders being chumps and deeply, unforgivably uncool. The boo birds got louder as the months passed, eventually evolving into chants of "Die Rocky Die!" He lost his Intercontinental title and suffered a knee injury in late April 1997 and vanished from television for over three months. He returned with close-cropped hair, now sporting all-black attire, and the half-black, half-Samoan Maivia joined with the reinvigorated Nation of Domination.

While the good guy version of Rocky Maivia was a retread at best, the new cocky, brash heel version of Maivia was a revelation—especially on the microphone. Immediately upon his return, he began referring to himself as "The Rock," eschewing the baggage of his lineage with the moniker foisted upon him when he entered the company. The Rock was loud, probably the most arrogant Superstar on the roster, and, most important, always lightning-fast with a retort or an insult. He loathed the fans for telling Rocky Maivia he should die, but he gave them what they wanted: The Rock couldn't have been further away in tone and in intent from the bouncing chucklehead who entered the company the previous year. As his first feud in his new persona, he went up against then–Intercontinental Champion Steve Austin, who treated The Rock as though he was beneath him, but the two men continued to be a thorn in each other's side right up until the time both wrestlers finished up their Attitude Era tenures with the WWF—and eventually main-evented three different WrestleManias against each other.

With his eye-popping, scenery-chewing facial expressions, his exactly the right amount of over-the-top theatrics in the ring, and his occasionally lifted but always entertaining promos that were unparalleled at the time for their combination of humor and irritation, The Rock eventually turned fans to his side—but not before he finally overthrew Faarooq, cast him out of the Nation, and claimed ownership of the stable for himself. Even in his first few years in the business—even in kayfabe—Dwayne Johnson played second fiddle to no one.

The self-proclaimed "Most Electrifying Man in Sports Entertainment" lived up to his own hype, extreme though it may have been. In hindsight, he may well have been the very first postmodern wrestler. Hollywood Hogan showed glimmers of the same reflexive commentary on a pro wrestler portraying a pro wrestler, and there have been many who have followed in the years since Maivia's reinvention of himself, playing in the sandbox of the medium and using the established rules of the art form to make a commentary on its own ridiculousness. (How's it going, Orange Cassidy?) But in trying to be the most obnoxious version of a pro wrestler, The Rock happened into a wrestling style that would become his trademark forever.

Looping open-hand-slap "punches," extravagant selling (especially when taking Austin's finisher, the Stone Cold Stunner), moves that didn't look quite right; The Rock's move set was not the traditional grouping of well-executed, legitimate-looking moves to which fans were accustomed; it was a pastiche. His version of Bret Hart's signature move, the Sharpshooter, debuted in the main event of the 1998 Survivor Series. Just one year after the Montreal Screwjob, The Rock's surging popularity led fans to believe he was the antidote to Mr. McMahon's iron fist during a one-night tournament for the vacant WWF Championship. But then, in the finals, Rock locked a half-assed, terrible-looking Sharpshooter on Mankind, and McMahon rang for the bell. The WWF had swerved the fans with a send-up of their own Screwjob on the symbolic anniversary of the most infamous wrestling event in modern history and had done so to crown a new "Corporate Champion" with a move that was so poorly executed as to be laughable.

Bizarrely, the Sharpshooter then became a signature part of Rocky's repertoire, and never once did it *look* like it was properly applied or hurt at all, although both he and his opponent always made sure to sell as though it did. The Rock's Sharpshooter wasn't a wrestling move; it was a representation of a wrestling move, and within the framework of pro wrestling as art, that amounts to the same thing. *Ceci n'est pas un Sharpshooter*, if you will. To that end, one of The Rock's most famous finishers—along with a standing *uranage* throw derived from judo, the Rock Bottom—was the People's Elbow (named after Rock's penchant for referring to himself as "the People's Champion," a boast lifted from Muhammad Ali at first out of delusion, but which Rock eventually grew into). Originally devised as a means to irritate the fans while also popping the boys watching in the back, the People's Elbow involved Rock standing over a prone opponent, kicking the opponent's splayed arm in tight to their motionless body, slowly removing his elbow pad, throwing it into the screaming audience, making a large strike-through gesture with both of his flailing arms, bounding off the ropes, leaping over his opponent, bounding off the ropes again, halting all momentum when approaching his opponent for a final time, swinging one huge leg over his now-incapacitated-for-many-seconds foe, and finally delivering a single, routine elbow drop straight to the sternum of the hapless chump foolish enough to tussle with The Rock.

The People's Elbow was derived from the fact that even back in the late 1990s, the routine pro wrestling elbow drop was shorthand for professional wrestling, period. If anyone, no matter how much of a nonfan they were, wanted to instantly convey or mock pro wrestling, they merely had to hold up an elbow, pat it twice, and drop it. There's never been as efficient or effective a signifier for the sport. It's like miming throwing a pitch or a football or swinging a bat, but more evocative—and it doesn't need a prop. The Rock, that bastion of postmodernism, took the most parodied and diminutive performative aspect of pro wrestling, added buckets of theatrics, turned it into a parody of a parody of a parody, and would routinely make the time between setup and delivery of said elbow longer and longer, taking it to absurd lengths—and it would regularly end matches. As recently as 2013, The Rock won his eighth and final WWE Championship with the People's Elbow, ending CM Punk's historic 434-day reign as world champion. Of course, by that point, the People's Elbow was on a nostalgia tour—but we'll get there. The point is, Rocky Maivia's heel persona, that bastion of brilliant postmodernism, was not a pro wrestler: he was a performance of every pro wrestler who ever existed before him. The Rock was a loving commentary on pro wrestling and how it worked, a wink through the cheesecloth-thin membrane that separates kayfabe from reality. Not only was it inspired, it was effective, and exactly what wrestling (and the WWF) needed at the time. Eventually, his multilayered act would turn him into one of the most popular and successful pro wrestlers in history, and then into one of the most popular and successful *people* in the entire world.

The agreed-upon "official" beginning of the Attitude Era is WrestleMania XIV, which took place on March 29, 1998. McMahon had scored a significant promotional coup by getting a post-ear-biting Mike Tyson (then serving what amounted to a suspension from boxing for chomping on Evander Holyfield) involved in the main-event story line pitting Steve Austin against D-Generation X's Shawn Michaels, who had held the WWF Championship since the Screwjob. Tyson was part of the match as a "special ringside enforcer" who had appeared on WWF television leading up to the event in league with DX. WrestleMania XIV had always been intended as the coronation for Austin as the company's new top star.

In a rare case of 1990s Shawn Michaels doing the right thing, the Heartbreak Kid entered the WrestleMania main event with his back being fucked six ways from Sunday, specifically so he could drop the title directly to Austin and not diminish the lineage of the world title. In January, Michaels had severely damaged three discs in his spinal column during a casket match against the Undertaker at the Royal Rumble. During that match, Michaels had taken a high back body drop over the ropes to the outside. In the process, his lower back smashed against the casket waiting at ringside. Two discs were herniated and a third was crushed on impact, but he toughed out the match and then made it all the way to Mania in April. Michaels got his comeuppance when Tyson revealed himself as being on Austin's side, and after Austin won the title clean as a sheet, Tyson laid out Michaels with a punch to the jaw. Michaels retired immediately following the match, and although he was convinced his career was over, he returned to wrestling after a four-year hiatus.

At WrestleMania XIV, Austin captured his first world title, Kane and the Undertaker had their first match against each other, and Michaels had his last match for a very long time. The next night, the status quo continued to shift as major changes were made on *Raw*, which was still solidly trailing *WCW Nitro* in the weekly ratings. In a very literal symbol of Mania XIV marking a new era for the company, Vince McMahon unveiled a new design of the belt representing the WWF Championship. The previous design—now referred to by fans as the "winged eagle" belt in a hilarious and oblivious dispatch from the redundancy department—had been in use since 1988. A full decade with the same title design made the belt truly iconic and legendary where

the contemporary WWF was concerned: the title belt that
went from Backlund to the Iron Sheik to Hulk Hogan was
introduced in 1983, and Hogan's first title reign underwent
complete changes in 1985 and 1986. The 1988 "winged eagle" design was in place for the heyday of Hulkamania and
the entirety of the New Generation, making it the definitive
image of the world championship for at least one generation
of WWF fans. As such, it was a huge deal when McMahon
opened up the March 30, 1998, episode of *Raw* by coming
down the entrance ramp with a sparkling new version of the
championship draped over his shoulder. He entered the ring
to a riotous crowd booing the Mr. McMahon character so
loudly that he couldn't hear himself. He introduced Austin,
who came to the ring holding the old title. Austin looked
at his title, then looked at the one over McMahon's shoulder. He plucked the new title from McMahon's hand, threw
the old one down, and posed with his new championship.
(When first introduced, the new "Big Eagle" championship
was mounted on a blue leather strap and sported the old
"block" WWF logo, but by the April 26 pay-per-view, Unfor-
given, it would have a standard black strap. Later in the year,
the new Attitude Era "scratch" WWF logo would replace the
previous logo and complete the belt most identified with the
entire Attitude Era—a design that would remain in place for
all of four years.)

After introducing the new title, McMahon congratulated
Austin on his victory and tentatively welcomed him as the
face of the company, not so subtly indicating that there was a
right and a wrong way to conduct yourself as WWF Champion, and that they could go along to get along. He offered
Austin a chance to play ball by toning down his image and

aligning with the corporate vision, allowing the power structure within the company to remain cordial. Austin shook McMahon's hand, then delivered a Stone Cold Stunner to his boss and flew one thousand middle fingers as the crowd issued a full-throated scream of delight and approval, nearly everyone in attendance waving a homemade sign—a trademark of the Attitude Era and a bane to anyone who attended events with the hope of a clear line of sight to the ring at any point in the evening.

The Austin-McMahon rivalry was officially underway and would serve as the anchor for the Attitude Era WWF during the Monday Night Wars: the no-nonsense, blue-collar, badass redneck butting heads weekly with his millionaire (soon to be billionaire) boss, who despised an employee who refused to fall in line but knew said employee was too valuable to his bottom line to outright fire. The story line was perfect and ridiculous and relatable, and it caught fire. The April 13, 1998, episode of *Raw* was a landmark for both the rivalry and for the WWF, as they teased an actual match between Austin and McMahon for the world title. This treated fans not only to the potential first match between boss and employee, but the WWF audience's first glimpse of Mr. McMahon out of his oversized suits. The spectacularly jacked Vinnie Mac was a stunning revelation to fans, but they still knew Austin could kick his ass with one hand tied behind his back (no, literally tied behind his back—that was the stipulation for the match that McMahon insisted upon). The match ended up being a bait and switch, as Austin's one-armed-ness led to an opportunistic attack by McMahon's camp, which included Dude Love, Austin's challenger at the next PPV. The tease of the match did its job, though, as the April 13 *Raw* ended

WCW Nitro's staggering eighty-three-week-long streak of winning the ratings war. The WWF continued to tweak everything about their product, as the Monday Night Wars raged on with both sides claiming victories (ratings and otherwise) over the next year, but McMahon vs. Austin was the ultimate key to turning around the fortunes of the WWF.

For better or for worse, Stone Cold Steve Austin vs. Mr. McMahon has colored the overriding story lines in WWE to this very day; more often than not since the Attitude Era, the main-event story lines tend to involve a hero railing against an oppressive authority figure, be it a general manager, commissioner, or board member—and said authority figure is usually a McMahon. It all just speaks to the lasting effect the Austin-McMahon rivalry had on wrestling history and the people who still have to write it every week.

Attitude Era Wrestlers

As an aside, and in the interest of making sure we're not looking at the Attitude Era through the rose-colored glasses usually used, here's just a slight smattering of some of the greatest and most abysmal creations that Russo, McMahon et al. came up with during this time:

VAL VENIS. Perhaps there is no better encapsulation of the Attitude Era than Val Venis, the wrestling porn star. He told dick jokes about his "Big Valbowski" (his dick; his dick was the Big Valbowski), sprayed people with a flesh-colored Super Soaker, fucked everything that moved, and ran afoul of villains by fucking their significant others. He also briefly had a shirt available for purchase that said COCKED, LOCKED . . . AND READY TO UNLOAD, with the lettering in a font meant to resemble spattered semen. This ain't your grandfather's wrestling show!

KAI EN TAI. While this was an imported faction of extremely good wrestlers who represented the Kai En Tai DX stable in Michinoku Pro in Japan, they're best remembered for getting into a feud with Venis over him fucking the wife of their manager, Yamaguchi-san. Yamaguchi-san threatened to "choppy-choppy" Val's "pee-pee," so it's almost a step up, racism-wise, that Kai En Tai eventually winnowed down to two members, Taka Michinoku and Funaki, who would cut promos in Japanese with their microphones muted, while a booming monotone from somewhere backstage "dubbed" them into English in real time. The promos would invariably end with Funaki cutting what appeared to be a lengthy tirade in Japanese, but the only English dubbing would be a summarizing "Indeed." (Of course, Funaki was later repackaged into "Kung Fu Naki," which isn't even ethnically or geographically accurate, racism-wise. I don't know whether that's worse, or better.)

THE ACOLYTES of Faarooq and Bradshaw were created when the Undertaker captured the former head of the Nation of Domination and the former one-half of a generic cowboy tag team and turned them into his ass-kicking, brainwashed minions. The Acolytes became the fearsome tag team of Undertaker's **Ministry of Darkness**, which also included such hits as the 500-pound Mabel who was brainwashed, wrapped in a garbage bag, and renamed **Viscera**, and the always crowd-pleasing **Naked Mideon**, one of the Godwinns who showed up wearing only a thong and a fanny pack, based on Mideon's real-life affinity for being nude all the time backstage. Art imitates life? Anyway, the Acolytes would eventually reclaim their personalities and become the fun-loving, cigar-smoking, beer-swilling mercenaries the **Acolyte Protection Agency,** or APA, known for their stance on ass and their preference for always pounding it.

THE HEADBANGERS. Mosh and Thrasher were a tag team that perfectly envisioned every sixty-year-old creative mind in the company's idea of what a "headbanger" was: a couple of bald guys in face paint who wore skirts and eventually conical bras. As headbangers are wont to do. The Headbangers gain bonus points for later turning Mosh into **Beaver Cleavage**, a *Leave It to Beaver* parody that only appeared in a series of vignettes focusing on how much Beaver—ostensibly a small child of some sort—wanted to fuck his mother. The skits were so unanimously poorly received that the final appearance of Beaver Cleavage featured him breaking character, saying that the whole thing sucked, and storming off. He would soon reappear as the next-best idea they could come up with for him after incest didn't work out: just a dude named **Chaz**. Crushing it all around, everyone.

THE ODDITIES. Well, if you're going to get the Insane Clown Posse into the company, I guess this is one way to do it. A group of strangely proportioned or otherwise "weird" wrestlers were all put into one stable. **Kurrgan**, the big guy from the Truth Commission, was put in a tie-dye shirt and was now a fun-loving rasta guy, I guess? **Giant Silva**, a giant, danced around with everyone as **Golga**, who was just Earthquake in a poop-brown mask, waved around a Cartman doll while wearing a Cartman shirt. I think his character was that he really liked *South Park*. **Luna Vachon** managed the group, **ICP** performed the theme music, and while their music was undeniably a banger, no one knew what the fuck the Oddities were trying to accomplish.

MEAT. Shawn Stasiak, son of former WWWF champion Stan Sta-siak, became the boy toy of Terri Runnels, Jacqueline, and Ryan Shamrock, who were known as the **Pretty Mean Sisters**, because misogynistic acronyms were allegedly *hilarious* in the 1990s. Meat was literally a human fuck toy. That was his gimmick. His trunks were made to look like Y-front jockey shorts. A wrestler named Meat. That's it.

THE UNDERTAKER. Yeah, I've put off talking about the guy long enough. It's a testament to the man behind the performance, Mark Calaway, that he's been able to capture and hold the attention and affection of the public given what he's had to work with over the years. Like Goldust, this is a prime example of the artist being able to transcend and manipulate the art and take it far above and beyond what's been given to him on paper. Starting out as an un-dead Old West mortician, he was granted imperviousness due to mystical and supernatural powers contained within a magical urn sometimes wielded by manager **Paul Bearer**. He later became a phantom, or perhaps a ghoul, and was replaced for a time by an impersonator Undertaker after being placed in a coffin and as-cending to heaven(?). During the Attitude Era, he really started to lean into the occult stuff, becoming a quasi-Satanist with lightning powers. (No one tells you that Satan will give you lightning pow-ers, but it's true.) He got real into goatees and runes and formed his **Ministry of Darkness**, and later just turned into a nonmystical biker who loved MMA and his country. **The American Bad-Ass** version of Undertaker is just as silly as everything else, but no one is booing the Undertaker under any circumstances. He eventually went back to being the **Deadman**, a hybrid of all his previous incarnations but really just a more reality-based version of the original Undertaker. Not only has the guy always, *always* made the gimmick work, he bridged the gap between all eras: he won the world title from Hulk Hogan, was one of the pillars during the New Generation, was one of the four or five very top guys in the Attitude Era, and settled in as being the established ace kicking veteran in the Ruthless Aggression and Reality Eras. But we'll get there. My point is, my hat is off to the Undertaker, but let's not kid ourselves that the character isn't silly as hell.

One thing can be said about this era, especially given the above: there was no shortage of personalities.

14

THAT'S GONNA PUT SOME BUTTS IN THE SEATS

While the WWF roster had a plethora of personalities contributing up and down the card during the Attitude Era, there was one person who was a surprising key to turning around their fortunes with one of the most intricate and involved story lines in history: Mick Foley.

Foley looked like a Southern "maniac" rassler but was nowhere near the type of person Vince McMahon would historically earmark for anything big. He made a name for himself in WCW, Japan, and a few other territories as Cactus Jack, an unhinged and risk-taking freak known for his wild brawls. After parting ways with WCW in 1994, Cactus Jack began doing regular tours in Japan with IWA while simultaneously becoming a fixture in ECW as they were beginning to establish a name for themselves and a following. Cactus Jack was a sensation in ECW, blowing fans away by being the best promo in the company while at the same time pissing off the die-hard and bloodthirsty fan base by refusing to take risks or engage in the gore they desired. This was particularly infuriating to ECW fans because, thanks to the 1995 IWA Japan King of the Deathmatch Tournament—one of the main foreign-market events to become an early sensation in tape-trading circles—Foley was already an established hardcore wrestling icon: this was a guy known for his willingness to fall onto thumbtacks or jump into barbed wire if it meant besting his opponent. For ECW fans, it was a slap in the face for him to not risk his own well-being for their enjoyment.

Foley signed with the WWF in 1996 and was given an all-new look and character: the enigmatically named Mankind, who wore an all-brown body suit and an asymmetrical leather mask. The backstory of the Mankind character was that he was a childhood piano prodigy who was abused by his parents and cast aside (almost like Oswald Cobblepot from Tim Burton's *Batman Returns*, but with more piano and less raw fish eating). Mentally unhinged, Mankind would squeal like a pig and pull his own hair out during matches. His main opponent for the first couple years of his WWF run was the Undertaker (with whom he would soon be inextricably linked), but his world title match against Shawn Michaels at the Mind Games pay-per-view in 1996 was a revelation to many fans: not only was Mankind a strangely compelling character and a fantastic promo, but he could *go* in the ring, taking the WWF Champion to the limit in one of the best matches of the past few years.

On May 19, 1997, *Raw* aired the first part of what ended up being a four-part weekly installment of a sit-down interview between Mankind and Jim Ross. It's still remarkable that the decision was made to film, edit, and air these stunning six-minute segments, and it's impossible to overstate just how important they were for completely transforming a character from "Undertaker punching bag" to "grassroots hero" in the span of just four weeks. The interviews delved into Foley's complete backstory, beginning with his childhood dreams of being a pro wrestler. Foley was a fan in the crowd at Madison Square Garden when Jimmy Snuka made his immortal leap from the top of a steel cage onto Don Muraco, which was foremost on Foley's mind when, as a teenager, he developed his first wrestling persona: Dude Love, a tie-dye-clad ladies' man hippie espousing peace and love. As a college student, Foley filmed himself, as Dude Love, making a leap from the roof of his mother's Long Island house onto an old mattress. That college student would never have dreamed that his ode to Snuka would end up inspiring legions of backyard wrestlers for years to come. The Jim Ross interview discussed Cactus Jack's time spent in WCW and Japan, his status as a deathmatch legend, and the character being "unwelcome" in the WWF. Adding another layer to the proceedings was Foley conducting the interview entirely in character as Mankind, wearing his mask, his head shaved in patches, and speaking in Mankind's trademark scream-shriek cadence. He was Mick Foley, but he had also been turned into Mankind by his travels and his unorthodox career. The interview series ended with Mankind finally snapping and attacking Ross, ostensibly to reestablish the character as a main-event (or at least prominent) heel.

The interview series landed like a bombshell among casual and die-hard fans alike. For WWF-only wrestling fans, the segments opened up entire new worlds of the medium: deathmatch wrestling; Japanese indies; the lingering vestiges of the territory system; ECW. Traditional fans were delighted Cactus Jack was getting a spotlight and were also impressed by the straightforward way the WWF managed to somehow entirely bust kayfabe while remaining completely in character. More than anything, the segments made this heel character universally beloved: Mick Foley was a fan just like them, a world-traveled journeyman dedicated to putting his body on the line for the fans' entertainment and for love of the game. As the weeks progressed, larger and larger segments of the crowd began cheering for this supposed bad guy. Shortly after the interview segments finished airing, Dude Love actually debuted on WWF television.

Steve Austin was in need of a tag team partner, but when approached by Mankind, said he had no desire to be paired with a freak. Okay then, said the character of Mick Foley: if you won't team with a freak, how about a bona fide fun-loving ladies' man? Dude Love appeared in the flesh: Mick Foley's teenage vision of suave sexuality given garish life by being draped over the half-broken body of a delusional thirtysomething man. Sporting tie-dye and a drawn-on tattoo, Dude Love "danced" for the fans by doing the "Bee's Knees" Charleston Crazy Legs made popular by Looney Tunes shorts and dads the world over. Later in 1997, Cactus Jack finally made his WWF debut, and the "Three Faces of Foley" began to exist concurrently in the company.

After failing to capture the title as Dude Love, the Mankind character began wearing an ill-fitting white dress shirt and poorly tied necktie over his full Mankind gear, completing the now-iconic Mankind look. The shirt would get increasingly tattered as the weeks wore on, but the Mankind character would continue to see the perfect corporate champion when he looked in the mirror, where McMahon saw only a freak he could use as gullible cannon fodder.

It was in his guise as a would-be corporate champion that Mankind faced his old foe, the Undertaker, in only the third-ever Hell in a Cell match on June 28, 1998, at the King of the Ring pay-per-view. The match—despite not being much of a match due to the nature of what transpired—ended up being one of the most well-known and famous matches in pro wrestling history and exposed many wrestling fans to a level of brutality they never could have imagined. The match began with Mankind climbing the cage and standing on the roof of the structure, daring Undertaker to come and get him. Undertaker followed, and after a brief exchange (during which the two men nearly fell through the roof of the not entirely reinforced Cell), Undertaker unceremoniously flung Mankind off the top of the 16-foot cage, where a horrified crowd watched Foley plummet through an announce table, which essentially exploded from the force of impact. Jim Ross's on-the-fly call of "As God is my witness, he is broken in half" was burned crystal-clear into the brains of all long-time wrestling fans.

The match would somehow continue from there, with Foley rising from a stretcher and rescaling the cage despite a separated shoulder, only to take an even more horrifying (although not as spectacular) bump when the Undertaker choke-slammed him through the flimsy roof of the cage and into the ring below. A chair followed Foley down, knocking him square in the face and knocking him out cold. Terry Funk and other officials had to stall the Undertaker while Mick came to. Mankind and Undertaker finally had a semblance of a match, which came to a merciful end when Mankind was hoisted by his own hardcore petard by being choke-slammed onto a pile of thumbtacks he had introduced into the bout.

For better or worse, the Hell in a Cell match between Mankind and the Undertaker is one of the most influential in wrestling history. It set the bar for all Hell in a Cell matches to follow (making it impossible for WWE to have the stipulation match without fans beginning endless speculation about who is going to fall off, fall through, or jump off the cage), but it also became the end-all, be-all for "epic" WWE-style grudge matches. Moreover, it definitively brought Mick Foley's Japanese deathmatch style to the United States— although Hell in a Cell 1998 placed an unfortunate premium on spectacle and outrageous stunts. Deathmatch wrestling would evolve from here in both directions, but this was the match that birthed a thousand "hardcore" promotions and ten thousand backyard wrestlers.

Always interested in zigging when people expect him to zag, Mankind parlayed enormous fan interest in him both as a sympathetic never-say-quit, tough-as-nails babyface and a hardcore legend post–Hell in a Cell by taking the character in a more comedic direction, becoming more of an irritant to McMahon than a suck-up (while still couching his being irritating in the interest of sucking up to the boss). When Steve Austin sent McMahon to the hospital, Mankind tried desperately to cheer up his boss with some hilariously unhelpful antics, including a hastily drawn puppet on a tube sock that he dubbed "Mr. Socko."

This new weirdo amalgamation of Mankind was desperate to win the approval of Mr. McMahon above all else and craved the few scraps of affection that Vince's character would dole out to him. One of these tokens of supposed affection was McMahon decreeing Mankind the first WWF Hardcore Champion and gifting him a special championship belt to go along with it. The belt was an utterly destroyed version of the "winged eagle" classic WWF Championship,* literally held together with duct tape and with the words HARDCORE CHAMPION hastily scrawled across the crumpled tape in permanent marker. It was actual garbage, but Mankind treasured it like one of his children. The Hardcore title would quickly become a cherished fixture of the Attitude Era, exclusively defended in the WWF's signature version of hardcore matches—no-holds-barred, no-disqualification contests that were heavy on trash cans, cookie sheets, stop signs, kendo sticks, and other items that were loud without being too damaging.

The hardcore division opened up the midcard to give even more members of the roster more things to do and a bigger spotlight by the company. Former job guys were elevated to become hardcore ass-kickers, most notably Al Snow and

---

* In one of the more clever self-reflexive historical nods WWE has ever pulled off, the Hardcore Championship belt certainly *appeared* to be the belt that Mr. Perfect stole from Hulk Hogan on a 1989 episode of *Saturday Night's Main Event* and smashed with a hammer, in a despicable act of disrespect. In truth, this was a different championship wrecked specifically for the Hardcore Championship, but the rumor—or mistaken belief—that the Perfect-smashed belt and the Hardcore title are one and the same has persisted to this day. The belt that Perfect wrecked has been sold between belt collectors several times over the years, and you can see some lovely close-ups of that belt on YouTube and elsewhere.

Bob Holly. It was the immense ego of Crash Holly (billed at 5 foot 8 but looking much smaller than that next to most other WWF Superstars and eventually billing himself as a "superheavyweight" who arrived at the ring with a scale rigged to show everyone he weighed "well over 400 pounds") that led to the most enduring wrinkle of the Hardcore Championship: the 24/7 Rule, which stated that the championship can be won or lost at any time, any place, provided there is a licensed WWF referee in the vicinity to officiate. The Hardcore Championship then began to change hands in hotel rooms, in parking lots, in playgrounds, and anywhere else the writing staff could imagine, keeping fans up to date with the latest changes via pretaped segments on the weekly programming. The 24/7 version of the Hardcore Championship explains why there ended up being 240 discrete reigns from the championship's inception until its dissolution in 2002.

Crash Holly himself was a twenty-two-time Hardcore Champion, and ECW and WCW mainstay Raven was the record twenty-seven-time titleholder for a championship that was in existence for less than four years. The legacy of the championship, however, was so enduring that WWE introduced a new title, the 24/7 Championship, in 2019, which played by the same rules, but eschewed most "hardcore" elements at play in the Attitude Era.

But back to Mankind. Mr. McMahon continued to butter up the poor beleaguered Mankind in late 1998, positioning him as an adoptive son against The Rock, who was riding a wave of fan support heading into Survivor Series. That Survivor Series included a one-night tournament to determine a new WWF Champion, as shenanigans in the four-way feud between Austin, Undertaker, Kane, and Mr. McMahon (and

McMahon's newly introduced son, Shane) had resulted in the company's top title being vacated. It appeared that Mankind was McMahon's next chosen one to hold the title, serving the role of the perfect lackey willing to do absolutely anything for the boss's approval. The finals came down to Mankind vs. The Rock, but in a deliberate parody of the Montreal Screwjob just one year earlier, McMahon gleefully called for the bell when The Rock locked in a shoddy Sharpshooter, revealing Rocky to be Mr. McMahon's choice of a perfect corporate champion. Vince, Shane, and The Rock celebrated and gloated, attacking Mankind after the bell before Austin ran down to clean house (including hitting a stunner on a recovering Mankind) to stand alone at the end of the event.

Mankind feuded with The Rock for months afterward, leading to three landmark moments for the WWF in the Attitude Era.

The first moment came on January 4, 1998, when—with the help of D-Generation X and a run-in by Steve Austin—Mankind won Mick Foley's first world championship, defeating The Rock for the WWF title on the main event of *Raw*. What makes this title change so legendary isn't just that it was Foley's first world title win, but that the match actually took place on December 29. At the time, *Raw* was still in the practice of only being live every other week, and WCW would regularly give away the results of the pretaped shows on *Nitro* in order to both mock the not-live-every-week *Raw* and to discourage viewers who might be tempted to change the channel. Keep in mind, of course, that WCW did not *need* to do this—they were winning more weeks in the ratings war than they were losing, and they had had that unmatched eighty-three-week stretch of dominating the television sets of wrestling fans (of who, across both companies' fan bases, over 10 million were tuning in every single week). Near the end of the January 4 episode of *Nitro*, lead announcer Tony Schiavone, acting on the orders of Eric Bischoff, sarcastically informed fans why they shouldn't bother watching *Raw* on this particular Monday. "If you're even thinking about changing the channel to the competition," Schiavone sneered, "do not. Because we understand that Mick Foley, who wrestled here one time as Cactus Jack, is going to win their world title." Schiavone barked a forced laugh, and then, to cap off a moment he has freely admitted he disagreed with and hated having to deliver, he said as a half-aside to his broadcast colleagues, "That's gonna put some butts in the seats."

As the WCW team chuckled off the idea of an also-ran winning the world title, Nielsen ratings showed that *several hundred thousand Nitro* viewers switched from *Nitro* to *Raw* in the next few minutes in hopes of being able to catch that Mick Foley title win as advertised.

Schiavone was far from the first person to break the news—in fact, as was the practice at the time, the WWF had announced the title change themselves on the company's official website after the tapings had concluded the previous week—but many were made cognizant of the fact that, hey, world title change happening on the other channel right now. Making matters worse for *Nitro* was that this was the same episode as the infamous Fingerpoke of Doom. WCW, never content to deliver on an announced main event fans wanted to see when they could bait and switch the fans instead, had advertised a rematch between Goldberg, who had just been robbed of the world title, and the new champ, Kevin Nash.

Instead, Goldberg was arrested halfway through the episode on charges of stalking Miss Elizabeth. Stepping up to challenge Nash was, of course, Hogan, who had claimed to have retired a month earlier and had handed leadership of the villainous nWo Hollywood (or nWo Black and White) stable over to Scott Steiner. Nash—leader of the virtuous nWo Wolfpac stable, which had split from Hogan's crew and included fan favorites like Sting—accepted the challenge, and the main event featured both men circling each other and stalling for a few moments before Hogan simply poked Nash in the chest. Nash flopped to the mat and allowed Hogan to pin him for the title, after which both men leapt up, hugging and cackling. It turned out that the entire nWo split had been a long con and that the entire unit was whole once again, free to run roughshod over WCW without fear of reprisal. WCW had made a cottage industry of swerving the fans and pulling the rug out from under them, but this was the final straw for many fans—one rug-pulling too many, and an exceptionally egregious and unnecessary carpet-tug—just to make Hulk Hogan the world champion yet again.

It was certainly a choice, and in a company overrun with massive contracts for performers who either had creative control or were the actual bookers of the story lines, it was this type of choice that WCW continued to make, over and over again. Confronted with these endless nWo circle-jerks and WCW failing to live up to their promises, the Fingerpoke of Doom was the last straw for many fans. WCW would win more weeks in the ratings war, but the mood among fans was different after January 4. Viewers switched over to *Raw* and saw the long-suffering, inarguably deserving Mick Foley hold aloft the world title while an emotional D-Generation

X paraded him around the ring. It was perfect, cathartic, and wonderful, and in stark contrast to the cynical middle finger they had seen on *Nitro*. WWE would eventually get into the "you fans are idiots for letting us trick you into caring about this" game many times in the following decades, but the disparity between the moods of the two programs on that night was glaring.

The next Mankind moment was far less heartwarming. During an "I Quit" match for the WWF Championship at the 1999 Royal Rumble on January 24, Mankind was handcuffed and walloped by an unthinkable eleven unprotected chair shots to the head by The Rock as Foley's horrified children looked on in the front row. The aftermath and reality of that brutal match was captured in the landmark *Beyond the Mat* documentary by director Barry Blaustein, which arrived in theaters at the height of the popularity of the Attitude Era and became one of the lasting documents of modern pro wrestling. This match was the first many fans really took notice of the line that wrestlers absolutely didn't need to cross for their entertainment.

In short order, Austin reentered the world title fray, pitted against forever-enemy The Rock. Rock vs. Austin was just behind (or ahead of, depending on who you're asking or what metric you're using) Austin vs. McMahon as the defining rivalry of the Attitude Era.

The most horrific tragedy of the Attitude Era hit the WWF shortly after the debut of a second weekly prime-time show. In the months leading up to the May 23, 1999, Over the Edge pay-per-view, Owen Hart had formed a partnership with Jeff Jarrett and was also working a comedy angle, appearing as the masked and bumbling Blue Blazer, the superhero persona under which he made his debut in the WWF way back in 1988. For Over the Edge, held in Kansas City, Vince Russo came up with an elaborate gag for Hart: prior to a match against the Godfather, Owen would be lowered to the ring from the rafters (half a spoof of superhero antics and half a spoof of WCW's Sting), but would get "stuck" above the ring, flail, and release himself from his harness, landing in the ring with a pratfall. As such, it was necessary for Hart's rigging to have a quick-release harness. Hart made the rehearsal runs without incident the day of the show, and had made similar entrances on prior events, albeit without the quick-release harness. The first three matches of the night aired on *Sunday Night Heat*, and Hart vs. Godfather for the Intercontinental Title was scheduled to be the third match on the PPV and the sixth match overall, on an eleven-match card.

As home viewers watched a pretaped interview, a malfunction caused Hart to plummet 78 feet from the rafters of the arena to the ring, where he landed on the top rope and was thrown into the ring like a rag doll from the force of impact. The arena was stunned, and the fall was so sudden and violent that many in attendance at first thought a dummy had been thrown into the ring. As a horrified crowd looked on, Jerry Lawler left his spot at the announce table and was one of several who immediately ran to check on Hart. When the pretape finished airing, the broadcast cut to Jim Ross at ringside, who informed the crowd that Owen Hart had just fallen to the ring in an accident that was "not part of the entertainment." When Lawler returned to his position, he and Ross spoke in understandably hushed tones, harrowed by what they had witnessed.* Hart, unresponsive, was taken by ambulance to the nearest hospital, where he died from internal bleeding caused by blunt force trauma.

The freak occurrence seemed eminently preventable. As Owen's widow, Martha Hart, would later and repeatedly point out, Owen had been put in a harness that was practically designed to result in a tragic outcome. When planning for the stunt, Martha says, qualified riggers and stunt performers insisted that the act be performed with secure mechanisms, which Owen would need to be helped out of and which wouldn't allow for the lightning-quick transition from descent to in-ring action that the WWF desired. Martha claims the WWF sent away those qualified riggers and instead used a quick-release mechanism designed for sailboats—and designed to release with only five pounds of pressure. Despite this negligence, Hart's death caused eternal backlash to WWE because of what happened immediately afterward: after halting the pay-per-view for fifteen minutes, McMahon made the decision to move forward with the rest of the Over the Edge event. McMahon and a few others have always insisted that Hart, the consummate professional, would have wanted the show to continue. Many more, however—including Owen's brother Bret Hart—have

---

* To this day, when a WWE announcer takes on a hushed and horrified tone for story line effect or in reaction to a worked injury or a large and scary stunt, fans refer to the announcer's using the "Owen voice," which is a crass knee-jerk response to the inferred crassness of announcers being made to use a serious voice and treat the entertainment as though it is real. This was a far more rational response in the years after Hart's death, but it's probably time to stop being indignant about wrestling announcers trying to use kayfabe to make a story line more impactful.

insisted Owen would in no way have wished to continue or to wrestle after a similar tragedy. It was a no-win scenario for the WWF, with a very short window for deliberation, but they opted to go for the scenario that depicted the company in a particularly cold and heartless light. Later in the show, Ross informed the television audience that Hart had passed away, but the still-stunned live crowd in Kansas City was not made aware of that fact until they returned home. The remainder of the matches featured performers who were understandably shaken and trying to do the best they could, in front of a crowd that had just seen a man sustain life-ending injuries. Over the Edge 1999 was the second and final event to be given that name and was never released on home video. The event remained unreleased until 2014, when it was uploaded to WWE Network.

Owen Hart, the only member of the Hart Foundation to remain loyal to Vince McMahon and not jump ship to WCW alongside Bret Hart, had died in a WWF ring under McMahon's watch. His widow, Martha Hart, sued the WWF for wrongful death, eventually settling out of court for $18 million, which she used to fund the Owen Hart Foundation in their native Canada.

The night after the PPV, *Raw* was turned into a special two-hour tribute show to Owen. Wrestlers were given the opportunity to wrestle if they cared to, and the episode featured ten short matches, free of story line. In between the matches were testimonials delivered to the camera in pretaped interviews with WWF Superstars, all talking about their experiences with Owen and what a wonderful human he was. There was no shortage of tears or emotion, and it remains one of the best episodes of television the WWF ever produced. The broadcast ended with Steve Austin, the company's biggest star—who was nearly paralyzed when his neck was broken by an Owen Hart piledriver in a match between the two at SummerSlam 1997, which likely contributed to Austin's early retirement—offered a wordless toast to his departed friend and rival, leaving a beer in the ring for Owen as he looked to a large photo of Hart projected on the TitanTron.

Bret Hart learned of Owen's death while he was flying to appear on *The Tonight Show,* and he has expressed regret that he was no longer in the WWF at the time to try and talk Owen out of doing the stunt. When WCW returned to Kansas City in October, he hand-selected Chris Benoit—a graduate of the Hart Family Dungeon—as his opponent in a tribute match to Owen, introduced by Kansas City legend Harley Race. The two men put on a clinic: the best match they could have, in memory of Owen. They delivered what was every bit an instant classic.

The Monday Night Wars continued after Owen's death, and that tribute match would be one of the few true main-event highlights in WCW in 1999, as Bischoff's company continued their incessant bait-and-switch tactics and returned to stroking Hulk Hogan's ego. The promotion of Kevin Nash to head booker in early 1999 also raised eyebrows among fans, who were still rankled at what they perceived as Goldberg having his legs cut out from under him at the height of his popularity. As Nash himself has pointed out several times in interviews, booking the shows was its own particular brand of hell. In order to book any given week's three-hour *Nitro,* you first had to know what you planned to follow it with on the subsequent three-hour *Nitro,* and that involved having to preplan Thursday night's two-hour *Thunder.* So, in order to book any Monday's three hours of television, you actually had to book eight hours of television.

What made it even harder was that many contracts in the company offered veto power or other creative control to individual performers. Even if the creative team managed to book the night's show, they constantly ran the risk of taking the proposed episode's events to any number of main event players, only to be told, "That's not gonna work for me, brother." It wasn't a great business model.

Any given week's five hours of television living and dying based on the touchy egos of the big contract-holders continued to raise the ire of the workhorses toiling away on the undercard. Chris Jericho, a world-traveled superstar who became hailed as one of the planet's exceptional in-ring talents, garnered a passionate following in Japan and ECW before signing with WCW, but languished as a white-meat babyface on the undercard until he started getting really, really weird.

While Nash and Hogan and Goldberg were playing backstage politics, Jericho was becoming a legitimate Monday night cult hero and potential breakout star after transitioning from virtuous "Lionheart" to a petulant, tantrum-throwing, top-knot-sporting, egomaniacal paranoiac. He was lights-out in the ring and a peerless heel on the microphone. With the booking committee so focused on stroking the egos of the main event players and nWo members, many midcarders were free to come up with much of their own characters and antics, and Jericho ran with it. During a feud with Dean Malenko, "The Man of a Thousand Holds," Jericho proclaimed himself the master of one thousand and *four* holds, unfurled a scroll, and began to read them off. "Arm bar," he began. *Nitro* went to commercial, and when the show returned,

Jericho was still reading from his list. This is the moment many fans fell in love with this unrepentant asshole, but he kept adding to his character. He began styling his facial hair and long blond mane in as many ridiculous ways as he could. He started sporting gaudy, sparkly shirts, rechristened *Nitro* "Monday Night Jericho," and gave himself a long list of nicknames, including "The Ayatollah of Rock 'n' Rolla." He decked out an obese, toothless man in a half-shirt and introduced him as Ralphus, his personal head of security. He tried to give himself impressive pyro, like Goldberg, but it just fizzled limply. Every week, more and more "Jerichoholics" started buzzing about their surprising new favorite, but behind the scenes, Eric Bischoff just didn't see any money in him. The major players in the company thought so little of Jericho, in fact, that despite Jericho calling out Goldberg for weeks at the end of 1998, they refused to give him what he really wanted: a two-minute squash loss to the stampeding world champ. Jericho began planning his escape, and he wasn't alone in that sentiment.

In the summer of 1999, a "countdown to the new millennium" graphic would appear as a bumper on episodes of *Raw*, with days, hours, minutes, and seconds counting down. On August 9, The Rock was in the ring cutting a promo when the countdown clock interrupted him and counted down to zero. The lights flickered, pyro exploded, a video began to roll on the enormous TitanTron screen at the top of the entrance ramp—and when the lights came up, there was Chris Jericho, in all his glory. The arena exploded with surprise and delight, as Jericho and The Rock traded barbs on the microphone. Jericho adopted yet another nickname,

Y2J,* and quickly found himself at home in the WWF. Of course, for Jericho, entering an all-new company with an all-new power structure came with its own set of bugaboos. McMahon thought that Jericho worked too fast and had too much of the WCW stink on him, so he paired him up against X-Pac for a time on the house show circuit to get him used to working the "WWF style." (X-Pac was McMahon's go-to guy for these sorts of assignments, as he could work with anyone, make all his opponents look good, and led by example, as he worked the exact pace and style that McMahon looked for in his wrestlers.) Jericho entered into a long series of extremely crowd-pleasing midcard feuds and began what eventually turned into a record-setting number of Intercontinental Championship reigns. He was given a big spotlight (no bigger spotlight than debuting opposite the then-hottest star in the company, The Rock), ample television and microphone time, title reigns, and sold a whole lot of merchandise, but fans were quick to lament when it took him over two years to finally enter the world title picture. Even after that, wrestling fans would often and loudly bring up Jericho as an example of wasted or "held down" talent that the WWF dropped the ball on. Of course, today, Jericho is firmly ensconced in the pantheon of no-doubter all-time greats: a six-time world champion, nine-time Intercontinental champ, seven-time tag champ, and the fourth ever Grand Slam Champion, in addition to continually reinventing

---

* This was a play on "Y2K," the year-2000 computer bug that threatened to wipe out civilization. Ask your parents about it, kids.

himself over the years and inspiring generations of fans. But if you can count on wrestling fans for one thing, it's being good at knee-jerk reactions.

This is the perfect time to talk about the last few members of the McMahon family: Vince's children. Shane McMahon first began working for the WWF when he was fifteen years old, helping to fill mail orders in the company warehouse. He quit after a couple years to find a different summer job, and he still points to quickly finding a construction job that paid twice as much as his previous WWF gig as the first time his father was truly impressed by his initiative. He attended Boston University and then returned to the WWF, working as a referee before transitioning to a backstage role and learning the business at his father's side. By the time Shane became an on-screen personality during the Attitude Era (first as a babyface referee defying his father and quickly thereafter his most well-known persona as a sniveling little entitled shit), eventually earning the admiration and love of pro wrestling fans by his willingness to take absolutely unnecessary risks with his body, it was widely assumed that he would one day take over the business as Vince's successor.

Things didn't quite work out that way. He moved to a largely backstage role once again in the mid-2000s, then returned to the ring for a while before finally departing the company altogether in October 2009, officially announcing his resignation from all duties. He would remain absent from the company until his return seven years later, in February 2016. In the interim, he acted as the CEO of a company that provided cable and on-demand services in China. He remains a member of the board of that company, China Broadband, Inc., to this day. He also founded and serves as vice chairman for a digital asset distribution company that is today known as Ideanomics, Inc. When McMahon returned to WWE, it was purely in a capacity as talent. He has acted as commissioner of *SmackDown Live* and an active wrestler and on-screen authority figure ever since, seemingly content to be relatively free of the business end of WWE. In 2017, Shane survived a helicopter crash, proving that McMahons remain nearly impossible to kill by normal human means.

Stephanie McMahon Levesque also worked for the WWF as a teenager, modeling wearable merchandise in the company's ads that appeared in programs and magazines. Like her brother, she also graduated from Boston University, after which she immediately began working for the WWF full-time. She hasn't left since, quickly rising through the ranks after beginning in 1998, as well as appearing on WWF programming as herself beginning in 1999. Behind the scenes, she was heavily involved in creative by 2002, becoming executive vice president of creative in 2007. In 2013, Stephanie was promoted to chief brand officer, and has since become a public face of the company both in business dealings and in its philanthropic and community efforts, such as founding the nonprofit Connor's Cure, and sitting on the board of the Children's Hospital of Pittsburgh Foundation.

On camera, meanwhile, Stephanie was the embodiment of the Madonna/whore stereotype, appearing first as a pure-to-a-fault, innocent boss's daughter who was drugged and corrupted by baddie Triple H, then revealing herself to be a duplicitous gold-digger, in on her own corruption all along to get the better of her father and wrest control of the company from him. Real life and kayfabe dovetailed as she and Triple H got engaged, then married in real life, much like their on-screen personae. With the exception of a handful of years where she would only make a few appearances on television each calendar year, she has remained a fixture of WWE programming, appearing whenever an authority figure, champion of the women's division, or established foil to any babyface is needed.

And finally, let's talk about Triple H. Best known by the abbreviation of his full WWE kayfabe name (Hunter Hearst Helmsley), his real name is Paul Levesque. As a wrestler, he's known for his massive physique, his role as a cornerstone of the Attitude and Ruthless Aggression Eras, and for nearly two decades he has rankled fans for his perceived propensity to appear far too often on television, insert himself into the main-event scene too often, and hold down more "deserving" stars and fan favorites. Ironically, after being promoted to Executive Vice President of Talent and Live Events in 2011, Triple H has set about redefining his legacy as the man who cultivates and launches the next generation of stars. Under Levesque, WWE created the Performance Center in Florida and a second Performance Center in the United Kingdom; cultivated NXT into a viable and beloved third brand (alongside Raw and SmackDown) with a passionate fan base; launched the Cruiserweight Classic tournament and the annual Mae Young Classic women's tournament; founded NXT UK as the company's British territory; and has overseen the development and main-roster promotion of scores of wrestlers, as well as given guidance to scores more recruits and signees to the Performance Center and *NXT*—many of who have been snatched up from the independent wrestling scene over the past several years.

Altogether, the McMahon family has been at the helm of

WWE since its inception. In the case of Vince Jr., he has been the sole visionary and sole aperture through which the final WWE product is oozed out into the world. On camera, the McMahon family have been, to varying degrees, the most powerful and important *characters* in canon on their television programming and in story lines. They're the bosses off camera, and they're the bosses on camera. For the majority of the time since 1998, there has ultimately (in kayfabe) been a McMahon behind any babyface being held down or any heel being elevated. A sizable portion of television time each week is dedicated to some combination of Vince, Shane, Stephanie, and Triple H. To make a pure sports analogy, it's tantamount to 30 percent of any NFL game being devoted to a camera trained on Roger Goodell as he orders Bill Belichick to bench Tom Brady for a pivotal fourth quarter, or as he barks at horrified cheerleaders to take their tops off, because that's what the people are here to see, dammit.

But back to the Attitude Era. Another major event happened in August 1999: Triple H's final elevation to main-event player. After turning heel and splitting from D-Generation X, Triple H unveiled a new look (one that, with the exception of his once-lustrous hair, remains in place today) and captured his first WWF Championship on August 23. At the end of the year, Triple H—who was feuding with a suddenly babyface Mr. McMahon—pulled off an elaborate scheme that ended with the kayfabe marriage of Helmsley and McMahon's real-life daughter, Stephanie. The McMahon-Helmsley Regime (or McMahon-Helmsley Faction, depending on which half of the Mandela Effect is currently affecting you), ended up becoming one of the central story lines in the company for the better part of two years.

But that Triple H–Stephanie wedding story line was concocted by a new creative team. By the fall of 1999, *Nitro* was consistently losing to *Raw* in the ratings, and WCW's ploys of doubling down on baiting and switching and relying on celebrity cameos failed to move the needle. On September 10, the Turner brass decided it was overhaul time. Eric Bischoff, who had overseen WCW since before *Nitro* even existed, was out. (Officially, he was relieved of his duties. Bischoff claims he intended to resign but was canned before he had a chance to.) One month later, WCW signed Vince Russo and his right-hand man, Ed Ferrara, and gave them complete control of the creative direction of the company. Chris Kreski took over as head writer in the WWF for the next year (eventually replaced by Stephanie McMahon) and the WWF didn't miss a beat, continuing to rack up huge gains in the ratings of both *Raw* and *SmackDown*. At WCW, meanwhile, well, the transition to the new creative team didn't go quite as smoothly.

Unchecked by the laser-focused and micromanager-to-a-fault oversight of Vince McMahon, Russo and Ferrara's "crash TV" ethos was a nonstop cavalcade of lessons in bad taste. If the behind-the-scenes chaos and unrest wasn't enough, Bret Hart's wrestling career came to an untimely end at Starrcade 1999 in December, when an errant kick by Goldberg caused a horrific concussion from which Hart would never fully recover.

As the year 2000 began, Russo and Ferrara found themselves suddenly suspended and supplanted by a booking committee headed up by Kevin Sullivan. For a large segment of long-suffering and underappreciated wrestlers, the latest WCW regime change was a bridge too far: Russo and Ferrara's TV might be overly sensational, but at least they were interested in pursuing and showcasing younger stars. To give the book back to Sullivan, who had overseen some of WCW's worst, Hogan-centric years, was just too much to bear. Earlier in 1999, a new faction called the Revolution had debuted in WCW. Comprised of Shane Douglas, Perry Saturn, Chris Benoit, and Dean Malenko, the Revolution was a stable of immensely talented midcard wrestlers, crying out for a fair shake in WCW. Benoit left the group before the end of the year, and at the Souled Out PPV in January 2000, right on the heels of Sullivan being put back in charge, Benoit won the WCW World Heavyweight Championship. That same night, viewing the title as nothing more than an empty gesture that didn't signify real change or appreciation, Benoit quit the company. Just fifteen days after Benoit won WCW's biggest prize, Benoit, Saturn, Malenko, and Eddie Guerrero all appeared in the front row on the January 31 episode of *Raw*. The new stable was dubbed the Radicalz, and they sent perhaps the most poignant message of the entire Monday Night Wars: WCW was a sinking ship with no one at the helm, and not even the world title was enough incentive to remain in the fold.

WCW was still kicking, but in every conceivable way, they had already lost the war.

15

CHYNA, SABLE, AND THE WOMEN OF THE ATTITUDE ERA

On February 16, 1997, on the WWF In Your House 13: Final Four PPV, Goldust and Hunter Hearst Helmsley threatened to come to blows over Helmsley's untoward advances on Goldust's valet and real-life wife, Marlena. A scream erupted from the ringside area, and the camera cut to the barricade separating the fans from the action. Marlena, grimacing, was caught in a deep choke hold from behind. She clawed at the enormous, beefy arm encircling her throat as she was pulled backward and off her feet. A security guard quickly appeared and tried to pull off the gigantic assailant.

"Who in the hell's that?" hollered Jim Ross on commentary. Then, in disbelief, he wondered aloud, "Is that—*is that a woman?*" Indeed, it was, and as a policeman and the security guard trundled the six-foot-plus monster off into the darkness, Marlena collapsed to the ground in shock and pain. Goldust came to her aid and screamed, "Throw her in jail!" before carrying Marlena to the back. The next night on *Raw*, Helmsley ambushed Goldust as he was doing an in-ring interview and left him lying with a Pedigree. Marlena jumped in the ring and delivered an emphatic slap across the face, when the humongous woman once again appeared from out of the crowd, sliding into the ring and grabbing Marlena in a bear hug. Lifting Marlena off her feet with ease, she swung her back and forth like a rag doll, the tiny blond woman's head snapping horrifically to and fro. It took two security guards, four referees, and officials Gerald Brisco and Rene Goulet to pull Marlena from the clutches of the individual Jim Ross described as an "Amazon."

As she was led to the back by the small army of personnel, fans stared in stunned silence. They had never seen anything like this woman before, and the soon-to-be-named Chyna was about to become one of the most iconic figures of an entire era of pro wrestling—male or female.

WWE began easing back into featuring women at the advent of the Attitude Era—although this time around, athleticism and in-ring work weren't prioritized. Two of the biggest stars of the era were introduced as valets for Helmsley, who would strut into the ring accompanied by a string of conventionally gorgeous bombshells. For his WrestleMania XII match against the Ultimate Warrior, Helmsley was accompanied by Rena Mero, a tall blonde with an impossible body. The announce team took turns salivating over her until

Helmsley lost. Backstage, the elitist snob began badmouthing his valet until her real-life husband, Marc Mero, made his debut in the WWF. (He had previously been a popular WCW wrestler under the name Johnny B. Badd, performing a Little Richard gimmick. As is the law any time Marc Mero is brought up in contemporary discussion, I am obligated to blow about 60 percent of readers' minds by pointing out that the man best known for being "wrestling Little Richard" is not black.) Mero came to the aid of the valet, who then became his valet under the name Sable.

With her skintight leather outfits and knockout looks (combined with Jerry Lawler audibly creaming his jeans whenever she appeared on-screen), Sable quickly became a supernova, one of the most popular and in-demand acts in the entire company. Her willingness to show skin endeared her to both the WWF and to the male viewers whose puberties she single-handedly jump-started. While WWF honchos tried to figure out how best to cash in on Sable's popularity, her polar opposite made her debut.

Joanie Laurer was born in 1969 in Rochester, New York. She overcame a tremendously turbulent childhood and managed to liberate herself at age sixteen. That same year, she began weightlifting and studied abroad. By the time Laurer graduated from college, she could speak four languages, was a classically trained cellist, and was bouncing from job to job while competing in fitness competitions, looking for a vocation that would inspire her. She stood nearly 6 feet tall and weighed close to 200 pounds, entirely muscle. In 1995, she began her wrestling training under Killer Kowalski, the same man who trained Helmsley. She took it up quickly, and since no one before her or since has ever looked quite like her, she soon came to the attention of the WWF. In a stroke of creative genius, Laurer became the logical endpoint of Helmsley's succession of supermodel valets: if no model was good enough to be on the arm of Hunter Hearst Helmsley, why not bring in a woman as muscle who could do his dirty work for him? The idea of a prissy heel with a woman as his muscle was inspired and of course served to rile up fans. Under her new WWF name, Chyna, Laurer loomed large during Helmsley's matches, and she wasn't afraid to stand toe-to-toe with any man in the company.

Billed as "The Ninth Wonder of the World" (in keeping with the sublime in-WWF-canon lineage that André the Giant was the eighth wonder of the world), Chyna handed out low blows to Helmsley's opponents, whacked them with weapons, or steamrolled opposing managers. As Helmsley became Triple H and transitioned from Connecticut snob to founding member of D-Generation X, Chyna came along for the ride. She was an integral part of the group, serving as the no-bullshit foil and straight woman for the dick-obsessed antics of Helmsley and Shawn Michaels. She was also, from the very beginning, positioned as a peer of the men in the company, not of the women.

That positioning was beneficial not only for Chyna and the growing number of her fans; it was also beneficial for Sable. WWF slowly began incorporating other women who could act as opponents for Sable, who transitioned to a wrestler while still keeping her screen time light on actual wrestling. Jacqueline Moore was brought in from WCW, where she could serve as a base, a guide, and a rival for the inexperienced Sable. Jacqueline won the vacant WWF Women's Championship by defeating Sable on September 15, 1998, reviving the title and becoming the first black women's champion in company history. Between 1998 and 2000, the women's division was rounded out by Debra (the former Debra McMichael in WCW, who served mostly as a manager in the WWF for Jeff Jarrett and her then-husband, Steve Austin); Ivory; Tori; Lita; the Kat; and in comedy roles, the Fabulous Moolah and her longtime compatriot, Mae Young. Young, who made her wrestling debut in 1939, was made the butt of many a joke as a horned-up woman in her seventies who disgusted wrestlers with her sexual advances. (She also gave birth to a hand on WWF television, but we're not going to talk about that.) Young and Moolah ingratiated themselves to a new generation of fans by their willingness to be power-bombed through tables by the Dudley Boyz at an advanced age (seventy-seven for Mae Young and a sprightly seventy-six for Moolah), in addition to other stunts.

The state of the women's division in the Attitude Era was a strange one, as it is remembered more for Jacqueline and Sable's bikini contest (essentially a nudity contest) than for any match in particular. Announcer Jerry Lawler and Debra collaborated on referring to women's breasts as "puppies," which meant any time a babyface woman wrestler appeared Lawler would squeal "Puppies!" in an excited falsetto, while presumably furiously masturbating just offscreen. Signs— which were nearly mandatory accessories for every attendee of a wrestling show in the late 1990s—began imploring the women's division to show their puppies. While Sable and Debra and the Kat served as eye candy for viewers, adept veterans like Jacqueline and Ivory were there to keep their matches grounded—while also serving as eye candy.

In 1999, the WWF kicked off a long-running partnership

with *Playboy*, as Sable agreed to do a nude pictorial spread and became the cover girl for the April 1999 issue, which remains one of the highest-selling issues in the history of the magazine. Over the next decade, a number of other WWF and WWE women would become *Playboy* Playmates and cover models—until the advent of the TV-PG Era.

Sable was the first woman on WWF television to refer to herself as a "Diva," doing so in early 1999. By the end of the year, "Diva" was the officially branded term for women signed to the WWF (apart from Chyna, who didn't compete in the women's division). Although the competitors vied for the WWF Women's Championship, they weren't referred to as women. Male WWF performers were Superstars; female WWF performers were Divas.

By early 2000, the Women's Championship was once again treated like something between a joke and an afterthought. On January 31, manager Harvey Wippleman, disguised as a woman named "Hervina," inadvertently won the title, becoming the first man to do so. In late March, the title wound up around the waist of Stephanie McMahon, a nonwrestler, who held the belt for nearly 150 days—mostly without defending it, and mostly just to keep it with her as a heat-generating prop.

On the subject of Wippleman, intergender wrestling had been treated as a special attraction and amusement ever since the introduction of women into wrestling in the late nineteenth century. In fine pro wrestling tradition, carnival acts delighted in bringing hapless marks into the ring who believed they could best a lady wrestler, only to be sent packing, roundly humiliated. In Memphis in the early 1980s, comedian Andy Kaufman (a lifelong wrestling fan and devotee) became one of the biggest all-time heel acts in the region by proclaiming himself the Inter-Gender Wrestling Champion of the World and trash-talking Southerners while only agreeing to wrestle women who he had obviously planted in the crowd. (Ironically, Kaufman pitched the idea of his act, playing off his celebrity as a cast member of the sitcom *Taxi*, to Vince McMahon Sr., who thought the idea belittled the prestige of professional wrestling. Said angle, of course, became national news for the Memphis territories, peaking with an appearance on David Letterman's *Late Night* in 1982, wherein Kaufman's blood rival, Jerry Lawler, slapped the famous Hollywood actor out of his chair in an angle that fooled the entire world for a decade or more.)

ECW, WCW, and WWE all dabbled in intergender wrestling during the 1990s, but it wasn't until 1999 that anyone thought to take the concept seriously in one of the Big Three U.S. companies. Chyna, having been presented as a legitimate threat since day one, began competing in the men's division. She became the first woman to qualify for the King of the Ring tournament as well as the first woman to become No. 1 contender for the WWE Championship. Already having gained fans during the initial DX run and among women who found her stature inspiring and admirable, Chyna finally became a full-fledged babyface by becoming blood rivals with Jeff Jarrett. Jarrett derided Chyna as having no business competing against men, and the feud culminated in a no-disqualification "Good Housekeeping Match" that marked Jarrett's final bout for the company. Chyna prevailed, winning the Intercontinental Championship. In doing so, she became the first woman to win any nonwomen's title in the company. She later became co–Intercontinental Champion with Chris Jericho. After losing the title for the final time, neither she, nor any other woman in company history, ever challenged for the Intercontinental Championship again.

As Chyna's popularity exploded, her appearance began to change. During her time in the WWF, Laurer underwent several cosmetic procedures, including plastic surgery on her jaw and breast implants, as well as leaning up considerably. Chyna was still more muscular than any other woman in the company, but she was no longer treated as a singular freak of nature. She began to be treated more and more like a sex symbol, beginning an immensely popular and successful pairing with Eddie Guerrero, who became a Lothario as a result of an overabundance of Latino Heat. To go along with her new image, Chyna—for the first time in her career—was moved into the women's division. In November 2000, Chyna appeared on the cover of *Playboy* for the first time.

After her appearance in *Playboy*, Chyna entered into a feud with Ivory, who at this point was Women's Champion and part of Right to Censor, a moral majority/Puritan/prude faction that was an overt parody of (or more accurately, a big "fuck you" to) the Parents Television Council, which had been open in their disdain for WWF programming. Chyna prevailed over the modesty crusader at WrestleMania X-Seven, winning her first and only WWF Women's Championship. Chyna was taken off television in late May and never returned, officially vacating the title when her contract expired in November 2001. There are conflicting reports about the circumstances around her departure from the company, but at least on some level, her relationship with Triple H had to have played a factor. Chyna and Helmsley began dating almost immediately upon her debut in the company, which turned into a five-year relationship. At some point between 2000 and 2001, the on-screen pairing between Triple H and Stephanie McMahon turned into a real-life romance, which likely involved some level of overlap with Triple H's existing relationship with Chyna. The split between Chyna and Triple H was a messy one, and with the boss's daughter involved, it became painfully easy for people in power within the company to pick sides.

Chyna passed away in 2011 as the result of an overdose, and was finally returned to WWE canon when she was inducted into the Hall of Fame in 2019 as part of D-Generation X. She remains one of the most important, if not the single most important, woman in the history of WWE. She inspired a generation of wrestling fans and had one-of-a-kind crossover appeal. No other woman in wrestling history had ever been, nor has been depicted as being, across-the-board equal to all competitors, male or female. Even wrestling purists admit that there was never any suspension of disbelief at the "unreality" of intergender wrestling when Chyna was involved.

16

A MONOPOLY ON EVERYTHING BUT PANDA BEARS

WWE Closes Down the Competition and Gets the F Out

The final episode of *Nitro*—just like "Black Saturday" for Georgia Championship Wrestling all those years earlier—opened with a shot of Vince McMahon speaking to the home viewers. He did just what he set out to do: drive a stake through the heart of WCW, then put his leering face all over the show, to celebrate his greatest personal achievement. In his biggest professional accomplishment to date at that time, he gleefully presented himself as exactly what his detractors always thought of him: a ruthless businessman who drives his opponents out of business and then gets his rocks off to the fullest by making sure as many people as possible are unhappy. Mr. McMahon, the villain, is one of the purest characters in pro wrestling history, and it succeeds precisely because it is entirely in line with what most observers and nearly all wrestling fans believe Vince McMahon to actually, *truly* be like. To his credit, McMahon has also gone out of his way in numerous interviews and public appearances—ostensibly out of kayfabe—to allow people to continue to believe the very worst about him. Since the birth of the Mr. McMahon character, Vince is happy to play the part of the heel. By the time of the publication of this book, the question is always exactly how self-aware he is—and how much he's working us all.

As I noted early on, you don't have to do more than type "Vince McMahon" into Google to get a bevy of autocomplete questions or stories about endless employees, peers, coworkers, rivals, and even friends who will talk at length about the outlandish character that Vince McMahon actually is in real life. The sneeze-hating, steak-chomping, burrito-unaware, airplane-aisle-fighting Vince McMahon is all too real, but it's precisely because of his particular brand of mania that his company ended up on the winning end of the Monday Night Wars.

Well, it's a combination of McMahon's drive and megalomaniacal micromanaging and authoritarian rule over WWE—combined with WCW's fatal combination of budgetary ineptitude and a creative team that was sorely lacking in creativity while also having to juggle a half-dozen of the biggest creative-control prima donnas in pro wrestling history. McMahon has never and would never allow any of his subordinates to have the final say in story lines without his approval, and that ended up being one of the most important differences in the fates of the two companies. McMahon's need for control above all is why WWE continues to pump out McMahon-approved history—even if it tends to clash with the facts.

The overwhelming popularity of the Attitude Era was also partly a miracle of timing, as great characters arrived just as the company tapped into the zeitgeist by pushing the envelope with tawdry story lines and the juvenile humor that passed for "adult" at the time. But the rise of the WWF during the Monday Night Wars owed just as much to simply not making the mistakes that WCW made.

The "buck stops here" command of Vince McMahon proved to be the thing that kept the ship on course, as WCW's many cooks and clashing egos, all with creative control, just led to a clusterfuck that only kept getting more clustered and more fucky as the weeks and months wore on. Granted, McMahon had plenty of help from all corners, both in the ring and behind the scenes, but his single-minded drive to win against WCW kept him willing to take risks and push the envelope—while still maintaining the final word on all content that made it onto the air. Within years, he would find himself without legitimate competition, would buy out his rivals, and would begin writing the official company revisionist history, which is still being revised and generally lands on a scale somewhere between "charitable" and "laughably false." But the winners make the rules, and in McMahon's history, he will always—*always*—be the winner.

As WWF barreled headlong toward WrestleMania 2000, they could seemingly do no wrong. Even with Steve Austin out of action since November 1999, the company wasn't missing a beat. Behind the white-hot Rock; a blood feud with Mick Foley that cemented Triple H as a main-eventer once and for all; a reinvigorated tag team scene with the Hardy Boyz, Edge and Christian, and the freshly arrived from ECW Dudley Boyz; a burgeoning star in the obnoxious Olympic gold medalist Kurt Angle; and the quintet of Jericho and the Radicalz, WCW's previous hottest under-the-radar stars, in addition to the usual cast of ne'er-do-wells making up the lower card and the hardcore division, the WWF was lacking in neither star power nor creativity.

Contrast that with WCW at the time, which was nothing short of an absolute dumpster fire. To this day, there is a not-insignificant subset of people who believe that Russo and Ferrara intentionally tanked WCW—moles acting on orders from McMahon. Of course, there are also large segments of fans who believe the Montreal Screwjob is a work. If you *were* going to intentionally tank and bankrupt an entire company, you probably couldn't do a better or more efficient job than Russo and Ferrara did—at least in the eyes of fans. Creating story lines that were impossible to parse; endless rebooting of story lines and allegiances; ramping up the game of hot potato in story lines; taking mean-spirited jabs at beloved characters like Jim Ross; and making two middle-aged wrestling writers the focus of national wrestling shows were all on Russo and Ferrara's agenda—and viewers began tuning out in droves.*

After putting Sullivan in charge of booking hadn't set the world on fire, WCW removed him once again and called both Bischoff *and* Russo back into service. The two men decided to take one of the most drastic measures a major pro wrestling company had ever seen at that point: a hard reboot of WCW. It's as if their big solution to pitch to leadership was "have you tried turning it on and off again?"

The new regime had a spectacular new high-profile stumble on deck, however. WCW had recently attempted to get into the multimedia game by coproducing a major studio motion picture that was heavily WCW-branded: *Ready to Rumble*, starring David Arquette, Scott Caan, and Oliver Platt as washed-up main-eventer Jimmy "The King" King. Arquette, who was a massive and lifelong wrestling fan, was approached and offered a chance to be WCW World Heavyweight Champion. Arquette tried to explain that he wasn't a wrestler, and that fans would hate it, but WCW insisted, coming up with a finish where he would "accidentally" win the title, and explaining that it would be good for everyone: him, the company, and the box office for *Ready to Rumble*. Put in a position that every wrestling fan has thought of and no wrestling fan would realistically be able to turn down, he acquiesced.

On the April 26 episode of *Thunder* (taped the night before), Arquette and Page faced Jarrett and Bischoff in a tag

---

* I absolutely don't believe Russo and Ferrara were moles tanking WCW on purpose. The biggest tell of all is their track record and arm's distance from WWE after WCW folded.

team match, where the winner of the fall would leave as world champion. After Bischoff was knocked out, Arquette pinned him to win the world title of DDP, his own partner. To say that wrestling fans shat on this result would be an insult to shitting: over the course of Arquette's twelve-day reign as world champion, fans went ballistic and flipped to the competition in disgust.

This story does have a happy ending in at least one sense, though: Arquette never lost his love for wrestling, and decided to do it right nearly twenty years later. He began real pro wrestling training and in 2018, at age forty-six, he debuted as a real pro wrestler on the independent circuit. He continues to take bookings and takes his role as a pro wrestler very seriously, and his willingness to sacrifice his body for sheer love of the craft has flipped fan sentiment on him 180 degrees, to the point where there is a legitimate groundswell to get him involved in a major WWE event like Royal Rumble or WrestleMania. It just goes to show you that anyone can win the love of wrestling fans. All it takes is dedication and, like, nineteen years!

The New Blood vs. Millionaire's Club feud persisted for a time after the Arquette debacle, but if you were thinking it sounded a lot like the nWo vs. WCW feud, you're correct. Fans quickly felt fatigue from the same old "our company hates your company" faction warfare. Finally, even Hogan jumped ship, in a worked-shoot-turned-actual-shoot two-for-one. The agreed-upon story line was that Hogan, frustrated with a lack of story line ideas and with the direction of the company, would flex his creative control muscle and refuse to lose a match to current world champion Jarrett. After this, Hogan grabbed the microphone and berated Russo, saying, "This is why this company is in the damn shape it's in; because of bullshit like this." That was all part of the edgy worked shoot story line, but both Hogan and Bischoff were apparently unaware of what came next. After Hogan left the arena, Russo returned to the ring and ran down Hogan as a prima donna he hated working with, publicly firing him from the company and stripping him of the title, promising you would never see Hogan in WCW again. Indeed, Hogan never returned to WCW television and attempted to sue Russo for defamation of character. (The lawsuit was dismissed in 2003, because courts were savvy enough to realize you couldn't defame a pro wrestling heel for pro wrestling comments on a pro wrestling show. There go my dreams of suing the estate of Freddie Blassie for his referring to wrestling fans as pencil-necked geeks.) Bischoff, never having been much of a fan of Russo to begin with, also left WCW as a result of the swerve.

Meanwhile, the WWF was mostly firing on all cylinders in 2000, despite a derided WrestleMania 2000 four-way main event that boasted "a McMahon in every corner" and mostly served up a world title match as a backdrop to a Vince vs. Stephanie vs. Shane vs. Linda McMahon feud. Triple H retained the world title, marking the first time in the sixteen-year history of WrestleMania that a heel was victorious in the main event. The majority of the rest of the year was focused on a feud between The Rock and Triple H and Stephanie McMahon-Helmsley in the main event, while the undercard remained white-hot with feuds involving Chris Jericho, Chris Benoit, and Kurt Angle; the tag team division being revolutionized by the Dudley Boyz, the Hardy Boyz, and Edge and Christian; and the spectacular romantic pairing of

"Latino Heat" Eddie Guerrero and Chyna. Angle entered the main-event mix late in the year and captured his first world title in October, just as Steve Austin returned from a nine-month rehabilitation from neck surgery.

The years 1999 and 2000 had been huge for the WWF from a business standpoint, and the McMahons responded by announcing a bevy of outside ventures. On October 19, 1999, the WWF became a publicly traded company and made Vince McMahon a billionaire for the first time. (McMahon would see his personal value fluctuate for years based on the stock price and WWE's ventures, but he returned to billionaire status in 2014 and has only gotten richer each year since.) The following month, WWF New York opened in Times Square. The WWF-themed restaurant and night club (and merchandise store, of course) became a fixture of WWF programming for the next few years, with many special events held there and secondary host segments beamed in via satellite on nearly every episode of *Raw* and each PPV for months. The restaurant was renamed the World in 2002 before closing the following year. The former site of WWF New York is now the location of the Times Square Hard Rock Café.

In February 2000, McMahon announced his largest non-wrestling undertaking ever: in conjunction with NBC and Dick Ebersol, the XFL football league was launched. McMahon proclaimed the NFL to be the "No Fun League" and promised smash-mouth football with a lack of penalties and other distractions, insisting he was returning the love of American football to fans who were longing to see hard-hitting, no-nonsense action. The XFL was, of course, a notorious failure, although much of that had largely to do with the short lead time between the announcement of the league and its debut the following spring. Lack of preparation and planning and knee-jerk reactions by both the WWF and NBC sides when ratings began plummeting led to a bizarre product, which McMahon then tried to revive with hasty titillation tactics like promising a camera in the cheerleaders' locker room. When the XFL folded after just one season, the NFL was happy to steal certain innovations—like the over-the-field Skycam, which is now a staple of the league—but for nearly twenty years, the most lasting memory of the XFL came from running back Rod Smart. The XFL allowed players to have nicknames rather than surnames on the backs of their jerseys if they so desired, and Smart—who broke off big plays in the XFL's first nationally televised game—opted to have his jersey say HE HATE ME. For many years, "He Hate Me" became a shorthand for the league. Against all odds, the XFL made a return in 2020, with a lot more lead time and a much more fleshed-out plan. Despite doing solid (for 2020) ratings and being universally praised for its myriad fun new football innovations, the 2020 season was cut short due to the pandemic caused by the COVID-19 novel coronavirus. A month later, they laid off nearly everyone in the company and filed for bankruptcy. Despite there being a television deal for 2021, there's no guarantee the league will return.

Even if WWF television and story lines hadn't been far more good than bad in the year 2000, it would have taken a Herculean effort to do a worse job or turn off more fans than WCW was doing on a weekly basis. Around the time Austin returned to the WWF, Russo departed WCW once again—this time for good—after suffering a concussion while winning the WCW World Heavyweight Championship. No, that's not a typo.

WCW returned to a more traditional booking committee following Russo's departure, but there were more serious issues looming than who was booking the shows (although the questionable booking definitely helped lead to this point).

Ted Turner had remained fiercely loyal to WCW during his time running TNT and Turner Broadcasting, partly due to Jim Crockett and WCW having been the anchor of his first national television station, TBS. Turner was perfectly happy to keep pro wrestling on his station, even during the many years it operated at a loss. Following the Time Warner buyout in 1996, the new executives were less thrilled about WCW being a loss leader, but Turner still had pull. That all changed when Time Warner merged with AOL in 2000, as Turner no longer had any say at all at TNT. AOL Time Warner opened the books on WCW and likely nearly fell on the floor when they learned that not only had WCW been losing an average of more than $14 million a year, they had lost $60 million *in the year 2000 alone*. Handcuffed by numerous guaranteed big-money contracts (including Hogan's, who was currently sitting at home in protest), the parent company began cutting back costs wherever they could, including running shows exclusively in the Southeast near WCW's Atlanta base of operations, while quietly looking for someone who might be willing to purchase the WCW albatross.

Around the time it became clear within WCW that its days were likely numbered, the WWF managed an end-around to eliminate its next-closest competitor, ECW, simply by signing a contract to be the premier wrestling show on TNN (later Spike). Paul Heyman and TNN executives butted heads throughout their short tenure at the network, so when *Raw* needed a new cable channel in 2000, the network was all too happy to scoop up the biggest wrestling company in the world and kick Heyman's baby to the curb.

Two months after TNN dropped ECW, wrestling fans were stunned when Paul Heyman walked down the entrance ramp on an episode of *Raw* and joined Jim Ross at the broadcast desk, becoming the official replacement for longtime color commentator Jerry "The King" Lawler, who had quit the company after his then-wife, Stacy "The Kat" Carter, had been fired. ECW officially closed on April 4, 2001. Many members of the ECW roster didn't know just how dire the situation with their company had become until Heyman showed up, without warning, on *Raw*. As lawyers began picking up the pieces of what was once ECW, the company was estimated to have a value of about $1.4 million—against nearly $9 million in debt. Shane Douglas, who was under WCW contract at the time, was still owed tens of thousands of dollars by ECW.

ECW was dead, but despite its own woes and its years of bleeding money, WCW remained a much bigger monster, and Vince McMahon still wanted nothing more than to drive a stake through its heart.

Bischoff, who never stopped believing in the value and marketability of the WCW brand, put together an investor group called Fusient Media Ventures, with the express intent of obtaining the rights to WCW. Bischoff's group believed they had a deal firmly in hand and was preparing to publicly announce the sale when Jamie Kellner, the head of Turner Broadcasting, announced the cancellation of all WCW programming on TNT and TBS. Bischoff's Fusient partners backed out of the deal despite Bischoff's pleas to purchase the company and shop it to other networks. The value of the company plummeted without a guaranteed weekly time slot, and that allowed Vince McMahon and the WWF to swoop in and put a stake in the heart of its longest-running and most public adversary.

For the bargain basement cost of $3 million, the WWF purchased outright all WCW trademarks and the entire WCW/NWA tape library on March 23, 2001, in addition to buying out two dozen contracts of wrestlers that seemed a good value to McMahon. The final TNT broadcast of *Nitro* was slated for March 26, 2001, as the news made headlines and landed like a solid punch to the solar plexus for every wrestling fan the world over. Even the most adamant and loyal WWF fan was blindsided and stunned by the news; what did being a wrestling fan even mean if there wasn't another side to kick around anymore?

The final brain trust of WCW—led by bookers John "Johnny Ace" Laurinaitis and Terry Taylor (unfortunately, to this day, still best known as the former Red Rooster in the WWF)—hoped to send WCW out with a bang, showcasing the best of what World Championship Wrestling had always had to offer. For the most part, they were allowed to, as the WWF of course had its own show to promote that night.

Pretty much everyone knew ahead of time that the deal had been completed and that the WWF was the buyer. But no one had *officially* handed down the news to the WCW employees, nor informed anyone what would happen next. Since McMahon was tied up with *Raw*, he sent Shane McMahon to Florida and that evening's episode of *Nitro* as an emissary—and also to be the person to break the news to the WCW locker room. In a hastily assembled meeting of the entire roster and the WCW booking committee, Shane delivered the announcement as he had been instructed.

"I remember walking in and addressing everyone," Shane recounted on an episode of *Table for 3.* "A lot of the guys I [already] knew, obviously, through different iterations of [them] being through [WWF]. I said something along the lines of, 'Those that want to be on board, we're very open arms and welcome. Those that don't, we completely understand your position. If you don't want to be involved with [us], we understand that as well. As of right now, just to let you guys all know, [the WWF] has purchased WCW.' And everyone—that's the first time they heard it. I looked around that room at [the] faces. Some were awestruck. Some were shocked. Some were angry. I could see it. I said, 'Oh boy, I don't know if I'm getting out of here.'"

Which brings us to the very last episode of *WCW Monday Nitro.*

Raw was in Cleveland that evening, and McMahon opened the show by appearing via satellite on both *Nitro* and the simulcast of *Raw.* After the McMahon segment, *Nitro* continued to air independently, although the concurrent episode of *Raw* featured multiple backstage segments of McMahon watching both shows on side-by-side televisions, gloating about his purchase of WCW and how much better a show *Raw* was putting on. (He also listed a number of WCW wrestlers who he may or may not choose to fire, possibly judging crowd reactions at mentions of the names by the WWF fans in attendance—and he specifically singled out Jeff Jarrett as someone who would emphatically *not* be welcome in the WWF, announcing he would be fired at the end of the night.) WCW wrapped up with WCW's greatest rivalry: Sting vs. Ric Flair for the last time ever. Flair wrestled the match wearing a WCW shirt, and after Sting got the submission victory, the two men shared an emotional embrace. It was WCW at its best, with no "crash TV" hijinks beyond what the WWF brought in.

To that point: Flair and Sting embracing was not the final image of *WCW Monday Nitro*. The final image was a simulcast of two McMahons bickering with one another. Shane McMahon appeared live in Panama City, getting in the *Nitro* ring and explaining to his father (in a WWF ring via satellite in Cleveland) that although a McMahon had indeed purchased WCW, it now belonged to Shane. As Vince performed his famous bug-eyed theatrical swallow of surprise, McMahon promised to lead WCW back to glory. It didn't quite turn out that way.

For years, fans had fantasized about an "invasion" of one promotion by the other—it was a huge reason why the original "invasion" of WCW by Hall and Nash had caught on like wildfire. Unfortunately, since AOL Time Warner was still on the hook for a large number of ridiculously pricey pay-or-play contracts, it was just sound business to let AOL continue to pay those wrestlers while they sat at home. Smart business, but terrible for story lines and for television. The invasion of the WWF by WCW did indeed happen, but not in the way anyone wanted, and missing many of what should have been the key players. Hogan, Hall, Nash, Goldberg, Sting, Flair, Mysterio, Steiner, Savage, Lex Luger—none of these people appeared in WWE until years after the buyout—or in the case of Savage and Luger, never again. The initial idea for the acquisition of WCW was to continue to run "WCW" as a weekly, "competing" television show, but the WWF quickly found out that no network was willing to give a time slot to something calling itself "WCW." Once the plans for WCW as an active additional brand were scuttled, the "Invasion" began in dribs and drabs in late May, with WCW wrestlers making run-ins during WWF shows, at which point the WWF locker room would empty and run them off. Further hope of WCW gaining respect was jettisoned after Booker T and Buff Bagwell had what was meant to be a "showcase" match and (not surprisingly for most who had seen Bagwell matches), shit the bed in front of an anti-WCW audience in the Pacific Northwest. The overall story line of the Invasion was quickly flipped; Shane's WCW contingent were no longer underdogs and were now a bunch of undeserving, entitled villains who sought to sabotage the WWF to make up for their own short-comings as a failed company. To make matters worse, in addition to the extreme lack of top-level WCW stars who were sitting out their contracts, key players like Triple H and Chris Benoit suffered injuries, and Eddie Guerrero entered rehab for a painkiller addiction before being released by the company that November. A hasty second invasion by top ECW stars (headed by Rob Van Dam and Tommy Dreamer) created an ECW/WCW alliance to run opposite—and eventually be thoroughly trounced and embarrassed by—the WWF.

After the Invasion limped to an end at Survivor Series, a series of Rube Goldbergian stipulations revealed that the returning Ric Flair had become an equal owner of the entire WWF/WCW/ECW enterprise, alongside Vince McMahon, giving McMahon an equally powerful authority figure to play off and freeing him up to lean fully into the Mr. McMahon character for the first time since the WCW buyout. The December 9, 2001, Vengeance PPV—the last PPV event of the calendar year—featured a one-night tournament to unify the WWF and WCW Championships. The two-round tournament featured precisely zero combatants who were working for WCW at the time of its demise. In the main event of the tournament, WCW Champion Chris Jericho defeated WWF Champion Steve Austin to become the first-ever Undisputed WWF Champion. The victory was huge for the ever-increasing subset of fans who were hip to the inner workings of the wrestling business thanks to the internet. At that time, there was an ever-increasing lament that Jericho—the hottest free agent and hottest act in wrestling when he made the jump to the WWF in 1999—hadn't been permanently elevated above the upper midcard in the intervening two years. Jericho had received oodles of airtime, high-profile feuds, and held a half-dozen championships, but had never managed a world title reign until he won the WCW Championship for the first time at the WWF No Mercy PPV on October 21, 2001. His becoming the first undisputed champion was huge, as it included his first WWF Championship—which of course was the first world title he held for a nondefunct company. Jericho fans were dismayed once more when it became clear in January 2002 that he was only holding the undisputed championship in order for the returning Triple H to win it at WrestleMania X8 that year—which is what came to pass.

Prior to WrestleMania X8, those lucrative WCW contracts for several of the dead company's top stars finally ran out. Mr. McMahon, so incensed about having to share ownership with Flair, became determined to kill his own company. As such, he introduced the original nWo of Hall, Nash, and Hollywood Hulk Hogan—the first time Hogan had appeared in the company that made him a household name in nine years. The nWo story line was nonsensical, made even worse because it came months after the Invasion story line had been put to bed. But it did lead to one of the most undeniable and memorable moments of the early 2000s: an icon vs. icon match between Hogan and The Rock at WrestleMania X8. The crowd at the Skydome in Toronto went absolutely apeshit for the entirety of The Rock vs. Hogan showdown, turning Hogan back into a babyface for the remainder of his WWF/WWE career. Unfortunately, the beyond white-hot crowd completely burnt itself out, leaving the true main event of Jericho vs. Triple H lackluster (in addition to the match being the culmination of a strangely emasculating love triangle story line that included Jericho taking care of Stephanie McMahon-Helmsley's dog to curry her favor).

With the addition of the WCW and ECW rosters and the return of former stars whose WCW contracts were expiring, there were far too many Superstars on the payroll to really showcase everyone. Since the WWF had two prime-time weekly shows in *Raw* and *SmackDown*, and since plans for a discrete WCW brand had fallen through, the company conceived the idea of a "brand extension." Raw and SmackDown held a talent draft the week after WrestleMania X8, where they selected wrestlers to be exclusive to each brand. This was the first major change that would define the early 2000s following the death of WCW.

The second major change came on May 6, 2002, when the World Wrestling Federation was officially renamed World Wrestling Entertainment. Since 1979 (predating Vince taking over the company), both the World Wrestling Federation and the nonprofit World Wildlife Fund (also known as the World Wide Fund for Nature, well known for its minimalist panda bear logo) had shared joint trademark rights to the initials "WWF," periodically rejiggering their agreement as both organizations grew in scope and prominence. In August 2001, a court ruled that the World Wrestling Federation had violated a 1994 contractual agreement about using the WWF initials in the United Kingdom. McMahon's lawyers initially appealed the decision, but ultimately decided to yield and change the name of the company, thereby circumventing any similar issues in the future.

WWE was born, alongside a creative ad campaign built around the slogan "Get the F out." At the same time as the rebrand, the company launched another quasi-outside venture: WWE Studios. McMahon apparently never got over the movie bug following *No Holds Barred*. Beginning with a trio of films starring The Rock, the studio began pumping out theatrical releases regularly, including *See No Evil* starring Kane, *The Condemned* starring Steve Austin, and *The Marine* starring John Cena. Still chugging merrily along to this day, WWE Studios now jointly produces or distributes a wide swath of films, many of which are direct to video and many that either feature a Superstar in a tertiary role or, occasionally, no WWE talent at all.

Two very different companies would spring up in 2002 in the wake of WWE's monopoly and the vacuum left by the complete death of WCW and ECW.

The first of these two new companies was NWA: Total Nonstop Action. Formed by Jeff Jarrett and his father, Jerry, upon Jeff's public dismissal from WCW by Vince McMahon, NWA (a member of the National Wrestling Alliance, but most often referred to as just TNA) started with a unique concept: rather than a weekly network or cable television show, TNA began as a weekly *pay-per-view* offering. Fans could buy the weekly two-hour show for $9.99, which was a steep

price—especially considering the content of those early offerings, including a midget wrestler jerking off while inside a
trash can and later pulling a gun on people inside the ring—
but it paid off, perhaps emphasizing how badly fans craved an
alternative product at the time. TNA survived off the revenue
of those weekly PPVs until it finally secured a television deal
in 2004. Some incarnation of TNA has been on the air ever
since, despite all odds, and today the company is known as
Impact Wrestling.

The other company that made its debut in 2002 is perhaps even more important to the trajectory of modern-day
WWE: Ring of Honor. The company was founded by Rob
Feinstein, who conceived of a company that would present
direct-to-DVD events exclusive to RF Video and would place
a premium on the very best in-ring work available. The Era
of Honor Begins featured a three-way main event between
Christopher Daniels, Low Ki, and Bryan Danielson, which
was a technical, hard-hitting classic the likes of which most
North American wrestling fans had never seen before. Ring
of Honor continued to pump out DVD releases at least once a
month (and often more) long after Feinstein was forced out of
the company after an underage sex solicitation scandal. ROH
is still in existence today, currently owned by Sinclair Broadcast Group—and a good portion of the current WWE roster
came up through the ranks of Ring of Honor at one point.

In the meantime, WWE set about business as usual being
the only real game in town, with a new name, new logo, and
a creative new brand extension. Vince McMahon had taken
over the world of professional wrestling. But his sins were
about to catch up to him.

17

CENA RISING

The Ruthless Aggression Era

Where the fuck was Vickie?!"

Eddie Guerrero let out an anguished wail seconds after being pulled off a ladder by Rey Mysterio and landing hard and awkwardly on the canvas. He pounded the mat in frustration, screaming again at the top of his lungs. His fury was clearly picked up by the ringside cameras and microphones and broadcast to the approximately 570,000 viewers who had purchased the 2005 SummerSlam pay-per-view. "God damn it!" he yelled to referee Charles Robinson at ringside. "Where the fuck was she?!"

While the commentary team tried to cover for Guerrero's

profanity by saying he was frustrated with how his match against Mysterio was progressing, the camera cut to a young boy with frosted hair sitting in a front-row seat. The boy, Dominick, had a supremely worried look on his face, and for good reason: he had the best seat in the house for the match that would determine which of these men would gain custody of him.

Dominick, the real-life son of Rey Mysterio, had been roped into a story line where Guerrero claimed to be his true father. The story line, which further employed Eddie's real-life wife, Vickie Guerrero, eventually proved Guerrero to be a liar, but culminated in a "Custody of Dominick Ladder Match," where documents for legal guardianship of a young human's life were suspended above the ring in a briefcase, with the first man to claim said briefcase emerging with the win— and a son! The match was notable not just for the legendary and timeless "Custody of Dominick" match graphic, featuring a forlorn Dominick and a ladder Photoshopped between the two combatants, but also for a flub leading to Guerrero's outburst: Vickie was meant to run in and get involved on Mysterio's behalf, but she missed her cue entirely.

The story line was derided at the time—how could it not be? A match for the custody of a child? What judge would sign off on that? But the work of the two Superstars involved elevated it, and the match was of course a classic. Today, the Custody of Dominick Ladder Match is a beloved high point of what had become known as the Ruthless Aggression Era. In retrospect, the Dominick saga is a perfect encapsulation of this stretch of WWE's history: extremely talented, underappreciated performers who were given something impossible to work with and creating magic with it against all odds.

Or at least "creating magic" was when things worked at their best. Often, the story lines and matches and performers all bled into each other, with gems scattered throughout. But maybe those years of homogeneity were to be expected. With no competition left, a new paradigm sprang up within WWE: competing with itself. While McMahon and the top brass chose to view this new dynamic as being guaranteed a victory every time, it also meant they lost every time. Fifty-fifty booking—it's baked right in.

For decades upon decades, professional wrestling had powered itself by the nonstop drive and single-minded focus of wrestlers who desired to be the very best. Politicking, backstabbing, and shit-stirring were long-standing themes inside countless dressing rooms around the world. Main-eventers had pulled many an underhanded tactic to get ahead. Vince McMahon believed that every member of his roster should be willing to scratch and claw and brownnose and shove his own grandmother into the mud in a pursuit to reach the very top. After WCW went out of business and the roster swelled, WWE slowly began amping up the in-your-face aggressiveness of their characters,* turning all Superstars (especially the babyfaces) into bullies who ridiculed their opponents and got angry about absolutely *everything.* The characters largely all began looking and sounding the same—wrestling

---

* It was manufactured aggressiveness, and in lip service only. Don't let the literal label of the Ruthless Aggression Era fool you; this was a far less wantonly violent period than the Attitude Era. There were moments of intense violence, yes—Eddie Guerrero's infamously blood-soaked battle with JBL springs to mind—but the focus shifted from the tits-and-chair-shots chaos of the Attitude Era to the more ringwork-and-emotion simmering intensity of the Ruthless Aggression Era.

fans believe that McMahon, without serious competition, allowed his own personal ego and idea of what a "real man" or "real hero" should be to begin bleeding through. His micromanaging stepped up a notch and everything started having his fingerprints—a far cry from the "let's see what sticks," fly by the seat of your pants approach that led to the varied characters of the Attitude Era. Of course, supplanting attitude with aggression ended up being an extremely bad look when wrestling's darkest day came at the apex of the Ruthless Aggression Era.

With *SmackDown* and *Raw* both firmly locked in with their exclusive rosters (and with the company alternating brand-exclusive PPVs each month with the exception of their "Big Four" events like Royal Rumble and WrestleMania), McMahon decided the time was ripe to officially transition the company away from its reliance on megastars like The Rock and Steve Austin and have the product itself be the selling point.

To announce the company was starting a new chapter, McMahon stood in the ring on *Raw* and addressed the roster, most of whom stood on the ring apron, listening to him. McMahon's speech leaned into the fan assumption of where the real Vince McMahon overlapped with the Mr. McMahon character, filled with kayfabe-blurring statements, as well as a glimpse into the inner workings of what the real-life CEO demanded of his Superstars.

"There's no question that each and every one of you knows that I, Vincent Kennedy McMahon, am an unqualified success," he began, as Jerry Lawler agreed vociferously on commentary. "Many of you in the past have asked me, 'Mr. McMahon, what's your secret? What is it that makes you the successful man that you are?' And tonight I'm going to share that very secret with each and every one of you.

"More than any one quality that makes me the successful man that I am—I would have to say that one quality is . . . *Ruthless Aggression.* Years ago, I took on every wrestling promoter throughout North America. I kicked every one of their asses. And why?" At this point, the arena erupted into a large chant of "Asshole!" and McMahon didn't miss a beat. "Not because I was an asshole, no, no. Because of Ruthless Aggression." He then boasted about kicking the ass of the United States of America in a court of law, and about kicking the ass of WCW. "He kicked the ass of the government, J.R.!" Lawler squealed. "That's ruthless!"

After hammering home the "Ruthless Aggression" catchphrase a few more times, he began addressing the wrestlers directly. "As you stand here on my ring, which one of you has that quality? Who among you has that one single ingredient? Who has enough Ruthless Aggression to reach for the stars as you never have before? Who has enough Ruthless Aggression to make the necessary sacrifices of mind, body, and soul in order to be a success in this company?"

That last line would prove to be more and more foreboding over the next few years. "The necessary sacrifices of mind, body, and soul." As a scripted line for a character, it's perfect. But it also kicked off the start of what critics see as the cookie-cutter Superstar and the micromanaged, scripted-to-death, "Vince McMahon's singular vision above all else, up to and including when it operates against the company's best interest" modern-day incarnation of WWE. Do you want to be in the main event? Do you want to be the world champion? You will have to make sacrifices—even if it means selling yourself out.

And that vision proved to be tailor-made for the man who would largely carry the company for the next fifteen years. While there's no specific codification of what "Ruthless Aggression" entails, it became an iconic way for the biggest star of this era to make his first impact.

Days after McMahon told the *Raw* roster that he desired more aggression (particularly of the ruthless variety) from his Superstars, John Cena answered an open challenge from Kurt Angle. Cena, who was making his WWE debut, had been wrestling in the company's developmental promotion, Ohio Valley Wrestling (OVW), as "The Prototype," a wrestling cyborg. Cena, a charismatic bodybuilder who had been declared too small for bodybuilding yet too big to be a fitness model, was originally recruited into pro wrestling by Rick Bassman at California's Ultimate Pro Wrestling (UPW). Virtually no one who watched WWE television had ever seen Cena before, so when he strode to the ring to challenge Angle, no one was sure what to make of him. Wearing dick-hugging bicycle shorts and sporting a bizarre high-and-tight haircut that looked like a tarantula had died on his head, Cena entered to generic rock music and stood eye-to-eye with Angle. After Cena introduced himself, Angle laughed, scoffed, and then asked him, "You tell me: what is the one quality that you possess, that makes you think that you can walk out here and come into the ring and face the very best in the business?"

With every vein in his body bulging and his eyes wide, Cena shook with energy as he barked his response: *"Ruthless.*

Aggression." This was immediately followed by a full-force slap to the face that sounded like Barry Bonds's home run off Francisco Rodriguez in Game 6 of the 2002 World Series. Despite never having seen this guy before, the slap and the fast-paced, energetic match that followed brought the crowd to their feet. Cena lost, but was congratulated by other Superstars backstage and began a middling run as a babyface who made sure to wear different color-matching tights and boots each week. WWE seemed to lose interest in Cena in the months that followed his debut, but that all changed when he dressed as Vanilla Ice in a series of backstage segments on the Halloween episode of *SmackDown*. Cena—who was an amateur rapper and hip-hop enthusiast predating his time in the wrestling business—entertained the Superstars backstage with "freestyle" raps that he had written himself, and they caught on with both the live crowd and the viewing audience. The next week, Cena began new life as a rapper, cutting rhyming promos (largely written by himself) on his opponents. Christening himself "The Doctor of Thuganomics," Cena began to get over more and more each week, and the groundswell of support would increase over the next two years.

In those intervening years before Cena became the biggest star in the company, *SmackDown* gained notoriety for being home to what fans lovingly referred to as the "SmackDown Six." Angle, Eddie Guerrero, Chris Benoit, Edge, Rey Mysterio, and Chavo Guerrero had all been drafted to *SmackDown*, and as they invariably wound up in orbit of one another, they continually put on some of the best matches in years, week after week, despite the opponent. *Raw* remained home to Triple H and Stephanie McMahon (and largely to the rest of the McMahons), and most of the story line focus and ridiculousness of pro wrestling would be seen on *Raw* each week. Fans tuned into the Blue Brand, *SmackDown*, for the wrestling of it all. For Guerrero and Benoit in particular, this was their first real opportunity to be the focal point of a pro wrestling show, after being lauded by fans for years for being the best in the world, but never getting the screen time or attention their adoring audience felt they deserved.

Over on *Raw*, things were pretty weird. For starters, in July 2002, the company hired Eric Bischoff of all people to be the brand's on-air general manager. During his tenure he introduced innovations like the Elimination Chamber match and the far less successful Raw Roulette, and we're not going to talk about Hot Lesbian Action.* He also presided over the era of Triple H as undisputed top dog of the Raw brand. If the McMahon-Helmsley Era had worn thin the patience of fans with regard to Triple H, the year after his return from injury outright broke it. While Triple H was undeniably welcomed back as a hero upon his return from injury in January 2002 (and had bulked up so much in the interim that a popular internet joke construct suggested he should change his name to "Quadruple H"), he began being booked more and more like someone who was absolutely unbeatable the majority of the time. At the advent of the brand extension, the only Superstars who weren't exclusive to a brand were the Women's Champion and the Undisputed Champion, who floated between the two. After SummerSlam 2002, the Undisputed Championship became exclusive to *SmackDown*, leading to speculation about what would become of the *Raw*

---

* No, really; we're not going to talk about it.

main-event scene without a world championship to chase. Fans raised their eyebrows when Bischoff created the WWE World Heavyweight Championship (using the same mold as the iconic WCW "big gold belt") and presented it to Triple H. Ostensibly, Triple H was awarded the title for being the No. 1 contender at the time, but to pretty much everyone watching, it came across like Triple H was made world champion of *Raw* just because he was Triple H. For any wrestler, this kind of singular focus as top dog would have been (and was— and continues to be) subject to derision from the fan base. As Triple H happened to be Vince McMahon's son-in-law in real life, that derision was ratcheted up to an all-time high.

Meanwhile, Paul Heyman was the head creative in charge of *SmackDown* at this time, and he knew what he and the fans wanted to see. One thing Heyman *definitely* wanted to see was an athletic specimen, the kind that only comes around once a generation. Brock Lesnar, a farm boy from South Dakota, was a freak of nature. Standing 6 feet 3 inches tall and weighing somewhere in the neighborhood of 280 pounds, Lesnar had been the NCAA amateur wrestling heavyweight champion before being recruited to pro wrestling by pretty much every old-timer who laid eyes on him. Lesnar looked like a monster who ate other monsters for breakfast, with freakishly long arms, a lat spread as wide as a Buick grille, and traps that made you involuntarily hand over your lunch money. In addition to his physique and his world-class amateur wrestling background, he was villain-in-a-slasher-film fast and could do absolutely anything within the context of pro wrestling. During his time at OVW developmental, he would routinely hit a Shooting Star Press: a forward leap off the top rope that included a backflip before landing on your opponent—a maneuver that, at the time, would never even be considered as a part of the repertoire of someone his size.* Lesnar made his debut on March 18, 2002, and won his first WWE Championship five months later, becoming (at the time) the youngest WWE Champion ever, at just twenty-five years old. He attempted his mythical Shooting Star Press just once in WWE: in the main event of WrestleMania XIX, when he whiffed when attempting to deliver it to Kurt Angle in what was supposed to be the finish to the match. Lesnar nearly broke his neck and severely concussed himself. He never went for the move again.

The company was undergoing its biggest shift at the top of the card since Hogan had left for WCW, kicking off the New Generation. In the year between WrestleMania X8 and XIX, Steve Austin took several extended breaks from the company, at first citing exhaustion and later walking out of the company twice due to disputes over the direction of his character.

The Rock, meanwhile, had been on a very different path. Prior to WrestleMania 2000, he hosted *Saturday Night Live* for the first time. It was only the second time a pro wrestler had hosted the Saturday night institution and the first time since Mr. T and Hulk Hogan jointly hosted in 1985 to promote the first WrestleMania. His turn as *SNL* host was a substantial revelation to many in the entertainment industry,

---

* It's difficult to emphasize just how batshit fucking crazy it was at the time that a 300-pound muscleman would do a Shooting Star Press, especially in this era when everyone from Keith Lee to Jeff Cobb to Brian Cage and others who outweigh Lesnar can do standing Shooting Star Presses and Phoenix Splashes and everything else under the sun. Trust me: Lesnar doing a Shooting Star was like turning the corner and seeing two unicorns fucking while a leprechaun filmed it.

as his natural charisma and versatility oozed off the screen. That year he was cast in 2001's *The Mummy Returns* as the Scorpion King—a massive, half-a-billion-dollar-grossing film that led one year later to WWE Studio's first release, the spinoff prequel *The Scorpion King*. *The Scorpion King* tripled its budget and spawned its own inexplicable series of direct-to-video sequels, and The Rock had his first bona fide hit as a leading man. While The Rock would make a couple other WWE appearances in 2004, he departed that year after his contract expired. WrestleMania XX marked the last pro wrestling match The Rock would have for seven years.

The heel side of the top of the card was strong when Wrestle-Mania XX rolled around. Big Show was a monster heel (or monster babyface) able to be slotted in whenever and wher-ever needed. Triple H had formed the Evolution stable along with Ric Flair and future world champions Batista and Randy Orton. Kurt Angle was still around and performing at the top of his abilities. Kane, now unmasked, was an unstable menace and still usually the focus of the Undertaker's wrath. But with the gradual departures of Austin and The Rock, it was necessary to elevate some fresh new stars on the baby-face side. Shawn Michaels had made an unexpected return to the ring in 2002 but was nearing forty and couldn't be expected to carry the company long-term at that point.

WrestleMania XX was tabbed as the big night to ce-ment two newly minted main-event stars—stars who had a longstanding groundswell of intense fan support. At the final PPV before WrestleMania XX, No Way Out, Eddie Guerrero (who had been rehired by the company in 2002) took advantage of Goldberg's interference to defeat Lesnar for the Undisputed Championship—his first world title. His best friend and onetime Radicalz stablemate, Chris Benoit, was long considered by fans to be the very best wrestler in the world, one they desperately wanted to see attain world champion status. But apart from the WCW Championship he won and vacated on the night he walked out of the company, he had never held a world title and had rarely been in the main-event mix since coming to WWE. Benoit got the hero treatment at the 2004 Royal Rumble, becoming just the second man (at that point) to enter at No. 1 and win the Royal Rumble match, guaranteeing him a world title shot at WrestleMania XX. He challenged Triple H for the World Heavyweight Championship, and Michaels was later added to the mix to make the main event of WrestleMania a Triple Threat match. At that point, fans assumed that the addition of the Heartbreak Kid meant Benoit was there to eat the pinfall for whoever won the match, thus yanking the rug out from under longtime fans who dared to once again get their hopes up that someone other than Triple H or his friends would be the top dog on *Raw*.

Backtracking for just a second, let's talk about the strangest match on the WrestleMania XX card and one of the most bizarre WWE matches of all time. Goldberg became an absolute supernova for WCW during the Monday Night Wars, reeling off a worked and inflated "undefeated streak" with a series of singularly dynamic and intense squash matches for months.* WWE declined to buy out his contract after

---

* WWE proved that this formula still worked in the 2010s with Ryback's streak of squash matches, but of course they ultimately deemed him "too popular" and failed to capitalize, undermining and hamstringing his momentum.

WCW folded, and by the time Goldberg made it to WWE for the first time in 2003, the company failed to utilize him in any way that really showcased what made him popular in the first place. His lackluster one-year run in WWE ended at WrestleMania XX with his battle with Lesnar.

While it was public knowledge that the Goldberg vs. Lesnar match would be Goldberg's last for the company, as his contract was now up, rumors began flooding the internet during the week of the show that Lesnar was walking away from WWE and his long-term, big-money guaranteed contract in order to attempt an NFL career. This meant that their match would be both men's last night in the company, in front of a rabid Madison Square Garden crowd that was intimately familiar with the inner workings of pro wrestling, well aware of the rumors and contract situation of both men, and considered both of them to be "traitors" to varying extents: Goldberg was never a WWE guy anyway and was now bailing, and Lesnar was showing disrespect and disloyalty to the company and the industry that had made him rich and famous. Both men were well known for their fast-paced, explosive, hard-hitting matches, but that night, in front of a white-hot crowd bursting at the seams to shower hatred and abuse on these two turncoats, they delivered a plodding and methodical thirteen-minute-plus affair filled with jockeying, stalling, and rest holds, while guest referee Austin watched bemusedly. During the match, the crowd decided that Lesnar's departure from the wrestling business was a degree more despicable than Goldberg's contract ending, which made it a bit more tolerable when Goldberg finally won with a Jackhammer. Lesnar gleefully gave the fans both middle fingers and catharsis finally arrived after the match, when Austin delivered stunners to both men and left them laid out.

The opening match on the WrestleMania XX card gave John Cena his first singles championship in the company. He defeated Big Show for the United States title after delivering his finishing move, the F-U (named in response to Lesnar's finisher, the F5) in a Herculean display of freakish strength. It was Cena's arrival, and his celebration in the crowd was just a hint of things to come, as his first world title would follow at WrestleMania 21.

In the WWE Championship match, Guerrero defended against Angle and retained due to wholesome cheating tactics, when he loosened his boot to slip away from Angle's dreaded ankle lock. In the penultimate match of the evening, the Undertaker—who had evolved his look into a biker nicknamed "The American Badass" (or Booger Red, if you prefer) in recent years—returned from a six-month hiatus in his old "Deadman" persona to best—who else?—Kane and improve to 12–0 at WrestleMania. And in the main event, all three men delivered an undeniable instant classic. Fans waited with their breath held for eternity until the one finish they thought would never in a million years take place actually transpired. A bloody Triple H, locked in the Crippler Crossface submission hold, tapped out in the middle of the ring to Chris Benoit, giving the Rabid Wolverine his first—and ultimately only—world championship in WWE. His best friend, Guerrero, joined him in the ring for his celebration. As confetti rained down on the two men and Madison Square Garden lost its collective mind, WrestleMania XX ended with the good guys winning. The two most unsung, beloved, and talented men in the company had reached the top of the mountain together, after wrestling with and against each other for over a decade all around the world. It was a perfect night for wrestling fans, and if you want to enjoy that thought and that moment for a bit, whatever you do, don't look at the title of the next chapter in this book.

Benoit held the title until August, when he lost it to make Randy Orton the new youngest world champion in WWE history. Guerrero lost his world title that year in the middle of a blood-drenched feud with JBL, the former Acolyte and self-proclaimed Ass-Pounder known as Bradshaw. JBL's lengthy title reign led to Cena's first title reign, and Guerrero and Benoit faded to the periphery again as a trio of other homegrown WWE main-event stars were elevated: Orton, Batista, and Edge.

In February 2005, news leaked that Edge (real name Adam Copeland) and Lita (real name Amy Dumas) were in a relationship. Since Lita was well known to be in a long-standing relationship with Matt Hardy—who was at home rehabbing from a knee injury—and Edge had only been married to his second wife for a few months at the time, this relationship was, uh—I guess we'll go with "frowned upon." Hardy began making numerous public comments venting his anger at the situation and was released from WWE after Wrestle-Mania. A few weeks after winning Money in the Bank, Edge was paired with Lita on-screen, as the duo parlayed the real-life animosity from wrestling fans into a hot angle for the company. Hardy spent a few months wrestling on the independent circuit, including for Ring of Honor, before being brought back in July. He jumped Edge on *Raw*, calling him by his real name and yelling for fans to watch him in Ring of Honor before being muted and restrained by security. The angle got fans' blood pumping—a rival company being yelled out by a scorned star on live television?!—but ultimately led to a series of one-sided victories by Edge before Hardy was moved to *SmackDown*. Edge, meanwhile, won the first of many world titles by cashing in his Money in the Bank briefcase against a bloody and exhausted John Cena at the 2006 New Year's Revolution PPV. Edge and Lita celebrated the following night with a "live sex celebration" on *Raw*.

Speaking of Cena, his character evolved from the Doctor of Thuganomics hip-hop head caught on like wildfire with fans and made him a veritable sensation. Upon winning the WWE Championship from JBL, Cena had a custom "spinner" version of the belt made; the absolute epitome of hip-hop ca. 2005. It featured a WWE logo in the center that, for a few years, spun, and generally it looked like a Hot Boys album cover. Edge periodically replaced the center logo with his "Rated R Superstar" logo and The Miz affixed the WWE logo to be an "M" during his title reign. Weird belt or not, that "spinner" championship was in use for the company's top championship for a surprising eight years—only two years less than the "winged eagle" belt that presided over the first few years of WrestleMania, all of the New Generation, and the advent of the Attitude Era. It was a symbol of the Ruthless Aggression Era and beyond . . . and so was Cena.

Following his first world title run and his starring turn in *The Marine*, Cena's character morphed into a general "support our troops" everyman and quasi-military type. He dropped the rapping that made him so popular and the edgier aspects of his character—beyond the ubiquitous and inevitable childish taunting of his opponents that rarely rose

above the level of "Hey y'all, this guy eats dog doo-doo!"—
and became, for the most part, an abject goody two-shoes.

It's likely that Eddie Guerrero would have rejoined the
main-event mix of Cena, Edge, Orton, Batista, Undertaker, Triple H, and Shawn Michaels if not for his sudden, shocking,
and untimely death at the age of thirty-eight on November
13, 2005. His nephew, Chavo, found Guerrero unconscious
in a Minneapolis hotel room the morning before a joint taping of *Raw* and *SmackDown*. The official cause of death was
acute heart failure caused by cardiovascular disease, with the
widespread understanding that his heart had been weakened
by heavy steroid and drug use over the years in combination
with a twenty-year career of wrestling nearly every day. His
was the most high-profile in a string of untimely deaths of
pro wrestlers at that point, drawing heavy scrutiny of WWE
and their business practices—and their lapse in drug testing in the intervening years since McMahon's 1994 steroid
trial. Two months after Guerrero's death, WWE instituted
its wide-reaching Wellness Program, which is meant to be a
comprehensive and regular testing regimen for drugs, alcohol, and cardiovascular disease. Superstars in the Wellness
Program testing pool (which notably excludes executives
and part-time performers) are subject to random drug testing by an outside agency. As an extension of the Wellness
Program, WWE allows any former employees in need to attend rehab programs on the company's dime. This marked
the first company-wide testing policy in a decade; the previous highly publicized steroid and drug-testing policy, so
important in the advent and wake of the 1994 steroid trial,
had been discontinued in 1996.

The *Raw* and *SmackDown* taped on the night of Guerrero's

death were tributes to Eddie, just as the *Raw* tribute to Owen Hart had been, and at WrestleMania 22, Rey Mysterio won the World Heavyweight Championship in Guerrero's honor, becoming the smallest world champion in company history. Benoit was said to be devastated by the loss of his best and longest-standing friend in pro wrestling.

Shortly after Guerrero's death, Vince McMahon found himself dealing with more allegations in the thick of the Ruthless Aggression Era. In 2006, an employee at a Boca Raton, Florida, tanning salon accused that McMahon arrived at Tanzabar on January 28—the day before the 2006 Royal Rumble in Miami—after the shop had closed and showed her nude photos of himself on his cell phone, before cornering her in a tanning booth and kissing and groping her, and attempting to remove her shirt. According to a police report, as she fled the room, he said that he was "only trying to have some fun." On March 25, local newspapers reported that the charges against McMahon had been dropped due to "insufficient evidence," but in 2018, the Boca Raton Police Department's initial report on the case was published online. Notably, this report contained the line, "There is probable cause to believe that Vincent McMahon did actually and intentionally touch against the will of [redacted], contrary to Florida Statute 784.03 (1)." This report was typed by the lead investigator on the case and reviewed by a supervisor before the State Attorney's Office in Palm Beach County determined on April 6 that there was lack of evidence to support the allegations.

Also in 2018, a witness named in the report, William Robert Wells, stated on the record that the Tanzabar employee came into an adjacent Papa John's where he was working on January 28, 2006. The victim was crying, and the witness saw Vince McMahon leave as she asked Wells to come into Tanzabar while she phoned the police. Wells claimed that McMahon sat in his car while they waited for the police for "a good forty-five minutes," staring at both of them the entire time. He eventually drove away shortly before the police arrived. Wells spoke about how unnerving the situation was and that the victim was scared and intimidated by McMahon's calm stare down.

While the Ruthless Aggression Era was actually focused much more on pure wrestling than the era that preceded it, the violence and excesses of the Hulkamania, New Generation, and Attitude Eras was adding up, and performers were beginning to pay the price in droves.

18

THE CHRIS BENOIT MURDERS CHANGE EVERYTHING

The June 11, 2007, episode of *Raw* was billed as "Mr. McMahon Appreciation Night," and throughout the episode many pretaped video messages to McMahon were aired, all heavily sarcastic or outright nasty. McMahon himself appeared nervous and paranoid, acting as though someone was out to get him. To end the evening, McMahon walked timidly to the ring—very out of character—and hesitantly took the microphone. He offered a faint and shaky "Thank you" before dropping the microphone and exiting the ring once again. He took one last look back at the crowd in the arena, then walked all the way out of the backstage area as the entirety of the WWE roster looked on. McMahon made his way outside and into a waiting limousine. Immediately after the door closed, the limousine exploded in a giant fireball.

For far too long, the late 1990s and early 2000s seemed

to be marked by the regular and horrifying rash of early deaths among professional wrestlers. Prior to the death of Eddie Guerrero in 2005, and beginning from the 1994 drug-induced death of Guerrero's tag team partner, Art Barr, here is just a sampling of the wrestlers who had died of overdose, suicide, medical issues, or organ failure before the age of fifty:

Eddie Gilbert, age 33 (1995, heart attack)
Big John Studd, age 47 (1995, liver cancer)
Dick Murdoch, age 49 (1996, heart attack)
Brian Pillman, age 35 (1997, heart disease with cocaine as a contributing cause)
Louie Spicolli, age 27 (1998, overdose)
Rick Rude, age 40 (1999, accidental overdose)
Jumbo Tsuruta, age 49 (2000, liver transplant complications)
Gary Albright, age 35 (2000, heart attack)
Yokozuna, age 34 (2000, heart attack)
Russ Haas, age 27 (2001, heart failure)
Terry Gordy, age 40 (2001, blood clot)
Big Dick Dudley, age 34 (2002, kidney failure)
Rocco Rock, age 49 (2002, heart attack)
British Bulldog Davey Boy Smith, age 39 (2002, heart attack)
Curt Hennig, age 44 (2003, cocaine poisoning)
Pitbull #2, age 36 (2003, overdose)
Miss Elizabeth, age 42 (2003, overdose)
Road Warrior Hawk, age 46 (2003, heart attack)
Crash Holly, age 32 (2003, suicide)
The Wall, age 36 (2003, heart attack)
Hercules, age 47 (2004, heart disease)
Big Boss Man, age 41 (2004, heart attack)
Chris Candido, age 33 (2005, pneumonia following a broken leg)

In the years following Guerrero's death, these dead wrestlers were joined by Earthquake, Brian Adams, Sherri Martel, Bam Bigelow, Mike Awesome, Test, John Kronus, Johnny Grunge—and Chris Benoit.

Many of those names represented wrestlers who had come up through ECW, the Philadelphia-based company that represented excess in all things in pro wrestling and was still passionately loved and missed by many fans. ECW had been known for its unfettered violence, profanity, and titillation, and it all worked because ECW honcho Paul Heyman understood how to use these tricks to help maximize the strengths of his performers while minimizing their weaknesses. For a fan base growing weary of the lack of viable competition and already growing nostalgic for the Attitude Era just a few years after its peak, the legend of ECW continued to grow as more and more people were able to gain access to DVDs and footage of prime Extreme Championship Wrestling.

Just a few short years after the death of WCW and the end of the Attitude Era, fans were tiring of the homogeneity of the WWE product. WWE was widely derided for hiring nonfans onto their creative team, preferring to bring aboard experienced scripted television writers over former wrestlers, bookers, or people with a deep knowledge and love of the wrestling business. (Or at least that's how fans perceived it. While it's true WWE preferred—and still prefers—to hire television writers for their scripted television show, many of these writers were wrestling fans.) More and more, wrestlers were told to stick word-for-word to prewritten scripts, rather than cut promos off the cuff—as wrestlers had been doing for decades. Backstage segments, talk show segments, and vignettes were seen as overly cheesy or cringe-worthy, and the company started to place more of an emphasis on the main-event scene, leaving many undercard and midcard wrestlers off television or languishing in endless retread feuds. Jobbers and squash matches were no longer used; everyone on WWE television was now a Superstar, which meant that some of the under-the-radar stars of the Attitude Era turned into the jobbers of the Ruthless Aggression Era. That homogeneity extended to the visual presentation of WWE television in 2003. Kevin Dunn, who had worked under Vince McMahon Sr. and was hired as a full-time WWF employee by Vince Jr. all the way back in 1984, was made an executive vice president and member of the Board of Directors in 2003 and was put in charge of all television production across the board. A slick-looking product became even slicker. As the product continued to look more polished, more fans were turned off—particularly fans who used to tune into WCW and ECW, where wrestling was largely about two men punching each other in the goddamn face because they hated each other's guts. Particularly in ECW, wrestling was about *combat*. These people ostensibly fight for a living; just fight each other, already.

After the success of an ECW compilation DVD that was released mostly as an afterthought, WWE realized there was a lot of money to potentially be made off the nostalgia of the defunct company's passionate cult following. The ECW reunion PPV, One Night Stand, was an authentic love letter to Paul Heyman's brainchild and was an unequivocal success. Far less successful was the relaunch of ECW on the Sci Fi Channel (later renamed Syfy).

WWECW (as it would forever become known) debuted on weekly television on June 13, 2006, and the show immediately felt strange originating from the same 10,000-seat arenas of *SmackDown*, rather than the intimate settings where ECW had always thrived. Crowd responses were often muted as well, owing to the fact that most weeks, the majority of the fans in attendance were there to see *SmackDown*, and depending on the time zone, either had to sit through an ECW taping to get to the stars they wanted to see, or filed out of the building during ECW as *SmackDown* went off the air. Initially picked up by Sci Fi for a thirteen-week run, the final incarnation of Extreme Championship Wrestling (and this may be surprising for some people to realize) ran weekly for almost four years. The shows were written by Paul Heyman, but ultimately Vince McMahon had final say in every story line and on every episode—a practice that has always been true and remains in place for all WWE products and programs. As the months progressed, fans began to perceive more influence from McMahon and less from Heyman: big guys Test and Mike Knox appeared and were featured prominently; Big Show became the focus of the title picture; Kevin Thorn, an incongruous "vampire" character, appeared; weekly time was devoted to Kelly Kelly, who proclaimed herself "an exhibitionist" and constantly threatened to get naked but never did. (In truth, many of these concepts and characters were Heyman concepts or pet projects, but fans were determined to dislike everything under the glossy WWE relaunch, despite his stamp of approval.) Over the summer, a couple of big blows were dealt to the ECW main-event scene: in July, RVD and Sabu were pulled over and arrested for drug possession. After dropping his WWE Championship and ECW title on consecutive nights following his arrest, Van Dam was suspended for thirty days. Sabu was fined but not suspended, but both men were in the doghouse for the foreseeable future. RVD never won another world title in WWE. In August, citing exhaustion, Kurt

Angle asked for and was granted his WWE release. Angle was suffering from an intense painkiller addiction at the time and it's possible WWE viewed him as a liability. When his no-compete clause was up, Angle immediately signed with TNA, where he wrestled full-time for the next decade.

A "New Breed" stable sprang up featuring characters who were new to WWE altogether. Backstage, Heyman and Mc-Mahon began to butt heads more often as their visions for the ECW brand diverged. By the time the ECW December to Dismember PPV rolled around, Heyman was burnt out. The main event of the pay-per-view was an Elimination Chamber match for the ECW Championship, meant to feature three "Heyman guys" as well as three traditionally WWE Super-stars: CM Punk, RVD, and Sabu would be in the cage along-side reigning champion Big Show, Test, and Bobby Lashley, a freakishly huge amateur wrestler in the Brock Lesnar mold* who had moved to ECW a month prior after a lengthy show-case run on *SmackDown*. Lashley had been in the midst of one of those pushes that fans occasionally perceive as "too much, too soon" and a "chosen" WWE wrestler being pushed down fans' throats (see Cena, John; and Reigns, Roman). Heyman came up with what he thought would make for the most exciting match: have CM Punk start out with Big Show, tap out Big Show with the Anaconda Vise, cementing Punk not only as a major player but also getting the crowd buzzing

---

* For the bulk of his initial WWE run, Lashley was unfortunately tarred with the fan nickname "Black Lesnar," as viewers convinced themselves that Lashley only existed as a hastily cobbled-together replacement for the departed Brock Lesnar. Maybe they weren't wrong! But Lashley rarely received a fair shake from longtime fans, despite his ability.

with the unexpected elimination of Big Show and the guarantee of a new champion walking out of the Chamber.

Unfortunately, McMahon hated the idea and nixed it, and despite Heyman's repeated and insistent protests—with both Heyman and Big Show pointing out that the crowd would turn on McMahon's proposed finish—the boss had final say. Sabu was "attacked" early in the PPV and removed from the main event, replaced with through-and-through WWE guy Hardcore Holly. Instead of sending Big Show packing, Punk was eliminated first. That took most of the air out of the match, and the rest of the air was taken out when Van Dam was eliminated third, by Test. Lashley ultimately won the match and the title, ending what had been, by every metric, a disastrous PPV. As predicted, fans shit all over Lashley's title win, and to this day December to Dismember is widely considered to be the worst WWE PPV of all time. (Objectively, it isn't close to the worst one, but it's definitely not what you'd like to call "good.") Heyman quit the company the next day and remained gone from WWE for six years. December to Dismember was the final ECW-branded pay-per-view.

Mr. McMahon began appearing on ECW television, which became involved in the biggest WrestleMania main event in history. Leading up to WrestleMania 23, television personalities Mr. McMahon and Donald Trump became engaged in a public feud that would be dubbed "the Battle of the Billionaires." The two longtime friends traded barbs on and off WWE television, and it was quickly decided that the two men would select proxies to do battle at WrestleMania. If McMahon's proxy lost the match, he would be shaved bald, while the same would happen to Trump if his chosen combatant took the loss. Steve Austin was naturally selected as the special guest referee. McMahon chose Umaga, the "Samoan Bull-dozer," as his proxy, while Trump selected ECW Champion Lashley. Lashley, naturally, emerged victorious, although the contest did feature Trump tackling McMahon outside the ring and delivering likely the worst worked punches in the history of our great sport. (He also took the worst Stone Cold Stunner ever after the match, but that's less notable.)

Following WrestleMania, Mr. McMahon—now sporting a do-rag to hide his recent Trump-induced baldness—actually won the ECW championship from Lashley in a handicap match where he was assisted by Shane McMahon and Umaga. Vince McMahon was the ECW World Heavyweight Champion. The ratings didn't suffer much, and ECW remained on television for years to come, but the last remaining original ECW fans finally gave up on Heyman's dream. Lashley won the title back on June 3, only to vacate it on June 11 when he was drafted to *Raw*. In that 2007 WWE Draft, ECW selected The Boogeyman, Chris Benoit, Viscera, The Miz, and former *Tough Enough* winner turned Eric Bischoff lackey turned one-half of the red-carpet-walking, paparazzi-seeking tag team MNM, Johnny Nitro.

And then Vince McMahon's limo blew up.

The following evening on ECW, flags outside the WWE headquarters in Stamford were shown flying at half-mast, as Vince McMahon was reported as "presumed dead" following the explosion.* If that weren't enough, ECW began with

---

* While never presented as anything other than a story line, at least one notable individual was fooled by the news of Vince's passing. According to Triple H, McMahon's good friend Donald Trump called the WWE offices concerned the following day, to see whether it was true that Vince had died.

a ten-bell salute and a tribute graphic to "the memory of Mr. McMahon." The ten-count salute was met with good-natured boos, and I have to stress that this *probably* would be remembered as a good-natured and out-of-the-box story line if not for the unforeseen tragedy that followed. The following week's *Raw* continued the story line and ended with Stephanie McMahon promising Vengeance (the name of the upcoming PPV) when they find out who is responsible for the exploding limo and explaining that next week's (post-Vengeance) *Raw* would be a celebration of Mr. McMahon featuring all three brands.

The June 19, 2007, episode of *ECW* featured a pair of singles matches to determine who would compete for the vacant ECW World Heavyweight Championship at Vengeance. Chris Benoit defeated Elijah Burke and CM Punk defeated Marcus Cor Von, setting up the PPV title match: Benoit vs. Punk. It was a big moment in the career of Punk, who hadn't been near the world title scene much since December to Dismember and who had—like nearly every other pro wrestler his age—long considered Benoit to be an inspiration and a true legend.

Chris Benoit grew up in Edmonton, Alberta, and trained at the renowned Hart Family Dungeon in Calgary. He broke into the business in 1985 and modeled his career, his style, and his very body on Tom Billington—the Dynamite Kid, one-half of the British Bulldogs and the *other* greatest graduate of the Hart Dungeon. Standing at somewhere between 5 feet 8 and 5 feet 10, Benoit knew early on that he didn't have the stature to be viewed as a top guy, so he'd better pack on the muscle. Dynamite Kid and Davey Boy Smith combined world-class ability with copious amounts of steroids, which brought them to the WWF and thus worldwide acclaim, so Benoit got on the gas early and often. Benoit joined the New Japan dojo in 1986 and toiled in the harsh and cruel dojo for the better part of a year while continuing to ply his trade in New Japan and in Stu Hart's Stampede Wrestling in Calgary. In 1990, Benoit debuted as the masked Pegasus Kid in NJPW. By that time, he was already an absolute monster, jacked to the gills but due to his height still wrestling in the junior heavyweight division. The Pegasus Kid gained international acclaim and attention by winning the illustrious Best of the Super Juniors tournament in 1993 and 1995 and won the first Super J-Cup tournament in 1994. All three tournaments were favorites of early tape traders (just as the series between Tiger Mask and Benoit's hero, Dynamite Kid, had been) and also featured the first notable matches between Benoit and Eddie Guerrero, who was wrestling for NJPW as Black Tiger at the time. Benoit spent time in WCW in 1993 before joining ECW for a year in 1994, where he famously broke Sabu's neck with a release suplex. This gained him the "Crippler" moniker, coined by Paul Heyman. Benoit won the ECW tag titles alongside Dean Malenko before both men were signed by WCW.

In WCW, Benoit joined the Four Horsemen and began to turn the heads of North American wrestling fans by consistently delivering the best matches of the night, despite rarely being placed in a position of prominence on the card. In the first of many bizarre kayfabe-transcending incidents in Benoit's career, head WCW booker Kevin Sullivan conceived of a long-term story line where Benoit was revealed to be having an affair with Sullivan's real-life wife, Nancy, who appeared on WCW television as Woman. Sullivan insisted Benoit and

Nancy travel together and live the gimmick, which quickly turned into an actual, real-life relationship, which ended Sullivan's marriage. Despite animosity between the two men backstage following this revelation, the matches between the two never descended into anything ugly, and the feud culminated in Benoit winning a retirement match against Sullivan, as planned.

We've already covered the formation of the Revolution, Benoit's world title win, and the defection of the Radicalz, but it's important to understand that during Benoit's five years in WCW (on top of ten hard years mostly spent in Japan prior to that), he was driven by what many had described as a fanatical passion to always have the best match every night, to always wrestle harder and more intensely than everyone else, and to never phone anything in. His dynamic and hard-hitting style, which gained him so many fans year after year, included a nightly top-rope–diving headbutt (which would miss as often as it would hit) that he prided himself in never "pulling" so that it looked as real as possible, multiple rolling German suplexes (which involved him dropping himself on his own head while holding a 200-pound-plus opponent), and a litany of unprotected chair and weapons shots. On the rare occasion that he would make a mistake in a match, he would punish himself by doing thousands of squats backstage without stopping, yelling at himself that he would be better next time. This fanaticism never left him during his seven years in WWE, where he worked an even more hectic schedule, which involved even more head-drops and diving headbutts. He was like the wrestling Terminator, driven by nothing more than to be a perfect, ruthlessly efficient pro wrestling machine.

Benoit was also a no-nonsense and no-bullshit hardened veteran and locker room policeman who was subject to bursts of cruelty. He banned The Miz from using the men's locker room for six months at the beginning of Miz's WWE run when he caught the rookie eating chicken over his bag. In a public display of unnecessary brutality, Benoit, Guerrero, and Hardcore Holly all took turns taking liberties with MMA fighter-turned-*Tough Enough*-winner Daniel Puder during the 2005 Royal Rumble match. Puder had run afoul of the locker room by being told to treat his match against Kurt Angle during *Tough Enough* as though it were a shoot, and then nearly breaking Angle's arm with a Kimura lock when he did just that. When Puder entered the Rumble match facing the three veterans, they took turns delivering brutal chops and stiff shots and dropping the rookie on his head a bit before eliminating him unceremoniously. It was tough to watch at the time; it's much tougher now. Benoit had a history of laughing at wrestlers who were hurt or suffering; he was amused by the pain or discomfort of others.

Vengeance: Night of Champions took place on June 24, 2007, at the Toyota Center in Houston, Texas, with the central conceit of the PPV being that every one of the many championships in the company would be defended. While the preceding episode of *ECW* had gone off the air promising fans a Benoit vs. Punk match for the vacant ECW title, the match instead became Punk vs. Johnny Nitro. Nitro won the match—as Benoit had been booked to win it prior to his disappearance—and rechristened himself "John Morrison" on the following episode of *ECW*. During the match, fans loudly chanted "We want Benoit!" and reacted with underwhelmed silence when Nitro won. The rest of the PPV continued as normal, ending with Cena retaining his WWE Championship in a Five-Pack Challenge match that also included Lashley, Booker T, Mick Foley, and Randy Orton.

Benoit had been scheduled to perform at a house show in Beaumont, Texas, on Saturday, June 23, the day before Vengeance. Chavo Guerrero, Eddie's nephew and one of Benoit's oldest and closest friends, received a voicemail from Benoit on Saturday afternoon, stating that he had overslept and missed his flight, and might miss the show. When Guerrero was able to reach Benoit on the phone, Benoit talked about his stressful day: Nancy and his son, Daniel, had been suffering from food poisoning, he said, and now he was having issues getting a new flight through Delta. When another WWE employee contacted Benoit later that afternoon, he said Nancy's condition had worsened and that she was now vomiting blood.

Early on the morning of the PPV, text messages were sent to several WWE employees, including Guerrero and referee Scott Armstrong, from both Chris and Nancy Benoit's phones. The text messages repeated the same information, stating that "the dogs are in the enclosed pool area," and giving their home address in Fayetteville, Georgia, with the odd preface "My physical address is . . ." Guerrero was unable to reach Benoit that day, but Benoit placed a call to the WWE talent relations office saying that he was at the hospital with Daniel and Nancy and that he would be taking a later flight into Houston to appear at the PPV. In all likelihood, Benoit was probably dead by the time the PPV was over.

What had actually happened that weekend was that Benoit, on Friday, June 22, had murdered Nancy Benoit by strangling her with a cord. He then killed Daniel, his third child, after sedating him with Xanax. (Benoit's first two children, Daniel's half-siblings, were with their mother, Martina.) Daniel's cause of death is listed as "cervical compression" on the autopsy report, although it appears as "suffocation" on the death certificate. The former seems more likely, as the autopsy report was conducted by an investigative medical examiner. Benoit placed Bibles by the bodies of Nancy and Daniel. He spent Saturday making his strange phone calls and sending text messages before taking his own life on Sunday, June 24. According to Nancy's sister, Sandra Toffoloni, one of the final results from the search history on Benoit's personal computer was "the quickest and easiest way to break a neck." Toffoloni also revealed that Benoit had looked into booking flights to Houston on Saturday, after killing his wife and child—meaning there was at least a moment, however brief, that Benoit felt he might be able to perform on the PPV despite having committed two murders two days earlier.

Benoit, of course, did not book any makeup flights. He went to his house's basement gym, removed the bar from the lat pull-down machine, and fashioned a towel into a makeshift noose. He attached the towel to the cable where the bar had been and placed the towel around his neck. He released the heaviest weight on the machine, which killed him by strangulation. He was hanging from the weight machine when police entered the house on Monday, June 25.

When Superstars from all three brands arrived at the arena for *Raw* that morning in Corpus Christi, head of talent relations John Laurinaitis was made aware of the strange text messages that Guerrero and Armstrong had received. WWE contacted the Fayette County Sheriff's Office and asked law enforcement to check in on the family. At 4:15 p.m., hours before *Raw* was set to go live, WWE was notified that Benoit, Nancy, and Daniel had all been found dead inside their home, and that the residence was being considered the scene of a major crime.

As word of the deaths began to spread (and no one knowing exactly what happened), WWE quickly organized an all-hands meeting. In what many Superstars have since described as a surreal scene, they gathered in the arena amid props meant to be used for the mock funeral of Mr. McMahon—a coffin, candelabras, funeral wreaths—only to be told that their coworker and his family had been found dead. As the Superstars took in the unbelievable news, they were informed that that evening's episode of *Raw* would be canceled and replaced by a three-hour tribute to Benoit. Anyone who wanted to tape a tribute testimonial was welcome to participate. Many assumed the deaths were due to a carbon monoxide leak; some assumed a home invasion and triple murder.

The June 25, 2007, episode of *Raw* opened with the now-familiar black tribute graphic: a headshot of the deceased, accompanied by the words "In Memory of Chris Benoit, 1967–2007." The next shot was of Vince McMahon in the middle of the ring in an empty arena. Since his character was presumed dead for weeks and this episode was meant to be his funeral, it was a stark opening, an immediate signifier that this, emphatically, was *not* part of the intended show. McMahon spoke to the audience. "Good evening," he began. "Tonight, this arena here in Corpus Christi, Texas, was to have been filled to capacity with enthusiastic WWE fans. Tonight's story line was to have been the alleged demise of my character, Mr. McMahon. However, in reality, WWE Superstar Chris Benoit, his wife, Nancy, and their son, Daniel, are dead. Their bodies were discovered this afternoon in their new, suburban Atlanta home. The authorities are undergoing an investigation. We here in the WWE can only offer our condolences to the extended family of Chris Benoit, and the only other thing we can do at this moment is tonight, pay tribute to Chris Benoit." He explained that the show would feature highlights from Benoit's career, as well as tributes from his peers. The show featured video packages and clips from his *Hard Knocks* DVD set and full matches from his lengthy career, and confessional-style testimonial interviews from Steve Austin, John Cena, CM Punk, Dean Malenko, and others. During the show, there was occasionally a lower-third graphic with photos of Chris, Nancy, and Daniel. While most of Benoit's peers were glowing and emotional, William Regal (who worked with Benoit in WCW as Steven Regal before joining him in WWE) was pointedly cagey. "All I'm willing to say," he said, "is that Chris Benoit was undoubtedly the hardest-working man in professional wrestling. The most dedicated and totally absorbed in the business of professional wrestling above anybody I've ever met. And that's all I've really got to say at the moment."

It remains unclear at what point who within WWE knew what, but the decision to run a tribute was made very early after receiving news of the deaths. As the show began to air on national television that evening, news was trickling out that this was not some freak accident, but something unbelievably sinister. By the following day, it was clear to everyone: Chris Benoit murdered his wife and seven-year-old son. When the June 26, 2007, episode of *ECW* aired that evening, it opened with a drastically different message. In a pretaped talking-head statement, Vince McMahon addressed the audience once again. "Good evening, ladies and gentlemen," he began, as a lower third introduced him as WWE Chairman Vince McMahon. "Last night on *Monday Night Raw*, the WWE presented a special tribute show, recognizing the career of Chris Benoit. However now, some 26 hours later, the facts of this horrific tragedy are now apparent. Therefore, other than my comments, there will be no mention of Mr. Benoit's name tonight. On the contrary, tonight's show will be dedicated to everyone who has been affected by this terrible incident. This evening marks the first step of the healing process. Tonight, WWE performers will do what they do better than anyone else in the world: entertain you."

That "healing process" would take far longer than WWE likely imagined, but McMahon was true to his word: Benoit's name was never mentioned on WWE television again. All mentions of Chris Benoit were removed from the website and muted on future WWE home video releases. His name remains unsearchable on WWE Network (although his matches on WWE, WCW, and ECW events remain intact). But Benoit's name would be mentioned by everyone *else* in the world for months on end. WWE's business practices were suddenly in the public eye once again, as part of a much graver discussion than the 1994 steroid trial. Benoit's horrific actions led to the most abrupt and sweeping changes in the history of WWE, but not before the murders sparked outrage on a worldwide scale. In the eyes of the media, WWE had fostered and created a murderer—and now they would answer for it.

PART IV

TV-PG, THE REALITY ERA, AND THE MONEY ROLLING IN

19
THE EXPLODING LIMO THAT WASN'T

Transitioning to the PG Era

WWE had hit its lowest point in the cultural consciousness (if not its lowest point of popularity). It was now perceived as a haven of drugs, debauchery, steroid abuse, violence, and now outright murder. In a desperate attempt to change the image of WWE, Vince McMahon made the hardest and most abrupt pivot of his life, killing "ruthless aggression" and painting the company in a gaudy new "family friendly" coat of varnish. Those generations of die-hard traditionalist, Southern rasslin', and WCW fans were already gone and never coming back. The next wave of changes set about alienating the die-hard fans who the Attitude Era had cultivated for WWE itself, in the pursuit of making a product that appealed to kids. The gamble eventually enriched McMahon beyond most people's (although probably not his own) wildest dreams and made WWE a powerhouse and appealing brand for television companies, streaming services, and advertisers (not to mention rich despots), but it also began bleeding viewers year after year, as wrestling fans grew increasingly disenchanted with the only game in town.

In the immediate aftermath of the Chris Benoit double murder–suicide, every newspaper, magazine, and tabloid in the country—but especially the growing crop of sensationalist magazine–style news and true-crime programs in the Nancy Grace vein—ran abundant stories about the tragedy. As the twenty-four-hour news cycle continued to roll over, half-truths and rumors and misinformation proliferated. These stories continued through the autopsy reports—showing the sedatives in Daniel's system, the alcohol in Nancy's, and ten times the normal adult male level of testosterone in Chris's—and beyond.

WWE went on the defensive, with Cena and McMahon and others appearing on national news shows to be interviewed and tout the general culture of the company and the effectiveness of their new Wellness policy. Many outlets wanted to determine whether this was a result of "'roid rage." The district attorney for the case noted that injection marks were found on Daniel's forearms. This in turn led to some nebulously sourced rumors that Daniel was suffering from a condition known as Fragile X, which makes children undersized. Following that thread, the rumor was that Benoit had been injecting Daniel with steroids to make him bigger, and that perhaps a disagreement with Nancy over this tactic led to the murders. (All medical records and family statements insist, emphatically, that Daniel did not suffer from Fragile X.) Even further along in the reporting of the story, conspiracy theories began to pop up, some even persisting to this day, suggesting that Benoit was either framed or set up and had nothing to do with the murders.

The true motive or inciting incident is unlikely to ever be discovered. In his autobiography, Hardcore Holly talks about how Benoit would become much more cruel, violent, and irrational when drinking, and believes that alcohol could have had much more to do with the murders than steroids or testosterone. The couple's marriage was not without a history of violence. In May 2003, Nancy filed for divorce and to have a temporary restraining order placed on Benoit, citing prior domestic abuse. Nancy withdrew both petitions several months later, but friends of hers have claimed that the marriage was unhappy and that Chris had on several occasions gotten physical when unhappy.

One factor that almost certainly played a role in the murders was the state of Benoit's brain following years of brain trauma that was excessive even for a professional wrestler. Due to Benoit's intense and perfectionist style—and the fact that he was one of the few wrestlers in the world willing to take absolutely any form of unprotected chair shot, even, unthinkably, to the back of the head—his brain showed signs of advanced deterioration. Chris Nowinski's Sports Legacy Institute was able to obtain Benoit's brain for study, and they discovered not only severe chronic traumatic encephalopathy, but a brain that was so damaged in all respects—damage was detected in all areas of the brain, including the brain stem—that Julian Bailes, West Virginia University's chief of neurosurgery, likened Benoit's brain to that of an eighty-five-year-old Alzheimer's patient. This type of damage has been known to cause severe shifts in behavior, as has been exhibited in the sudden fits of rage and abrupt suicides in several former NFL players who suffered from CTE.

It's likely Benoit suffered hundreds of concussions over the course of his twenty-two-year wrestling career, and no one who watched a significant portion of his work would be surprised that he caused lasting brain damage to himself. Sandra Toffoloni, Nancy's sister, said the family was told that given the state of Benoit's brain and his heart—like Eddie Guerrero's, swollen to three times the normal size due to years of heavy steroid abuse and ready to fail or burst at any moment—it was highly likely he would have been dead within ten months of the murders regardless.

With Benoit's heavy steroid and testosterone use on full display, WWE garnered the attention of the United States government once again. The House Committee on Oversight and Government Reform, which at the time was once again on the warpath regarding performance-enhancing drugs in Major League Baseball, requested WWE turn over all documents and statistics related to the Wellness policy and that both Vince McMahon and Linda McMahon appear before the committee to testify. Both McMahons obliged, with their trusty attorney, Jerry McDevitt, in tow. Linda McMahon's testimony largely featured her failing to remember specific instances of any of their questions and saying she never had much direct contact with George Zahorian, while Vince and McDevitt were very feisty and combative during their appearance in Washington, D.C. McMahon refused to engage in what he deemed to be "gotcha bullshit" tactics by the committee, and the most telling portion of the appearance came when the WWE CEO was asked why the company provides former employees with access to rehabilitation programs if they feel substance abuse is not an issue.

"Two words," said McMahon. "Public relations. That's it. I do not feel any sense of responsibility for anyone of whatever their age is who has passed [away] and has bad habits and overdoses [on] drugs. Sorry; I don't feel any responsibility for that. Nonetheless, that's why [we've set up this program]. It's a magnanimous gesture."

In the wake of the investigations, committee chairman Henry Waxman recommended the government take a closer look at steroid use in professional wrestling. Waxman concluded that the records showed a whopping 40 percent of WWE Superstars tested positive for steroids or recreational drugs in the first year of the drug test being put in place in 2006—even when test subjects were made aware that they would be tested. The investigation also called into question the "shadiness" of wrestlers who were able to obtain exemptions for anabolic steroids, testosterone replacement, or other PEDs.

Immediately after Benoit's death, WWE began placing much greater emphasis on wrestler safety both inside and outside the ring. In the years that followed, WWE banned any chair shots to the head, regardless of whether they were protected, and limited moves that led to excessive head drops. German suplexes were strictly limited for a long time. Around the same time the NFL instituted a concussion protocol; so too did WWE. (WWE's concussion protocol came under scrutiny again after CM Punk's release, but WWE has made significant strides in pulling athletes due to injury in the past couple of years. There's still no off-season for wrestlers, of course.) Through stricter safety standards and a beefed-up Wellness policy, WWE was making changes, but the biggest one caused by Benoit was yet to come.

In 2008, WWE announced that all their television product going forward would be rated TV-PG. Blood, sex, and excessively wanton violence were downplayed drastically (and blood would soon be gone from the company altogether, except for rare occasions usually involving Brock Lesnar). Even John Cena's finishers weren't safe from the transition: his F-U got the much less interesting name "Attitude Adjustment" and the STFU finisher was once again referred to by its technical name: the STF. The "edgy" story lines of the past two eras were no more. And of course, no exploding limos. Shows, and especially wrestler promos, became even more tightly scripted. Once again seeking mainstream acceptance and synergy (and trying to get the stink off from Benoit), WWE began a long-running cross-promotional tactic in 2009 wherein every episode of *Raw* would be presided over by a guest host, usually a celebrity in the midst of promoting something or other. The guest host era occasionally led to absolute magic, as in the cases of Bob Barker, Betty White, and the Muppets. More often than not, it featured something more akin to three-fifths of the cast of *Entourage* stammering their way through getting the name of SummerSlam wrong.

D-Generation X re-formed, this time in the two-man iteration of Shawn Michaels and Triple H. In stark contrast to their original mission statement of being profane, transgressive edgelord iconoclasts, they were now family-friendly goofballs who made thinly veiled, forced dick jokes and threw glow sticks to fans. They even made continual meta-jokes about how Michaels's status as a born-again Christian meant he couldn't even partake in some of the new DX's more risqué material. (Which generally wasn't risqué at all.)

Longtime WWE fans, of course, lamented the departure of the Attitude Era, which had finally made wrestling cool and hip when many of those viewers had been kids and teenagers. To make matters worse, WWE began doubling and tripling down on only allowing the Superstars they had groomed. In the Attitude Era (and even in the beginning of the Ruthless Aggression Era), wrestlers up and down the card were allowed to experiment with stories, characters, catchphrases, and match structure, and if something caught on with the fans, that was one more thing that worked; everyone was able to get a chance to get themselves over where appropriate, which meant the product as a whole was more exciting. Fans could feel vindicated about helping something get popular and could be excited about seeing their favorites, even if they rarely won.

In the TV-PG Era, by stark contrast, Superstars were punished if they caught on with fans when they weren't "supposed" to. If a catchphrase caught on with fans, the wrestlers were told to stop saying it. If fans went nuts for a specific move or spot, the wrestlers were told to stop doing it. Everything became more tightly regimented, and WWE took pains to make sure the nails that stuck up got hammered down. At the same time, McMahon and other top executives still told Superstars to keep reaching for "the brass ring." He said he wanted all his wrestlers to have the confidence and belief that they can be the top guy and wanted all the members of his roster to aspire to main-eventing WrestleMania one day.

In 2008, the brand split necessitated the creation of a second women's championship—and the championship rankled fans, particularly female ones. Introduced on July 20, the Divas Championship was one of the gaudiest titles a pro wrestling company had ever presented. Said by many fans to resemble lower-back tattoos misogynistically referred to as "tramp stamps," the design of the belt's main plate was a large pink butterfly surrounded by curlicues and sparkly letters. The design was universally panned, reducing the entire division to a hodgepodge of feminine stereotypes. Despite the negative reaction, this became WWE's sole women's title in 2010 when it was unified with the WWE Women's Championship, and it remained in use until 2016.

Fans were also upset about the 2009–2010 feud between Mickie James and LayCool, the tandem of Layla El and Michelle McCool. During the feud, James was relentlessly mocked by LayCool regarding her weight and referred to as "Piggie James." James was, of course, essentially the same size and weight as every other Diva in the company, but the heels persisted, bullying her to tears on WWE television over this phantom weight problem. Everyone hated that.

ECW kept chugging along over on the Sci Fi Channel, now renamed Syfy. With the new TV-PG initiative, the central conceit of ECW was effectively neutered, so the ECW brand slowly became a repository for new and developing wrestlers to try out gimmicks and characters and get reps in on live and national television without the high stakes of being thrown directly onto *Raw* or *SmackDown*. In its final years, ECW became a highly entertaining, mostly developmental third brand. If the enterprise had been named literally anything other than "ECW," it might have been given a chance by fans and would likely still be beloved as a fun tertiary brand.

While longtime fans began tuning out en masse around this time, the company began finding value in marketing their brand over individual Superstars. Somewhere between WrestleMania 22 and WrestleMania 23, WWE's biggest show of the year really started to become a destination weekend not just for wrestling fans, but for sports fans in general. The annual spring supershow—for which people had always traveled, but not quite to such an extent as they would from about 2007 on—started to become a good reason to take a vacation on that particular weekend. Ring of Honor was the first company to latch on to WrestleMania weekend as a good time to run some shows in the same market, on the same weekend. Beginning in Chicago in 2006, ROH began running double shots in the same metropolitan area as WrestleMania each year, hoping to scoop up wrestling fans looking for something else to do that weekend.

WWE's main-event scene didn't offer much in the way of turnover as it entered the TV-PG Era. Cena, Randy Orton, Triple H, Michaels, Batista, Undertaker, and Edge were all still firmly entrenched atop the card, with Kane, Chris Jericho, and a returning Big Show slotted in when and where needed. Lashley, believed to have been groomed for a top spot in the company, suffered an injury in mid-2007 and was released in February 2008 without returning to television. Sheamus, an enormous Irish wrestler with ghostly pale skin and a bright orange goatee and shock of red hair, rose quickly to the main-event scene, but was derided by fans and not given a true fair shake when word got out that he was a workout buddy of Triple H's. At WrestleMania XXIV in 2008, Shawn Michaels retired one of the last stars of the Hulkamania era when he defeated Ric Flair. Two years later, Michaels himself would retire after losing the second of his consecutive instant-classic matches against the Undertaker.

While WWE purported to be the only real game in town, other companies rose and fell—or simply persisted. MTV debuted Wrestling Society X, an over-the-top and ambitious league from Kevin Kleinrock with an emphasis on tag team wrestling and lucha libre. Out of pure reflex rather than any real desire to smite the competition, WWE counterprogrammed WSX in its early weeks, putting Undertaker on *ECW* in an attempt to draw WSX viewers' eyeballs. MTV never really knew what to do with Wrestling Society X and moved it all around the schedule without advertising it was doing so. MTV only aired the first nine of WSX's ten taped episodes, the last of which provided a true culmination of the season of pro wrestling. Fans finally were able to watch that final episode on a complete WSX DVD set, which sold shockingly well.

Jeff Jarrett's TNA, meanwhile, continued to plod along week after week, even after splitting from the NWA. The product received a significant boost when Kurt Angle came aboard in late 2006, instantly becoming one of the faces and main focuses of the company. Creating a stigma that would stay with TNA for a decade to come, the company often placed a premium on former WCW and WWE stars rather than elevating their homegrown talents.

The indie scene continued to grow, spurred by ROH on the East Coast and Pro Wrestling Guerrilla—a collective founded by six Southern California wrestlers—on the West Coast. In Philadelphia and neighboring states, Combat Zone Wrestling (CZW) and IWA Mid-South kept hardcore and deathmatch wrestling alive, but still very much underground. Fans who became disgruntled with WWE began to use the internet to find the flourishing network of independent promotions and discovered that they were able to easily find lots of quality wrestling to appeal to any preference or proclivity.

In early 2010, after nearly a year of using the ECW brand to introduce talent from WWE's newly consolidated developmental territory, Florida Championship Wrestling, Vince McMahon finally decided to shutter the still-breathing corpse of Paul Heyman's Extreme Championship Wrestling. Taking the place of ECW in the Syfy time slot was a bold new venture that McMahon proudly boasted would be groundbreaking. WWE called the new venture NXT, which didn't stand for anything at all. Over the next ten years, fans would eventually find in NXT hope for the future of the company. And in 2011, a singular hero emerged on the main WWE roster to further inspire and enthrall a diminishing fan base desperate for a new megastar to cheer.

20

PIPE BOMBS AND ANGER MANAGEMENT

The New Hope of the Reality Era

WWE continued to act like the only game in town (because for all intents and purposes, it was) and reduce its version of sports entertainment down to its lowest common denominator and most broadly palatable product. The grind of never having an off-season and having no threatening competition to spur creative juices meant that the "WWE style" of professional wrestling settled in: matches followed a specific pattern on the undercard and another in the main events, with gimmick matches and gim-mick PPVs like Elimination Chamber, Extreme Rules, Money in the Bank, Hell in a Cell, and the tried-and-true annual Survivor Series and Royal Rumble (although even Survivor Series became largely devoid of what were now called "tradi-tional" Survivor Series elimination matches) to break up the monotony. A continuing emphasis was placed on WWE, the entity, above the WWE Superstars. In stark opposition to how pro wrestling had operated for a hundred years or more, WWE was seemingly operating as though it was the com-pany itself that people were coming to see, rather than the stars as the attractions to "talk them into the building." In this respect, WWE was ahead of the curve of the entertain-ment industry's next big shift to tent-pole franchises above all else. The difference was that WWE began making more and more money despite fans never being more displeased with the product—or at least, the fans who cared enough about wrestling to yell loudly about how much they wanted something different than what WWE was giving them every week. How they did that was by resisting fan favorites and then, once those same populist heroes rose to the top, ignor-ing or dropping them—trying instead to channel the audi-ence's energy toward corporate champions. This was never more obvious than with Bryan Danielson and CM Punk.

The "talking into the building" tenet of years gone by was also diminishing, as WWE shows became more tightly scripted with each passing year, and with the exception of a very select few established top stars (like Triple H), promos were scripted word-for-word before the shows and Super-stars were expected to follow those promos to the letter or risk strong admonishment afterward. The stories and characters grew more generic. Wins and losses stopped mattering much as the company began relying more on "50/50 booking." Main-event programs would stretch on for months with the opponents trading wins on PPVs in matches with varying conditions or stipulations, until a final match with ultimate stakes. Sometimes, the two rivals would start feuding again just a few months later.

The first in a string of unthinkable WWE returns came in 2010, when Bret Hart (who had been on speaking terms with McMahon since 2005 and was inducted into the WWE Hall of Fame in 2006) returned to WWE television. He feuded with his old boss and had a "match" against Mr. McMahon at WrestleMania XXVI that was really more of a one-sided, glorified beating (as Hart wasn't medically cleared to take anything resembling a bump) of McMahon by most of the extended Hart family, which must have been extremely cathartic for all involved.

The contest was McMahon's final match to date, the last in a series of violent and punishing brawls against his biggest stars at WrestleMania (following blood-soaked affairs against Shawn Michaels at WrestleMania 22 and against Hulk Hogan at WrestleMania XIX). Hart was made the general manager of *Raw* for a time before giving way to a year-long concept that fans are still trying to puzzle through: the anonymous *Raw* general manager.

After relieving Hart of his duties, McMahon introduced the concept on an episode of *Raw*. A laptop was placed on a podium near the announce team, and periodically throughout the show, the default iOS text alert sound (of all sound cues) would echo through the arena. Play-by-play announcer Michael Cole would get up from his position at the announce table, walk to the podium, and read the latest missive from the anonymous general manager, usually a command for certain Superstars to engage in fisticuffs immediately (or in the main event, if the laptop was feeling saucy). The idea was phased out in July 2011, but a year later, a one-off joke insinuated that the anonymous GM had been DX mascot and erstwhile purgatory-dwelling unbathed "leprechaun" wrestler Hornswoggle. In the tradition of the concept of the anonymous *Raw* general manager, I have no follow-up or natural segue away from this topic.

While WWE was settling into its lack of variance and while TNA was doing whatever it is that they did at that time (which was have a bevy of thrilling and innovative stars and memorable characters in their midcard X Division while surrounding it with aging main-event players and whatever Vince Russo–adjacent nonsensical claptrap gimmickry and head-scratching story lines), Ring of Honor continued to lead the charge of the independent scene.

It's difficult to overstate the influence that ROH had on the modern pro wrestling world. From WWE on down, most major stars either passed through or were products of the ROH vanguard. One of the company's greatest strengths was being a curator of the top wrestling talent in the world at all times, and in finding ways to replenish its roster when top stars were inevitably snatched away. Some of Ring of Honor's top early stars were Low Ki, AJ Styles, Samoa Joe, and Christopher Daniels. When all those wrestlers signed with TNA and were told they could no longer appear on ROH DVDs or iPPVs, the company turned to its next wave, headed by Austin Aries, CM Punk, Nigel McGuinness, Davey Richards, and "The American Dragon" Bryan Danielson. When that batch was snapped up, the company turned to Tyler Black, Kevin Steen, Roderick Strong, El Generico, and Adam Cole. And so on. You might notice that with the exception of Daniels and a one-off *NXT* appearance for Richards, every one of the wrestlers I just mentioned either had a run-in with, or is actively part of, WWE as you read this.

Like I said, the influence is hard to overstate.

Arguably the most successful crossover star Ring of Honor ever produced was CM Punk. Paul Heyman had worked with Punk prior to the relaunch of ECW and viewed him as the perfect up-and-comer to take up the torch of ECW and get the new iteration legitimized in the eyes of fans. Punk had a notable and passionate following from his days on the independent scene, where he was known as the best promo, bar none, outside of WWE and TNA—but also had the in-ring skills and natural charisma to go along with it. Punk made the biggest name for himself at Ring of Honor, where he had a trilogy of Matches of the Year against Samoa Joe (including Joe vs. Punk II, one of the first—if not the first—sixty-minute time-limit draws—known in the business as "a Broadway"—many indie fans had ever seen) and served as the head trainer of the ROH wrestling school for a while. Punk's character began life as a heel—his real-life status as a practitioner of straight edge (a punk subculture proscribing drug and alcohol use) was exhibited as arrogance. "I'm straight edge; that means I'm better than you," he would proclaim to irate fans in attendance at ROH, IWA Mid-South, and CZW events, and elsewhere. By the time he finished his trilogy with Samoa Joe, he was beloved by all independent wrestling fans for his ability combined with his passion for the business.

Shortly before Punk left the indie scene, he clearly seemed like a person in transition: he beefed up (naturally) and switched from his trademark satin boxing shorts to traditional wrestling trunks. He dyed his bleach-blond hair black. Fans knew he wrestled a tryout match with WWE and that he was on their radar. In June 2005, news broke that Punk had reportedly accepted a deal to sign with WWE, although he was set to challenge Ring of Honor world champion Austin Aries at Death Before Dishonor III on June 18. On social media and elsewhere, Punk made a plea for fans to come out to the show, intimating it would be his last night with the company. An emotional Punk thanked the audience and stunned everyone in attendance by actually winning the world title. After the match, Punk appeared to begin a farewell speech before essentially calling everyone suckers for getting duped into caring about him. It was a final, sublime Ring of Honor heel turn that was ratcheted up at the next ROH event. Entering to Living Colour's "Cult of Personality" as his new entrance theme, a suit-clad Punk gloated and taunted the fans, taking delight in signing his official WWE contract on the ROH title itself and promising to take the world title with him when he left the company in a few months. This kicked off what is lovingly referred to as "the Summer of Punk" (trust me; this will be important later) as he embarked on a spectacular farewell tour of red-hot title defenses before finally losing the title in a multiperson match and having a chance to leave the company as a hero once more in his final ROH match, a beyond-emotional affair against his best friend, Colt Cabana, with whom he had broken into the business.

Punk excelled at OVW, but the anti–independent wrestler

bias was still a very real thing in those days. Punk had WWE employees tell him he'd never be called up or put on television. Heyman and ECW ended up being his saving grace and his ticket in.

In ECW, CM Punk was about the only thing that continued to click with longtime ECW fans as the ECW Originals faded from television more and more. Punk was a known entity to WWECW fans exactly because of his Ring of Honor work, which former fans of the original ECW happily sought out and eagerly consumed and followed because of its early focus on dream matches and its company aesthetic of having the best in-ring work anywhere in the world, purely out of passion for the art and the sport of wrestling and a belief that the best performers competing to the best of their abilities should be the driving force behind the platonic ideal of professional wrestling. Punk, however, was one of the few ROH stars of that era who was signed by WWE as opposed to TNA. WWE seemed to have a stigma against the super-workers of the indies, who were perceived by executives and trainers to have developed "bad habits" wrestling in "bingo halls" and may be good at having matches but were largely devoid of charisma. Again, these beliefs didn't have a whole lot of truth to them, but this was the company line for years.

Punk was one of the few who got the nod from WWE, largely because of his reputation as the biggest personality and the best promo among the independent circuit. Paul Heyman and many others went to bat for Punk (and WWE was the only destination Punk was interested in, as he was always driven to become the biggest fish in the largest possible pond) and he was eventually brought into the OVW developmental territory and then to ECW, but always seemed halfway in the doghouse, or perpetually lingering just outside of being the focus of any main-event interest, despite more and more fans getting on board with what he was doing.

Punk's first big break in WWE came at WrestleMania XXIV, when he managed to capture the Money in the Bank briefcase, guaranteeing him his first non-ECW world title shot. Three months later, Punk cashed in on the ultimate opportunist, Edge, in a pique of irony after Edge was decimated by Batista on an episode of *Raw*. Punk became World Heavyweight Champion, but to say his first reign was disappointing is an understatement. WWE treated Punk's status as champion as an afterthought, to the extent that he lost his title in a match he wasn't even a participant in, being jumped backstage by Randy Orton's Legacy stable and replaced by Chris Jericho. Punk was shuffled back down the card, and most fans assumed that was that, the rug having been pulled out yet again by WWE's lack of confidence in a performer without ever fully committing to giving them a fair shake in a prominent position.

Shockingly, they tried the same thing again a year later. Punk became the first-ever back-to-back winner of the Money in the Bank match at WrestleMania 25, and on June 7, 2009, he became a despised heel when he cashed in his contract to win the World Heavyweight Championship from Jeff Hardy, the longtime fan favorite who had just won the world title moments earlier in a ladder match at Extreme Rules.

Playing off Hardy's public and storied struggles with substance abuse, Punk really leaned into the assholish aspect of his straight edge persona (which wasn't a persona) for the first time in WWE. He ruthlessly mocked and belittled Hardy, taking cheap shots drawn from real life, and fans were *pissed off about it.* Punk finally proved to WWE that his ideas and his positioning as world champion could succeed with audiences and at long last began to receive something resembling support from the company. The feud with Hardy led to the formation of the Straight Edge Society, a stable of devotees that Punk had "liberated" from substance abuse. Punk painted himself as a Messiah—he was effectively Straight Edge Jesus—and in the yearlong run with the SES, he alternately delighted and infuriated fans with his unrelenting gift of gab. Punk was not afraid to tear up the scripts he was handed by writers before shows and became one of the very few performers in the company who was given freedom to craft his own promos.

With that in mind, let's put a pin in CM Punk's WWE journey for just a moment and turn to one of the founding fathers of Ring of Honor: "The American Dragon" Bryan Danielson.

Danielson, who broke into the wrestling business in 1999, was one of the first trainees at Shawn Michaels's Texas Wrestling Academy. Briefly signed to a WWF developmental contract at the advent of his career due to his ties with Michaels, Danielson competed in the landmark 2000 and 2001 King of the Indies tournaments and then rounded out his training in the New Japan dojo. It was quickly apparent to anyone who laid eyes on his in-ring work that he was a spectacular talent. He main-evented the first Ring of Honor event in a three-way match against Christopher Daniels and Low Ki, and as one of ROH's founding fathers, his career was off and running. Within a year of joining ROH, it was clear that he wasn't just exceptional, but was a generational talent. While anchoring many of ROH's events, Danielson traveled the entire world, remaining in high demand for years due to his unparalleled in-ring work. It was often said that Ric Flair could wrestle a good match with a broomstick; in similar fashion, it was nearly impossible for the American Dragon to turn in a bad match, no matter his opponent. When ROH suffered through its first and second roster raids, Danielson held the line with thirty-eight successful world title defenses as part of a fifteen-month reign as the company's top champion.

Danielson gained one of the most passionate fan bases in the world during his time in the indies, where he was unanimously regarded as the best wrestler, bar none. Not only did Danielson fundamentally *get* wrestling and what makes it work on a level that few others in history have, he was also constantly seeking ways to push the boundaries. He and Austin Aries tried to convince ROH to let them have a ninety-minute match but settled for a seventy-four-minute classic at the aptly named Testing the Limit event. Danielson's feud with Nigel McGuinness over the unification of the ROH World and Pure titles was notorious for its brutality, including multiple unprotected and shoot headbutts and a ghastly sequence where Danielson repeatedly drove McGuinness's head into the steel ring post. (For their part, both men now regret leaning so hard into basing this series of matches around intense and very real brain trauma.) McGuinness and Danielson both departed Ring of Honor in 2009; McGuinness signed with TNA, where he was renamed Desmond Wolfe, and Danielson was tabbed once again by WWE.

By 2010, WWE had consolidated its various developmental territories into one location: Florida Championship Wrestling in Tampa. WWE ended its partnerships with Ohio Valley

Wrestling, Deep South Wrestling, Heartland Wrestling Association, and a few others and moved all its wrestlers who were signed to "developmental" contracts under one roof.

It was from FCW that WWE drew the roster for its ECW replacement, the optimistically named *NXT*. Conceived of as a competition-based reality show under a season structure, it was a combination of *Tough Enough* and the current WWE product, and combined kayfabe and reality, although the "reality" usually took place in the form of curveballs that the contestants weren't aware of ahead of time. The first season paired eight FCW wrestlers as "rookies" with eight established "mentor" WWE Superstars. The rookies would compete in weekly challenges as well as matches and would be eliminated at regular intervals, with the ultimate winner of the season earning a spot on the roster as well as a title shot of their choosing.

Bryan Danielson was tabbed as one of those initial eight *NXT* rookies, infuriating independent and hardcore wrestling fans in three distinct ways with one fell swoop. First, the American Dragon was given the WWE-trademarked name of "Daniel Bryan," which seemed particularly uninspired. Second, the labeling of Bryan as a "rookie" when he was more experienced than half the mentors on the show. But most infuriating of all to anyone who had followed Danielson's career was his being paired with The Miz as his mentor. The Miz was the alpha and omega of what a manufactured, in-house cookie-cutter WWE Superstar represented to most longtime fans. The Miz had only ever aspired to be part of WWE, so he was snatched up based on his *Real World* celebrity and turned into WWE's ideal of what a Superstar looks like. Casting Bryan as The Miz's supposed protégé was taken as a "fuck you" to fans—which in retrospect must have been WWE's intent all along. They used Bryan as a way to rile up the diehards, and that first season of *NXT* played it to the hilt.

Bryan main-evented the first episode of *NXT* with an instant-classic dream match against Chris Jericho (who was the mentor of rookie Wade Barrett, quickly determined by fans to be WWE's pick to win the show, given he was tall and had an immaculate haircut). Bryan lost that match while being ranked first on the initial coaches' poll (a weird concept that never got easier to understand) and then proceeded to go 0–10 through the first twelve weeks of the show. Bryan consistently half-assed the physical challenges and sub-improv-class impromptu promo competitions while running rings around everyone else in the ring, and fans assumed the whole while that Bryan was being made an example of for being the "indie guy" and was continually embarrassed solely to make fans unhappy. That was the state of die-hard pro wrestling fandom at the time: they were conditioned to believe WWE wouldn't let them have nice things, because WWE hated pro wrestling and everyone who watched it.

After another loss in Week 12, host Matt Striker asked Bryan who he would cut if the decision were up to him. Bryan named himself, due to a failure to get the job done, and the *NXT* higher-ups obliged. Bryan's departure was shocking, but his exit interview raised eyebrows the world over. Striker tossed out the scripted question he was given, a pointed barb at the independent circuit (which itself was a metatextual sending up of fans' *perceptions* of what WWE thought of the indies). "I gotta ask," Striker began, "do you regret leaving the independent scene—where you were a big fish in a small pond—to ultimately drown in the sea that is the WWE?"

"Well, that's funny," responded Bryan. "Because Daniel Bryan never wrestled on the independent scene. If you go on YouTube, 'Daniel Bryan,' all you ever see is Daniel Bryan in the WWE. But there was this guy—man, he was out there, he was kicking people's heads in. People called him the best in the world, the best technical wrestler in the world. He was a champion in Japan, and Mexico, and Europe." Now more animated than he had been in any interview in the previous twelve weeks, he turned to Striker. "You might know this guy," Bryan continued.

Striker cut him off there, asking his final question: "What's next for this guy?" he said, pointing at Bryan.

Bryan turned to the camera. "For Daniel Bryan, I don't know, man," he said. "That might be the end of him. He's eliminated from *NXT.* I mean, he can't even beat rookies. What's wrong with this guy? He can take Batista to the limit, but he can't beat rookies." He inhaled sharply, wincing at the very thought of that reality. "Daniel Bryan might be done," he continued. "But Bryan Danielson . . . god knows what's gonna happen to him." The crowd roared its approval while Striker beamed ear-to-ear at the masterful promo that Bryan cut. Fans had always been told that the company line on Bryan Danielson was that he didn't have a personality, even though anyone who had followed his Ring of Honor career—from all-American babyface to evil Jedi wrestling master to shit-head passive-aggressive wrestling hero to violent, vindictive asshole—knew that couldn't be further from the truth. With his exit interview, Bryan showed off his abundant personality *and* charisma, and went from indie darling to a plucky underdog that absolutely every WWE fan could get behind.

On the June 1 season finale of *NXT*, Wade Barrett did indeed win the competition over runner-up David Otunga, but no WWE fan predicted what happened next. On June 7, the main event of *Raw* featured WWE Champion John Cena vs. CM Punk,* who won a fan vote to determine Cena's challenger. Around five minutes into their match, Wade Barrett appeared at the top of the entrance ramp and slowly began making his way to the ring. From all around the ring and through the crowd, the other rookies from the first season of *NXT* appeared, first attacking and taking out Punk and the Straight Edge Society before surrounding Cena in the ring. The eight men, all wearing black armbands with an *N* on them, dogpiled Cena and left him lying. They then turned their attention to the very infrastructure of *Raw*, attacking Striker and Jerry Lawler at the announce table. As Michael Cole fled the scene, the final ten minutes of *Raw* featured the *NXT* rookies beating up producers, the timekeeper, ring

---

* At this point, the Messiah of the Straight Edge Society was wearing a mask following a feud with Rey Mysterio. Punk's SES disciples showed their allegiance by having their heads ceremonially shaved in the ring, while Straight Edge Jesus CM Punk of course had resplendent, flowing locks. His loss to Mysterio resulted in his having to shave his own head, but since Punk's character was that of an egomaniacal hypocrite, he donned a mask while his hair slowly grew back. It's a decades-old gimmick that is sure to generate heat—Kurt Angle did something similar in 2002, when he lost a hair vs. hair match to Edge and paraded around afterward with a wig held on by amateur wrestling headgear—and it always works. It also allowed Punk to appear on weekly television with a big pentagram in the middle of his face. My point is: the Straight Edge Society ruled.

announcer Justin Roberts, and other officials, before tearing apart the announce table and dismantling the ring itself, removing the ropes and the canvas while still taking the time to return to the ring to hit a series of finishers on Cena. Without the benefit of commentary, the effect was immediate: it looked like absolute bedlam and like nothing that had ever been on a WWE show before. The show went off the air with Cena being stretchered out of the arena in front of a stunned crowd.

The story line behind the stable was every bit as innovative and intriguing as their explosive debut had been. Now calling themselves the Nexus, the stable of *NXT* rookies was formed in solidarity in response to how they had been treated in the first season of the show. They were expected to go tooth-and-nail against each other and be belittled by their more experienced peers every week, and their ultimate reward for this humiliation meant seven-eighths of them would ostensibly be out of a job when it was all over? The Nexus opted instead to rise up and fight back against WWE. It was the same fake-invasion story line/new stable takeover that had been performed many times in high-profile situations, including both the nWo and the WCW/ECW Invasion, but this metatextual spin spoke directly to the type of fans who had been turned off by WWE in the past decade. Intentionally or not, the Nexus was a reflexive and self-effacing jab not only at how WWE had stagnated and grown complacent, but at the gatekeeper and anti-outsider mentality that had permeated the sport of professional wrestling since its inception.

The Nexus ran into an issue immediately after their debut. During the out-of-control attack,* ring announcer Justin Roberts had his shirt and jacket ripped off, leaving his tie in place around his neck. Seeing a golden opportunity for drama and a fantastic visual (as he always did), Daniel Bryan choked Roberts with his own necktie, rearing back on it as Roberts clawed at his throat and the cameras caught the whole thing in a visceral close-up. An amazing moment for live television, but not in keeping with the company's TV-PG standards. Destroying a ring was fine for WWE and their advertisers. On-air strangulation was another matter altogether. Perhaps Chris Benoit was still weighing on the minds of company executives, but regardless of the definitive reason, Bryan was told that he went too far in the attack and that his contract was being terminated. Four days after the debut of the Nexus, Daniel Bryan was a free agent.

Bryan quickly took bookings all over the world, with every promotion dying to get a chance to promote a show featuring the returning Bryan Danielson. At wXw in Germany, he won a two-day tournament. At IWA, he won the Puerto Rico Heavyweight Championship. He main-evented shows in CHIKARA, Dragon Gate USA, HWA, SCW, EVOLVE, and at his old stomping grounds Pro Wrestling Guerrilla in California, where he was showered with neckties upon his entrance and won the company's world title, only to vacate it the same night. He wrestled TJP, Bobby Fish, PAC,

---

* Very few people at ringside and no one not involved in the *Raw* main event that night was clued in fully as to what the Nexus attack would entail. The mayhem was largely unscripted, as the members of the Nexus were just told to beat up and destroy anything they possibly could.

Shingo Takagi, Chris Hero, Jon Moxley, Shelton Benjamin, Roderick Strong, Eddie Kingston, and numerous others. It was one of the most eventful and prosperous two months in independent wrestling, but it came to an abrupt end when Daniel Bryan made his surprise WWE return on August 15 at SummerSlam, appearing alongside Cena, Edge, Bret Hart, Chris Jericho, John Morrison, and R-Truth as that team's secret partner to face the Nexus. Bryan was back in WWE to stay, although due to the abrupt nature of his rehiring, he continued to fulfill his indie booking obligations until October 1.

Meanwhile, John Cena wiped out the Nexus and created a new signature moment: "LOL CENA WINS." Hulk Hogan and Goldberg and many others may have had years of looking unbeatable to the point of infuriation, but Cena had innumerable moments when the deck was supposedly stacked against him, only for him to "overcome the odds" with ease and nearly every time. There were occasions when Cena defeated the entire WWE roster by himself, which really *sounds* like it should be hyperbole. Cena would be thrown off or through things, hit with weapons, cheated against, ganged up on, hit with every move in the book, and would still win. It took a stun gun for Goldberg's win streak to come to an end in WCW; John Cena couldn't have lost a match during the John Cena years if you shot him in the face with an elephant gun.

At least Bryan was able to get clear of the Nexus by sheer happenstance before they became a punchline. But that didn't mean he didn't still have a steep uphill climb due to the continued belief within WWE that he wasn't marketable or charismatic. He captured his first title in the company in

September when he defeated his former mentor, The Miz, for the United States Championship, but quickly found himself in the midcard shuffle, paired with the Bella Twins in a series of comedic love-triangle vignettes. He was set to defend the U.S. Championship against Sheamus at WrestleMania XXVII, but after being moved to the pre-show, the match descended into chaos after four minutes and turned into a Battle Royal that was won by the Great Khali, a 7-foot-1 giant from India who briefly won the World Heavyweight Championship in 2007. Continuing on with a trope that originated on *NXT*—which was one of the main things that rankled fans about WWE's treatment of Bryan—lead announcer Michael Cole would assume a disdainful tone during every Daniel Bryan match, deriding Bryan as a "nerd" and a loser and belittling his past accomplishments and his then-veganism. Fans were well aware that all announcers were fed talking points and lines directly from Vince McMahon in their headsets during shows, so the assumption was these were the company's actual feelings about Bryan, usually losing sight of the fact that if WWE truly didn't care about a wrestler, they just didn't put them on television—or didn't employ them at all.

NXT launched its second season, complete with its own indie darling in the form of fellow ROH founding father Low Ki, competing under his new WWE name, Kaval. In another tongue-in-cheek jab at the grassroots favorite, Kaval's mentors on *NXT* were the team of LayCool—Michelle McCool and Layla El. (LayCool was absolutely great and the pair were perfect foils to the far-too-self-serious Kaval, and if you disagree, you're wrong.) Other rookies featured third-generation wrestlers Joe Hennig, the son of Mr. Perfect, and

Windham Rotunda, the son of multiple tag team champion Mike Rotunda, aka Irwin R. Schyster, and named after his godfather, Four Horseman member Barry Windham. Naturally, Hennig and Rotunda were given the names Michael McGillicutty and Husky Harris, respectively, despite both being acknowledged as the sons of their famous fathers. Kaval actually won the second season and challenged Dolph Ziggler for the Intercontinental Championship in November but was gone from the company forever by December. The all-women third season of *NXT* introduced WWE audiences to the Chickbusters—AJ Lee and Kaitlyn—as well as WWE mainstay Naomi. By the fourth season, Daniel Bryan was part of the show once again, this time as a mentor to Derrick Bateman.

In the middle of the third season of *NXT*, the show moved from Syfy to an exclusive weekly webcast on WWE.com, and WWE basically stopped paying attention to it. The winner of the third season was Johnny Curtis, who appeared on WWE television only fleetingly before being taken off the road and repackaged as ballroom dancer Fandango.* The fourth season was *NXT Redemption*, with contestants pulled from prior seasons. Bryan was part of that season as well, once again paired with Bateman, but over the course of a whopping sixty-seven episodes, the season never actually came to a conclusion. Instead of being a competition show, it became

---

* According to one of Chris Jericho's memoirs, the Fandango character originated when Vince McMahon called Jericho to berate him for appearing on *Dancing with the Stars*, because in McMahon's mind, only losers danced. When Jericho told McMahon that the professional male dancers on the show got laid constantly, McMahon fell into a stunned silence. A short time later, Fandango—the dancer who fucks—was born.

an extremely loosey-goosey and very weird entity unlike any other WWE television—once the higher-ups took a more passive, hands-off approach to it. As a result, *NXT Redemption* became a passionate cult classic, with fans falling in love with these weirdo characters before the plug was finally pulled in August 2011.

Meanwhile, after losing the United States Championship to Bryan, The Miz became WWE Champion in November 2010. As much as fans hated John Cena and had grown weary of Randy Orton at the time (to say nothing of Triple H), they *despised* the idea of The Miz holding the top title in the company. They felt he didn't deserve it, that he was annoying, and that he was bad in the ring. In short, The Miz was a true heel. While Miz built toward a WrestleMania match against John Cena for the title, CM Punk busied himself by ditching the Straight Edge Society and forming a New Nexus, augmented with McGillicutty, Harris, and muscle freak Mason Ryan, while several original Nexus members instead opted to join Wade Barrett's new faction, the Corre. The New Nexus was even shorter-lived than its original incarnation, and Punk was once again a solo act by the summer.

Behind the scenes, Punk continually pressed McMahon and other higher-ups for a chance to really be given the ball as a new face of the company, citing the numerous "brass rings" that he had grabbed during his time in the company and pointing out his impeccable track record at getting fans to actually care about pro wrestling story lines in the new millennium.

The Miz successfully defended the WWE Championship at WrestleMania XXVII in an afterthought, when The Rock— who returned to WWE television after a seven-year hiatus to host WrestleMania—interfered to set up a Rock vs. Cena main event for the following year. Don't worry, everyone: The Rock beat up The Miz after the main event to make sure no one took the world champion seriously. John Cena won the title back on May 1, and at long last, CM Punk got to the fireworks factory.

Playing off the real-world fact that his WWE contract was set to expire, CM Punk started one of the hottest periods of the last decade. After winning the No. 1 contendership for Cena's title, Punk interfered in a Cena vs. R-Truth tables match on June 27, 2011. While wearing a vintage Stone Cold Steve Austin shirt, Punk walked to the top of the ramp, where he sat down cross-legged and addressed a prone John Cena, still in the ring. The unscripted promo began:

> **John Cena, while you lay there, hopefully as uncomfortable as you possibly can be, I want you to listen to me. I want you to digest this, because before I leave in three weeks with your WWE Championship, I have a lot of things I want to get off my chest.**
>
> **I don't hate you, John. I don't even dislike you. I do like you. I like you a hell of a lot more than I like most people in the back.**

The promo was already unusual for how it downplayed the reality of the feud between the two, but then Punk went a step further.

> **I hate this idea that you're the best. Because you're not. I'm the best. I'm the best in the world. There's one thing you're better at than I am and that's kissing Vince**

McMahon's ass. You're as good at kissing Vince's ass as Hulk Hogan was. I don't know if you're as good as Dwayne though. He's a pretty good ass kisser. Always was and still is.

He grinned, waved at the camera, and gleefully cried, "Whoops! I'm breaking the fourth wall!"

And so on he went, for all the world like a fan finally taking the company to task for how hidebound and safe it had become, excoriating Vince McMahon for refusing to let him advance, the company for undervaluing him ("I'm a Paul Heyman guy," he said, referencing another "Paul Heyman guy" who took his ball and went home—Brock Lesnar—before name-dropping the possibility of wrestling for New Japan or for Ring of Honor, then specifically waving to his then best friend and ROH employee, Colt Cabana), the entire pro wrestling corporate machine for only promoting stars who will suck up to the boss, his absence from appearing on souvenir cups and in the opening credits of *Raw*, and the audience for bothering him for autographs at the airport and being "too lazy to get a real job." Just as he was about to launch into "a personal story about Vince McMahon," his mic was abruptly silenced and his voice drowned in the roar of an astonished audience. He stood up, angrily gesticulating at the camera as the camera cut away.

The shoot-style promo was an instant sensation not just in the wrestling world, but beyond, because Punk had pulled back the curtain and blatantly shattered kayfabe, in between breaking long-held WWE mandates like not breaking the fourth wall, not addressing the camera directly, and not mentioning other wrestling companies. Within hours of the show-ending speech, national mainstream media outlets and sports networks had been clued in on the genre-defying monologue.

Vince McMahon must have been thrilled. Because it was, of course, a worked shoot, setting up CM Punk as an anti-heroic heel with tremendous heat with the company.

Over the next week, talk radio ran amok wondering whether it was actually part of the show (it was) and how much of what Punk was saying was true (nearly all of it). In the promo, Punk laid out what he intended to do when he finally got his title match at the Money in the Bank PPV: he was going to win the title, let his contract expire, and then go defend the belt elsewhere. In his opinion, that was exactly what the fans deserved for continuing to pour money into a company that was going to keep making money despite itself and with no regard for the people who watch it.

Punk was suddenly the hottest thing in pro wrestling, so naturally, as part of the story line, Vince McMahon suspended him for his tirade and kept him off television the following week. Cena insisted Punk be reinstated, so Punk returned on the go-home show for Money in the Bank to cut another all-timer, lights-out promo, which turned into a back-and-forth between him and Cena. Punk explained to the crowd that McMahon was now bending over backward to try and sign him to a long-term contract extension, which he found funny because all he ever wanted was a microphone on WWE television. "See, this," Punk explained, pointing to the mic in his hand, "is power. This voice is power. In anybody else's hands, this is just a microphone. In my hands, it's a pipe bomb—as I showed you two weeks ago." Fans were listening. The world was listening. In just two weeks, Punk had turned his match with Cena into the most anticipated bout in years. His initial speech, which retroactively became known as the "Pipe Bomb" promo, was already seminal. It was reported that his contract was legitimately running out. Adding to the intrigue was that Money in the Bank was taking place in Rosemont, a suburb of Chicago—not only was Chicago Punk's hometown, but the market was a notoriously clued-in and raucous one. Fans were invested in this match with all their hearts. Would WWE really risk a potential riot by having Cena win yet again?

On the evening of Money in the Bank, Punk signed a twenty-four-hour contract extension with WWE. In front of a crowd as hot as any in the history of pro wrestling, Punk and Cena proceeded to have the best WWE match in years. Dave Meltzer of the *Wrestling Observer Newsletter* rated it at five stars, making it the first five-star match in WWE since 1997. The crowd in the arena lived and died with every strike and maneuver by the two men, and it all ended with Punk hitting his finishing move, the Go 2 Sleep, and pinning Cena in the middle of the ring to become the new WWE Champion. He grabbed the belt, blew a kiss to a furious Mr. McMahon at ringside, and departed through the crowd. After riding bikes around town and celebrating with his close friends that night, Punk went home to his Chicago apartment and put the WWE Championship in his refrigerator. The Summer of Punk was about to begin, just as it had hit Ring of Honor several years earlier.

Punk's initial idea for the WWE iteration of the Summer of Punk was for him to actually leave the company, taunt WWE from afar, and even wrestle matches in other promotions. WWE went along with the idea at first; Punk made media appearances, attended an indie show, and popped up at the San Diego Comic Con to badmouth Triple H. But WWE quickly got antsy and wanted Punk back on television sooner rather than later. While Punk was off television, the Mr. McMahon character organized a tournament to determine a new champion. On July 25, Rey Mysterio captured the vacant title, but lost it that same night to Cena. As Cena celebrated, the guitar riff for Living Colour's "Cult of Personality" rang through the arena. Cena looked around, confused, before Punk emerged at the top of the ramp with the WWE Championship around his waist. He had a new long-term contract; he had his Summer of Punk theme music; the world was talking about what he was going to do next. It seemed the final pieces were in place for him to become the new face of the company. Are you ready for the big reveal that things didn't turn out that way?

Punk unified the WWE Championship and Cena's interim version at SummerSlam on August 14 but was attacked by Kevin Nash afterward and vulnerable to Alberto Del Rio, who cashed in his Money in the Bank contract to defeat Punk and become the new champion. The Summer of Punk sputtered out and turned into a three-way feud between Punk, Nash, and Triple H. The wind was out of the sails of the act that was the hottest in years just a few months after it began.

The *Raw* and *SmackDown* roster split and brand extension, which began to such fanfare in 2002, was officially ended on August 29, 2011. The single-branded PPVs had been out the window since 2007, and with ECW being shuttered, the pretense was not worth continuing. All champions and all wrestlers now appeared across both shows as time and story line dictated.

On the same PPV where Punk captured the company's top prize, Daniel Bryan won the *SmackDown* Money in the Bank ladder match. At this point, Bryan was playing the character of a delusional egomaniac. He vowed to be the first man to hold the Money in the Bank briefcase for one year and cash it in at WrestleMania XXVIII, but he instead tried to cash in several times in November and finally took advantage of Mark Henry rendering the Big Show unconscious to cash in and win the World Heavyweight Championship (at the time *SmackDown's* top prize) on December 18. After pinning an already-unconscious man, Bryan celebrated like he'd just won the Super Bowl. He hopped onto the announce table and waved the title in Cole's face, taunting him, before turning to the camera. "This is for everyone who's supported me for the past twelve years!" he yelled. He began slapping hands with fans and let out a loud "Yeah!" while standing on the ringside barricade.

Bryan began having television matches against lower-ranked opponents, winning one-sided matches and having over-the-top, way-too-enthusiastic celebrations afterward. He began celebrating his victories by pointing both index fingers in the air and exuberantly, repeatedly yelling, "Yes!" It was obnoxious. It was unnecessary. And it quickly caught on.

Late 2011 became beneficial to Punk as well. He recaptured the WWE Championship on November 20 at Survivor Series, kicking off a title run that became the longest in over two decades. During Punk's historic title run, he added Paul Heyman as his spokesperson and advocate, declaring himself a "Paul Heyman guy" to repay Paul for his loyalty and support during Punk's WWECW days. Over the course of his 434-day world title reign, Punk would consistently have fantastic, lengthy matches and continue to do spectacular microphone work—but the lightning in the bottle that was sparked with his Pipe Bomb promo was never recaptured after the Summer of Punk ended so abruptly. Punk had the longest unbroken title run since Hulk Hogan's initial reign that lasted from 1984 until 1988, but over the course of that 434 days, despite defending the title on every pay-per-view, Punk's match was rarely the main event.

After The Rock made his return to WWE following a seven-year hiatus from wrestling, he and Cena main-evented WrestleMania XXVIII in a match billed as "once in a lifetime." The Rock emerged victorious, while elsewhere on the card, Triple H and the Undertaker faced off in Hell in a Cell with special referee Shawn Michaels. That match was billed as "The End of an Era," with all three men taking a curtain call together after the Undertaker improved to 20–0 at WrestleMania. In truth, the billing for neither of those matches proved accurate; a Rock vs. Cena rematch for the following year was set in stone immediately after—if not before—WrestleMania XXVIII became the most purchased wrestling event in history. Triple H and Undertaker, meanwhile, continued to appear on subsequent WrestleManias, as did other returning Attitude Era stars.

But it wasn't just Attitude Era wrestlers who returned to the company at this time. The night after WrestleMania XXVIII, Brock Lesnar made his shocking return to the company. In Lesnar's eight years away from WWE, he had been released by the Minnesota Vikings after making their preseason squad and transitioned into MMA, capturing the UFC Heavyweight Championship. After retiring from MMA (for the first time) at the end of 2011, Lesnar signed a huge contract with WWE and reentered the company as one of the most legitimate and decorated performers to step foot in a WWE ring. He was treated as a big deal immediately upon his return and set about working in only main event–level programs while working a far more reduced schedule than nearly anyone else in WWE.

One final match worth noting on the WrestleMania XXVIII card is Daniel Bryan vs. Sheamus for the World Heavyweight Championship. The two men had been relegated to the pre-show and then their match had been usurped the previous year, so both were hopeful that they could show off their stuff in a competitive match. By this point, Bryan's sarcastic "Yes!" chant had caught on like wildfire with the larger WWE fan base, and when Sheamus and Bryan made their entrances as the first match on the main card, the WrestleMania crowd was littered with Daniel Bryan signs and yelling "Yes!" pretty much nonstop. The time was ripe for a star-making moment. Alas, what happened instead was an eighteen-second match, with Bryan getting caught by a Brogue Kick and pinned to lose the title after being distracted by kissing his on-screen manager and girlfriend, AJ Lee.

The following night on *Raw*, a raucous crowd made up of out-of-towners who stuck around after WrestleMania chanted "Yes!" throughout the evening, but particularly during Bryan's appearance in the main event. The crowd continued to chant after the show went off the air, and Bryan addressed them on the microphone after the show. "Last night was the worst night of my wrestling career," he told them. "But thanks to everybody here chanting 'Yes!' . . . I think you people have finally convinced them to make me a new T-shirt."

WWE did indeed make Bryan a new T-shirt, and he also

got a couple of chances at Punk's WWE Championship during his historic title run. After splitting from AJ, Bryan's character became more unhinged and angry, now finding the "Yes!" chants infuriating and constantly trying to drown them out or counteract them by instead shouting "No!" Bryan was forced to attend anger management classes alongside Kane. In a series of comedy vignettes, Kane and Bryan resisted their anger management training while being made to team together in matches. They invariably argued vehemently with one another and occasionally had prolonged, stalling "hug it out" sessions. The team became known as Team Hell No and captured the tag titles—which led to them shouting at one another, "*I* am the tag team champions!" The team quickly became beloved, turning Bryan into a babyface once again. He returned to the "Yes!" chants, and fans were eager to participate in full once again.

In order to build to a Cena vs. The Rock rematch with higher stakes (and for Cena to get his win back), it was necessary to get the world title onto The Rock. He was set to face Punk at the 2013 Royal Rumble, and during the buildup to that match, the man who became a supernova thanks to his gift of gab found himself thoroughly outclassed in promos. Maybe he was just rusty. Punk headed into the match with a secret weapon: a trio of enforcers collectively known as the Shield.

Conceived of by Punk, the Shield was comprised of three standouts plucked from developmental who operated as a paramilitary mercenary force. The "Hounds of Justice" sought to exact a measure of equity against those who held down or held back those they felt were more deserving, but they were really just operating as Punk's hired guns for the most part.

Punk had three specific men in mind for the role: former ROH compatriots Tyler Black and Chris Hero, and Les Thatcher trainee Jon Moxley. Like Punk, Moxley had gained a reputation during his time on the indies as being head and shoulders above all his peers in promo skill. Evoking a young Roddy Piper, Moxley had the gift of gab. He also supplemented his promo skills with an eagerness to participate in deathmatch wrestling. WWE signed off on Black and Moxley—who wrestled in FCW as Seth Rollins and Dean Ambrose, respectively—but they balked on Hero, who was signed to WWE under the name Kassius Ohno. Instead, WWE rounded out the trio with a different man as the powerhouse: Joseph Anoa'i, wrestling under the name Roman Reigns, a second-generation wrestler who was part of the most storied Samoan wrestling family in history and a cousin of The Rock.

Despite the Shield's best attempts to help Punk retain his title, The Rock prevailed at Royal Rumble, capturing his eighth WWE Championship. The following night on *Raw*, Rock unveiled a new WWE Championship belt, designed by Orange County Choppers. The new belt officially retired Cena's custom spinner belt, in use since 2005. The basic design of the Orange County Choppers belt continued to be refined over the next couple of years but is in essence the same title design in use today.

Punk moved away from the title picture, moving instead into a feud with the Undertaker heading into WrestleMania 29. Punk vowed to end the Undertaker's undefeated streak and infuriated fans by invoking the memory of the Deadman's deceased manager, Paul Bearer. Leading into their match, Punk poured the kayfabe ashes of Bearer over the Undertaker. The match played second fiddle to The Rock vs.

Cena rematch but ended up being the best match on the card—especially after The Rock tore his abdomen to shreds in the opening minutes of the main event title match. After WrestleMania, Punk entered into a well-received feud against Brock Lesnar, now managed by Punk's former advocate Paul Heyman. After years of nonstop grind trying to prove himself as a top guy, including "favors" to McMahon like hurrying back from injury or traveling to European tours at the last minute, Punk was rapidly burning out. A nasty staph infection late in 2013, which Punk wrestled through, didn't help matters.

Bryan continued to be the most popular wrestler in the entire company throughout the summer of 2013 and was finally given a chance to challenge Cena for the WWE Championship in the main event of SummerSlam. No one expected Bryan to actually win, especially after Triple H made himself the special referee for the match. Fans couldn't believe it when Bryan hit Cena with a running knee and pinned him, clean as a sheet, to win the title. What they *could* believe happened just minutes later, as Randy Orton interrupted Bryan's celebration and Triple H hit Bryan with a Pedigree to help Orton cash in Money in the Bank and capture Bryan's freshly obtained championship. The rug had been pulled out once again, but this one seemed to especially sting. Bryan recaptured the world title the following month, but was stripped the next evening by Triple H. It felt like there was a personal vendetta against Bryan—largely because of the on-screen vendetta against Bryan.

But because of that perceived holding down of Bryan, combined with the undeniability of the "Yes!" chant, his popularity only grew throughout the rest of 2013. He very briefly became a member of the cultlike Wyatt Family, but broke free in time for the 2014 Royal Rumble. Behind the scenes, Punk was loudly campaigning for Bryan to go to the main event of WrestleMania XXX and capture the now-unified WWE Championship, but WWE's plan was for that main-event spot to go to the returning Batista.

Despite Bryan not being advertised as participating in the Royal Rumble match that year—he instead had a singles match against Bray Wyatt—fans were clamoring for him to be the man to win and earn a spot in the WrestleMania main event. During the Royal Rumble, as the clock counted down to introduce each of the thirty participants, "Yes!" chants rang out in anticipation of Bryan entering. The crowd got increasingly irate as the number of remaining entrants dwindled and by the time the thirtieth man entered and was *not* Daniel Bryan, there were thunderous, vociferous boos—even though the entrant was the universally beloved Rey Mysterio. When Batista won the match to punch his ticket to Wrestle-Mania XXX, the crowd again voiced its displeasure. As good as both men were, Batista vs. Randy Orton was not high on the list of Mania main events fans were dying to see.

During that Royal Rumble match, Punk suffered a concussion. The next night before *Raw*, he again voiced his displeasure at Bryan, the most popular wrestler in the company, not being part of the main-event mix at the biggest show of the year. He also voiced his displeasure at a great many other things, including his concussion the night before and WWE's plans for him at WrestleMania: namely, a match against Triple H. "I don't need to wrestle you at WrestleMania," Punk says he told Triple H, who was now real-life chief operating officer of WWE. "You need to wrestle me." Perceiving his words were falling on deaf ears, Punk walked out of the company and didn't go back.

Regardless of the impetus—whether Punk's leaving the company was a wake-up call or not—Bryan was slowly integrated back into the world title picture over the next few months. The Authority of Triple H and Stephanie McMahon belittled Bryan on WWE television, saying he didn't have the stature or the personality to make it as a champion or the face of the company, tarring him with the epithets of being a "good hand" and a "B-plus player." On March 10, 2014, fans wearing Daniel Bryan T-shirts and calling themselves "The Yes Movement" filled the ring, swearing to "occupy *Raw*" if Bryan did not get a fair chance at the WrestleMania XXX main event. The Authority finally relented, offering him an opportunity: if Bryan could defeat Triple H at WrestleMania XXX, he would be entered into the main event match later that night.

The main card of WrestleMania XXX opened with Bryan vs. Triple H, and the two men delivered a certifiable classic. Bryan won the match to make the main event a Triple Threat, but the Authority ruthlessly attacked him afterward, injuring his ribs. Fans were cautiously optimistic about Bryan's chances—after all, WrestleMania almost *always* has a happy ending—but an emotional night was taken up a notch later, as the Undertaker's undefeated streak at WrestleMania came to a sudden and unexpected end when he lost to Brock Lesnar. The sound of the air leaving the Superdome in New Orleans isn't something I'll ever forget, and the slack-jawed, wide-eyed reaction of "stunned Undertaker guy," front-row fan Ellis Mbeh, became instantly iconic.

But the show being taken down a notch by Undertaker's

loss was just setting the table for the ultimate elation later that evening. Despite being stretchered out mid-match, only to make a heroic return, Bryan's underdog performance— intentionally or not—recalled the Triple Threat main event of WrestleMania XX one decade earlier, where another immense fan favorite no one thought would ever be allowed to win WWE's top prize in a WrestleMania main event did the impossible. It's not a certainty that WWE was intentionally doing a callback to Chris Benoit's greatest career moment, but the match did end with the underdog tapping out the perceived favorite to win—using a crossface. But despite the strange echoes, the elation was undeniable when Batista submitted to the Yes Lock, giving Daniel Bryan a win at WrestleMania. As 70,000-plus fans chanted along with him, Bryan held aloft two belts and screamed *"YES!"* in celebration. For the first time, his enthusiasm matched the occasion. Confetti rained down and fireworks went off, and Bryan celebrated with courageous young cancer patient Connor Michalek and his family.

As WWE slid toward what has been referred to as the Reality Era (due to the majority of fans being intricately familiar with the inner workings of pro wrestling, combined with Punk and Bryan's reality-blending story lines and Triple H and Stephanie's dual roles as on-screen and off-screen authority figures—and with the advent of crossover E! reality show *Total Divas*), Punk and Bryan dared to give fans hope for the future. But Punk was not around to see Bryan's greatest triumph—and once again, Bryan's greatest triumph was fated to not last nearly as long as anyone had hoped.

Just two months after winning the world title at WrestleMania XXX, Daniel Bryan was forced to vacate it due to severe neck injuries. To the surprise of no one, John Cena won the vacant WWE Championship in June 2014, but to the surprise of everyone, Cena was unceremoniously demolished by Brock Lesnar at SummerSlam, beginning the first lengthy modern-day Lesnar title reign, marked by a lack of Lesnar actually appearing on weekly television, and absolutely never wrestling except on PPV. After winning the title at SummerSlam, Lesnar only wrestled on one PPV for the rest of the year.

The Shield, which had become one of the very hottest babyface acts in the company thanks to their talent level, general badassery, and a pair of bangers-only feuds against the Wyatt Family and the reunited Evolution, dissolved in 2014 when Seth Rollins joined forces with the Authority and turned on his brothers Dean Ambrose and Roman Reigns. It quickly became clear to fans that Roman Reigns was being groomed as the new top babyface in the company, when all they really wanted was Bryan or Ambrose or Cesaro or any one of the many long-suffering and deserving undercard mainstays—or, yes, even CM Punk, for whom arenas full of fans continued to chant even after he signed with UFC and became involved in a messy lawsuit and countersuit due to disparaging remarks he made about WWE's in-house doctor on his friend Colt Cabana's podcast after being released.

Although they were cheering passionately for him a month ago as part of the Shield, there was a sense of too much, too soon for Reigns—especially in relation to any one of a number of wrestlers who fans would rather see in that spot. In previous years, they had watched runaway popularity for cult favorites Ryback, Zack Ryder, Damien Sandow, and others get nuked simply because they got popular on their own

and not because WWE desired them to be in prominent positions. Reigns was asked to speak more often, which meant
that he had to read awkward and corny lines word for word
each week. He stopped being "cool" in most conventional
senses and fans sensed another Cena in the making. They
didn't want another Cena, so they began booing him loudly
in every arena he entered, even though he was always supposed to be the good guy.

Reigns, of course, was well aware of the crowd reaction,
but felt that was just the sort of thing that came with being put in that "top guy" position. "I started as the silent but
deadly type," Reigns said. "Sort of a badass, not [having] to
say too much. It progress[ed] from week to week. Everybody
wants to be on top. Everybody wants to ascend, to be the top
guy. So, they start doing all the stuff that they have to do. Not
everybody wants to be busy every single day. I'm that guy. I'm
a workhorse. I'll take anything and everything I can get, and
I'll do it with a smile on my face."

That he would continually "overcome the odds" in the
grand tradition of Cena certainly didn't help matters. By the
time Reigns won the 2015 Royal Rumble, not even an appearance from cousin The Rock to raise his hand in victory
could stop the Philadelphia crowd from mercilessly shitting
all over Reigns's moment. (A major contributor to the poor
reception for Reigns was that in 2015, a freshly returned
Daniel Bryan actually entered the Royal Rumble match but
was unceremoniously eliminated by Bray Wyatt midway
through.) The knife was twisted the following month, when
he defeated Daniel Bryan to secure his spot in the main event
of WrestleMania 31.

Hilariously, while Reigns was getting booed everywhere

he went because people perceived him as the next Cena, the current and actual Cena spent 2015 reinventing himself on the midcard, becoming United States Champion and invoking a "United States Open Challenge." Each week he had showcase matches against a wide swath of the roster, almost all of them incredible. Cena made his opponents look like a million bucks while being taken to the limit against opponents like Cesaro, Ryder, Sami Zayn, and Neville (previously known as PAC). He even debuted a new move: a springboard stunner. Cena wasn't without his Cena-isms, of course. When Kevin Owens defeated Cena clean as a sheet in his first match on the main roster, it wasn't even an hour before it was announced on-air that there would be a rematch at the next PPV. Cena won that one, believe it or not.

WrestleMania 31 featured the first of four consecutive Mania main events for Reigns, and the strongly anti-Reigns crowd at Santa Clara's Levi's Stadium was the most courteous the reception ever got for him. He and Lesnar faced off in a powerfully hard-hitting match, wherein Lesnar continued his status as a meme icon by tossing Reigns with several suplexes before loudly taunting his opponent by saying "Suplex City, bitch." Fans braced for the inevitable Cena-esque Reigns to Hulk up and win his first WWE Championship, but fourteen minutes or so into the match, Mr. Money in the Bank, Shield turncoat Seth Rollins, raced down the long entrance ramp and into the ring, becoming the first person to cash in their Money in the Bank contract during the main event of WrestleMania and turning the match into a Triple Threat. After Reigns took out Lesnar, Rollins delivered a curb stomp to win the match and the WWE Championship.

The plan for months had been to crown Reigns, but the negative reaction from fans convinced WWE to hold off, with the decision for Rollins to win coming on the day of the show and kept top-secret from everyone except those directly involved in the match. The decision infuriated Reigns's father, Hall of Famer Sika of the Wild Samoans, who was sitting ringside. The import of the moment wasn't lost on Rollins, whose elated and subtle "Thank you so much, brother" to Reigns as he was pinning him was picked up by the in-ring microphone.

WrestleMania 31's main card opened with a death-defying multiman ladder match for the Intercontinental Championship, which was captured by Daniel Bryan. Bryan hoped to become the face of *SmackDown* after he returned, but the week after WrestleMania, Bryan suffered another concussion and other lingering injuries. By April 16 he was pulled from future dates, and when he returned to television on May 11, it was to vacate the Intercontinental Championship and let fans know he received bad medical news and didn't know whether he'd be able to return.

Bryan, who suffered multiple concussions in his long career (his repertoire, like Chris Benoit's, featured a diving top-rope headbutt and lots of suplexes), found little that interested him outside of being a wrestler. As documented on *Total Divas*, he had an extremely hard time dealing with WWE refusing to medically clear him and fell into a deep depression when it looked like his in-ring career would be over. He reportedly mulled sitting out his contract and leaving to wrestle elsewhere—any other promotion in the world would have gladly taken him and wouldn't have given a tinker's cuss about whether doctors advised against him competing*—but at the time, WWE had established a precedent, notably with Rey Mysterio, that there was a loophole in contracts that allowed them to freeze and extend wrestlers' contracts due to injury or inactivity. Bryan instead agreed to take an on-screen role as *SmackDown* general manager and retired from wrestling on February 8, 2016, in front of a *Raw* crowd in his home state of Washington. WWE fans were in disbelief. Bryan and CM Punk, the two underdog heroes in whom they put their hope for the future, were both gone and didn't appear to be coming back.

WWE fans had allowed themselves to be "talked into the building" by two shining lights that they screamed their voices hoarse for every night until they made it to the top. And for all the fans' passion and love, they were left with part-time champions who didn't bother to show up and a deeply uncool, manufactured star they never asked for. If you happened to be aware of online wrestling fans at the time, the mood was *bleak*. WWE was now about the brand above all else, and the fans couldn't help but take it personally.

---

* For all their storied history of poor business practices and lack of care for their "independent contractors," WWE remains the only pro wrestling company in the world with a strict and written concussion protocol. They have also proven to be the only company willing to keep performers from wrestling if they aren't medically cleared, even if it means scrapping long-term plans.

21
TOTAL DIVAS AND TOTAL EVOLUTION

Women Become Superstars

Things finally seemed to be changing for women in WWE. *NXT*'s women-only season three provided a jolt to the division by adding the Chickbusters best-friends team of AJ Lee and Kaitlyn, unrepentant dorks who loved pro wrestling and were easy to root for. Between 2010 and 2013, a number of established Divas departed from the company, including Phoenix, McCool, James, Kelly Kelly, and Eve Torres. Alicia Fox became the first black Divas Champion in 2010—the first black woman to hold a WWE championship since Jazz's final reign in 2003. Natalya, the daughter of Jim

"The Anvil" Neidhart and the niece of Bret Hart, became the established veteran and unsung ring general of the division.

When NXT transitioned from weirdo cult internet show to the company's official, developmental third brand, there were abundant NXT success stories, beginning with Seth Rollins and Braun Strowman and continuing through the Four Horsewomen of NXT: Charlotte Flair, Becky Lynch, Sasha Banks, and Bayley.

All four wrestlers became the focus of the revitalized WWE women's division and multiple-time champions on both brands. Ric Flair introduced his daughter, Charlotte, when she made her debut on NXT television, and the training team, in addition to visiting main roster women like Natalya, quickly helped these four pioneers take their in-ring game to another level. (It would have been hard to gain much more legitimacy for the NXT women's division than the tournament final match for the vacant NXT Women's Championship at the first TakeOver: Charlotte, with Ric Flair in her corner, versus Natalya, with uncle Bret Hart in hers.) While Paige and then Charlotte may have gained the early attention in NXT, it was a long-running blood feud between former best friends Sasha Banks and Bayley that really took the division to the next level. The pinnacle of the feud (though not the final match) was their landmark battle at NXT Take-Over in Brooklyn, where pure-of-heart Bayley, at long last, finally captured the NXT Women's Championship. It was a match that the "real" main event—a ladder match between Finn Bálor and Kevin Owens—had no hope of following. For the first time, fans began insisting that women should get a shot at the main event, especially when the competitors were able to bring the thunder like Bayley and Sasha had.

Women's wrestling, long a sideshow at best, was pushed to new heights in the ring. Outside of the ring, women became a huge focus for the company in an entirely different—but no less valuable—way.

In 2013, WWE and cable channel E! struck up a partnership that would end up being spectacularly influential not just for the future of women in WWE, but for the company's image in general. WWE announced the debut of *Total Divas*, the company's first true reality show in the contemporary sense. (*Tough Enough* had plenty of elements of the reality competition show, but *Total Divas* was fully in line with E!'s other reality offerings like *Keeping Up with the Kardashians*.) WWE hastily introduced two new (nonwrestler) Divas, JoJo and Eva Marie, as the show was about to premiere. Fans instantly hated Eva Marie, who played her role on the show as the scheming and backstabbing stereotypical "reality show two-faced bitch" to the hilt. The cast of the first season was JoJo and Eva Marie, Natalya, Nikki and Brie Bella, and the Funkadactyls, Cameron and Naomi.* The show was a hit for E! and for WWE and was instantly the platonic ideal of what a reality show should be. That it took this long for pro wrestling to have a true reality show was absurd. Pro wrestling was founded on kayfabe and all pro wrestlers are taught to live the exaggerated, kayfabe version of themselves at all times whenever cameras or civilians are around. Pro wrestlers are perfect subjects for reality television and

---

* The Funkadactyls served as backup dancers to "The Funkusaurus," Brodus Clay, who was the only living, breathing, rompin', stompin' Funkusaurus in captivity—which explains why he constantly, desperately pleaded for someone to get in contact with his mother, who was likely worried sick.

their ingrained dual lives and dual personae result in their coming across as real people, especially contrasted with the majority of nonwrestling reality show personalities, who are often unnatural as they try kayfabe on for size for the first time, awkwardly behaving unlike themselves for the benefit of cameras or producers.

Total Divas combined a tantalizing mix of behind-the-scenes WWE footage with (mostly staged, but mostly very well done) snippets of the Divas' personal lives away from the wrestling business. The show had the added benefit of including plenty of appearances from the Bella Twins' real-life significant others: Brie's boyfriend (and later, husband), Daniel Bryan, and Nikki's boyfriend, John Cena. The show is likely the single biggest contributor to bringing in nonwrestling fans to WWE television from its debut on.

Despite the popularity of *Total Divas* and the Divas themselves, women continued to get precious few minutes on *Raw* and *SmackDown*—particularly in the ring. Even the roster additions of NXT standouts Emma, Summer Rae, and Paige, who billed herself as "The Anti-Diva," didn't lead to more time for the women's division—in fact, quite the opposite. In early 2015, total Divas in-ring time lasted less than ten minutes on pay-per-views and was a fraction of that on television.

On February 23, 2015, a promising-looking tag team match pitting the Bella Twins against Paige and Emma lasted less than thirty seconds—and was the only women's match on the show. Fans had had enough and flooded social media with the hashtag #GiveDivasAChance for much of the next forty-eight hours. The issue was furthered the next evening, when Stephanie McMahon tweeted an inspirational quote from Academy Award–winner Patricia Arquette with the sentiment, "Thank you @PattyArquette for having the courage to fight for #WomensRights on such a grand platform. #UseYourVoice." AJ Lee replied that evening, taking the WWE CBO to task for not practicing what she was preaching. "Your female wrestlers have record-selling merchandise and have starred in the highest-rated segment of the show several times," Lee began. "And yet they receive a fraction of the wages and screen time of the majority of the male roster. #UseYourVoice." Stephanie McMahon responded a short time later, with a curt tweet reading, "Thank you, [AJ], I appreciate your opinion. #UseYourVoice." That same evening, Vince McMahon tweeted, "We hear you. Keep watching. #GiveDivasAChance."

Most fans assumed Lee—whose contract was up soon—would be punished or taken off television for publicly taking her boss to task, as had been the norm in the past. Most observers also assumed that the McMahons paying lip service to a proposed focus on the women's division was just that—lip service. In the short term, there wasn't a lot of sweeping change to the women's division, but that changed on July 13. Proclaiming that we are now in the middle of a "Divas Revolution," Stephanie McMahon introduced the *NXT* call-ups of three of NXT's Four Horsewomen: Charlotte Flair, Becky Lynch, and Sasha Banks. Women did begin receiving more attention and screen time.

WrestleMania 32—one of the most lackluster in years on the men's side of things—ended up being a landmark event for the women's division. On the *Kickoff Show*, *Total Divas* cast members Brie Bella, Naomi, Natalya, Eva Marie, and Paige defeated the team of Emma, Lana, Naomi, Summer

Rae, and Tamina when Brie tapped out Naomi using a rolling version of husband Daniel Bryan's Yes Lock. (Brie took an extended sabbatical after WrestleMania, taking both Bella Twins off WWE television.)

But the landmark news—which many fans predicted ahead of time—came prior to the eighth match on the card. Hall of Famer Lita unveiled a new WWE Women's Championship, which would be awarded to the winner of the Triple Threat match between Divas Champion Charlotte Flair, Sasha Banks, and Becky Lynch. Lita also announced that, henceforth, women in WWE would no longer be referred to as Divas, but would instead be branded as Superstars, just like their male counterparts. Flair won the match by tapping out Becky Lynch with the figure-eight leglock to become the inaugural Women's Champion (although the finish of the match drew criticism for Ric Flair, Charlotte's father, preventing Banks from breaking up the submission, needlessly inserting the machinations of a male interloper into a landmark match for women).

After the 2016 brand split, Becky Lynch became the first SmackDown Women's Champion, and Raw's women's division was marked by Flair and Banks trading the title back and forth multiple times. The feud between Charlotte and Sasha featured a number of highly publicized "firsts," including the first women's Hell in a Cell match, which was also the first time in WWE history that a women's match main-evented a PPV. While the women in WWE didn't receive anything close to equal time during the Divas Revolution (which became the Women's Revolution, and then the Women's Evolution), their plight absolutely improved. Women's matches became competitive and marked by excellent in-ring work, and the women's division kept being further augmented by talented NXT call-ups like Alexa Bliss, Nia Jax, Bayley, Carmella, Asuka, and the returning Mickie James.

Attitudes about women's and independent wrestling continued to shift and change in the years leading up to the Women's Revolution and during it. In the mid-2010s, the worldwide independent scene experienced the rapidly increasing popularity of intergender matches—specifically, intergender matches that were treated as competitive contests where male and female competitors were on equal footing. Many fans (unsurprisingly, nearly all of them male) thought that men and women being presented as athletic equals took kayfabe and suspension of disbelief too far and made a mockery of the business. For years, WWE shied away from signing women who participated in lots of intergender matches, and in several cases WWE talent scouts told women to stay away from intergender wrestling for several months before they could take a look at offering them a contract. Thankfully, that sentiment was out the window by 2018, as many women with extensive intergender experience were brought into NXT. In 2018, Becky Lynch even got to wrestle in an intergender match on *SmackDown*, defeating the diminutive comedy wrestler James Ellsworth. (In fact, before leaving the company that year, Ellsworth was routinely beaten up by the entire women's division every night at WWE live events.)

NXT's second women's golden age after the Four Horsewomen were called up belonged entirely to Asuka. Formerly known as Kana and regarded as the best woman wrestler in the world, the Japanese star was a force of nature in NXT. During her time on the developmental brand, Asuka was one of the most dominant wrestlers in history, male or female, and was the anchor of a depleted division, assisting the other NXT women in honing their craft by giving them a chance to work with the very best on a regular basis. Asuka never lost during her time in NXT, capturing the NXT Women's Championship at NXT TakeOver: Dallas in 2016 and defeating all challengers. After 510 days as champion, she finally vacated the title without having been beaten on September 6, 2017, and departed for the main roster. She continued her reign of dominance on *Raw*, extending her undefeated streak while winning the first-ever women's Royal Rumble match and running the table with her partner The Miz on the inaugural season of the Facebook Watch–exclusive Mixed Match Challenge.* She challenged Charlotte Flair for the SmackDown Women's Championship at WrestleMania 34 and, shockingly, tapped out to the figure eight. For 914 days in WWE, Asuka had been undefeated—an unprecedented reign in modern pro wrestling history. After that loss, Asuka floundered, even going months at a time without appearing on WWE television, but her dominance helped anchor NXT for the better part of two years and was a singular, landmark run for women's pro wrestling.

WWE's renewed attention to the women's division took

---

* While it probably didn't draw the viewership numbers they were hoping for, the first season of the Mixed Match Challenge was an unexpected and absolute delight. The round robin tournament comprised of intergender teams played out over the course of twelve weeks in a weekly twenty-minute episode that originated on Facebook. Superstars cut unscripted promos and let loose in the ring, just having a blast. Twenty minutes of pro wrestlers having fun is a fucking joy to watch, as it turns out.

another leap forward in 2018 when they finally landed a cross-over athlete they had been courting for years: former UFC champion Ronda Rousey, who was one of the most dominant fighters in MMA history. Although Rousey's MMA career had come to a strange and anticlimactic end, she remained a massive star and a household name. She made her debut at the end of the 2018 Royal Rumble and made her in-ring debut at WrestleMania 34, teaming with Kurt Angle in a mixed tag match against Triple H and Stephanie McMahon. Rousey's debut match—which was extensively rehearsed ahead of time—was a revelation and the highlight of the event. It was clear that Rousey was a natural, but the match was also booked perfectly. Rousey's hot tag was the crowd reaction of the night, followed closely by her mixing it up with Triple H and throwing strikes that made him retreat to the corner and cower. By the time Rousey applied an arm bar to McMahon for the submission victory, a new WWE star was born.

During Rousey's reign, WWE accidentally backed into finding their next massive star. For months, fans had been begging for Becky Lynch to be featured more often, as well as pointing out that Charlotte Flair's actions as a supposed babyface were extremely shitty—especially since Charlotte was playing against type, as she always did her best work as a heel. At SummerSlam, Lynch saw her hard-earned Smack-Down Women's Championship match turn into a Triple Threat just because Flair showed up and said she wanted in. Fans screamed about the precedent of preferential treatment that had begun to hound Flair at this point as she verged on becoming the women's division's own John Cena. Even more upsetting: Flair pinned *Lynch* in the SummerSlam match to capture the title. It was an infuriating and heelish tactic, and fans roared in delight when Lynch finally had enough and beat the stuffing out of Flair after the match.

Unfortunately, in WWE's mind, Lynch was the heel in this scenario, jealous of the success of her best friend. Creatively, the company was apparently blind to the fact that any normal human would interpret the situation as an overly entitled jerk taking advantage of her best friend, and her best friend finally standing up for herself and claiming her agency. WWE, however, stuck to their guns and had Lynch cut a heel promo on Flair on the following *SmackDown*. Fans rightfully continued to cheer Lynch and boo Flair, and slowly, WWE reversed course and brought the two women to their natural alignments. Lynch's star continued to climb as she was finally allowed to settle into a trash-talking, asskicking badass in the vein of Stone Cold Steve Austin. She carried that trash talking to social media as well, speaking her mind plainly and dragging everyone who crossed her. Fans adored all of it.

On October 28, 2018, WWE presented the first-ever all-women PPV, aptly named Evolution. In addition to the finals of the 2018 Mae Young Classic (where Toni Storm defeated Io Shirai) and a Rousey vs. Nikki Bella main event for the Raw Women's Championship, Lynch successfully defended her SmackDown women's title against Flair in a brutal, twenty-eight-minute Last Woman Standing match. After Evolution, Lynch taunted Flair by borrowing from her father's famous catchphrase "To be the man, you have to beat the man." After definitively defeating a Flair, Lynch declared herself "The Man." The moniker caught on and an iconic nickname was born.

Lynch's legend grew during the buildup to Survivor Series, when the SmackDown roster invaded *Raw*, beginning with Lynch attacking Rousey in the dressing room. During the roster-wide melee, Lynch was caught with an errant punch from Nia Jax that broke her nose, bloodied her face, and gave her a concussion. *Raw* went off the air with a grinning and strutting Lynch, blood smeared across her face, loudly proclaiming, "This is my show now!" It was a fortuitous accident in many ways. Beyond providing a generational visual on par with Austin's bloody face at WrestleMania 13, Rousey and Lynch had been scheduled to face each other for the first time at Survivor Series. Due to Lynch's concussion, she wasn't cleared to compete, pushing the match back. Lynch remained the company's hottest star and won the second women's Royal Rumble match in January 2019 to punch her ticket to WrestleMania 35, and WWE listened to their fans who said the Rousey/Lynch program should headline the biggest show of the year.

The match again turned into a Triple Threat after Flair defeated Asuka to become SmackDown Women's Champion. The main event was set: Raw Women's Champion Ronda Rousey vs. SmackDown Women's Champion Charlotte Flair vs. Becky Lynch for *both* women's titles. For the first time ever, women were main-eventing WrestleMania. The match delivered (although it was marred not only by a burnt-out crowd that had already watched a seven-hour wrestling show and Rousey accidentally getting her shoulders up on the planned finish of the match but the referee counting to three anyway), and Lynch became dual champion, declaring herself not only the Man, but Becky Two Belts. Rousey took an extended leave of absence after WrestleMania but reappeared as a cast member on the ninth season of *Total Divas*.

And so the WWE women's division continues to go, in fits and starts. Many times, the focus on the division reeks of crass opportunistic public relations, and there are occasionally episodes of *Raw* or *SmackDown* devoid of women, but the female WWE Superstars are in a fundamentally better place than they ever have been in the company. NXT's women's division continues to rank as one of the best in the world. Fans continue to dream that one day WWE will fix the disparity between how women are treated on *NXT* and how they're treated on *Raw* and *SmackDown*.

The trend in recent years has been positive but given everything fans—and women—have been through over the course of WWE's existence, you'll understand why no one is necessarily holding their breath that this upward trajectory for the women Superstars will continue.

PART V

WHAT COMES NXT

22

TAKEOVER

WWE Gets Global

Despite a number of technological misfires along the road, WWE's greatest stroke of innovation in the past decade has been the WWE Network. The over-the-top streaming service—up until its 2019 infrastructure change, at least—was the epitome of what a streaming service should be, beating services like CBS All Access, ESPN+, Disney+, and many more to market by several years. It also remains one of the best values of any streaming service, particularly to wrestling fans. The Network contains the complete PPV libraries of WWE, WCW, NWA, AWA, and ECW; every episode of *Raw*, *SmackDown*, and *Nitro*; many episodes of

WCW Thunder, ECW Hardcore TV, World Class Championship Wrestling, WWF Superstars of Wrestling; numerous other classic wrestling promotions; past seasons of *Total Bellas* and *Total Divas*; and of course every episode of *NXT*.

Pay-per-view carriers were less than enthused, and the majority of cable companies summarily stopped offering WWE PPVs for purchase, after the Network launched. While fans have reaped the benefits, the shift away from the traditional pay-per-view model has unfortunately impacted Superstars' pocketbooks: wrestlers who appear on PPV events no longer receive anywhere near the same share of PPV money they did in years past.

Since WWE Network hit the market, pro wrestling fans have been inundated with an embarrassment of riches from all over the globe in the form of *additional* streaming services.

Due to WWE's excellent experience with monetizing alternative platforms and finding new revenue streams, their company valuation has risen steadily in recent years, despite dwindling television ratings and viewership. In the current landscape of cord-cutting, multiplatforming, DVR-viewing, and so on, traditional television ratings are viewed across the industry as mostly an antiquity. Wrestling fans, more than just about anyone else, cling strongly to ratings reports every week, reading them like tea leaves to foretell WWE's fading fortunes. Ratings don't mean anything—*especially* to fans—but they *used* to mean something in the Attitude Era and during the Monday Night Wars, so it's fine if fans feel some measure of comfort hanging on to an outdated measure of success if it's something tangible that they can look at.

Due in part to their increasing coffers, WWE set its sights on expanding into other markets beginning in 2016. WWE television had always aired in most countries that were aware of pro wrestling, but thanks to the success of the Performance Center, the WWE Network, and the NXT brand, WWE executives believed the developmental model could work everywhere. Instead of being the only major pro wrestling company in the United States, what if WWE was the major pro wrestling company *everywhere*?

After the indie scene in Europe (particularly in the United Kingdom and Germany) boomed in the 2010s, WWE decided they should monopolize that market as well. NXT UK launched in January 2017 and snapped up nearly all the most notable talents from England, Ireland, Germany, and elsewhere, largely killing off what had been a thriving scene in the U.K. In 2020, the company is doing everything they can to launch NXT Japan, although breaking into the extremely traditional pro wrestling culture in that country has been more difficult than expected.

Other markets that WWE deeply invested in in recent years were India and, far more notably, their most lucrative partnership ever: on March 5, 2018, WWE announced a joint partnership with the Kingdom of Saudi Arabia and Crown Prince Mohammad bin Salman to run major events in Saudi Arabia for the next ten years. The notoriously oppressive and staggeringly wealthy country, which had committed a litany of human rights violations for decades, had been working hard over the past few years to change their global image and attract tourism, led by bin Salman's ambitious Vision 2030 plan. The fifteen-year plan seeks to overhaul and diversify the economy of the Kingdom of Saudi Arabia. In conjunction with high-profile but relatively minor changes to women's rights in the country, bin Salman's regime attempts to garner abundant positive press—something Saudi Arabia has had precious little of in recent years. One of the easiest, yet highest-profile ways to garner that press was through several deals with large sports entities and governing bodies.

The tactic has been used before many times by other countries with less-than-glowing reputations in the world at large, notably with locations for the Olympics, the World Cup, and other large tournaments. It has been called "sportswashing" by critics; sports fans uninterested in politics might feel a country can't be all *that* bad if major sports or leagues are holding events there, or a country can be thought of as "legitimate" if a major sports event is welcoming tourists.

Regardless, WWE was perfectly willing to do business with bin Salman and the KSA, especially with hundreds of millions of dollars at stake. The initial agreement between the two parties was for an annual event over the course of ten years, but that was almost immediately expanded to two events a year for a decade—with each event, based on WWE's quarterly earnings statements, worth at least $45 million per show and potentially upward of $60 million per show. The first event, the Greatest Royal Rumble, was heavily criticized by fans not just because of where it was taking place, but also because on WWE television during the buildup and several times during the show, WWE showed video packages gushing about the beautiful city of Jeddah and the glorious Kingdom of Saudi Arabia, which was making many strides for equality and a prosperous future. Throughout the evening, the announcers profusely thanked the KSA and praised bin Salman and his Vision 2030 plan. It was propaganda so thinly veiled as to be called "naked," and North American wrestling fans didn't care for it one bit.

Not making the initial trip to Saudi Arabia was the entirety of the women's division, as women competing in sporting events was prohibited by the country. (In fact, it was only in 2017 that women were permitted to attend sporting events—provided they were accompanied by a man.) Also not allowed to compete were Sami Zayn, due to his Syrian heritage, and Noam Dar, who was born in Israel. The women would eventually be allowed to wrestle on the Saudi shows (in special outfits to adhere to modesty laws), but the attempts at positive press for "progress" there fell woefully flat.

The WWE Saudi events also faced criticism and scrutiny for their high-profile usage of aging and previously retired wrestlers. It has been reported that bin Salman was a wrestling fan but had not paid close attention to pro wrestling since the 1990s. He reportedly requested names like the Ultimate Warrior and Yokozuna for the Greatest Royal Rumble but settled for Triple H and Undertaker (due to the fact that the Ultimate Warrior and Yokozuna were dead). Crown Jewel 2018's main event had Shawn Michaels in his first match in eight years, since retiring in 2010. Michaels had sworn loudly and often that he would never wrestle again because he didn't want to be one of the hundreds of wrestlers who made a big deal out of retiring only to keep getting in the ring. In the years prior to Crown Jewel, he had also declined offers to return to WWE for any number of dream matches that fans were dying to see, including against AJ Styles and Daniel Bryan. When it was announced he'd be teaming with Triple H to take on the Undertaker and Kane at Crown Jewel, it was clear that the comeback was all about money. (Michaels has since admitted that the payday was just too absurdly large to turn down.) The four aging Superstars turned in an absolute train wreck of a match, during which Triple H suffered a torn pectoral muscle. (Another main event in 2019 was a similar catastrophe, with the fifty-four-year-old Undertaker facing fifty-two-year-old Bill Goldberg in one of the worst WWE matches of all time. Goldberg visibly concussed himself during the match, and the two men took turns nearly killing each other by only being able to half-perform their moves.)

One month before November 2018's Crown Jewel, the entire world began watching Saudi Arabia when *Washington Post* correspondent and critic of the bin Salman regime Jamal Khashoggi went missing and it was soon revealed that he had been assassinated by Saudi agents. WWE's high-profile dealings with the Saudi government and promotion for Crown Jewel immediately came under scrutiny, especially given Linda McMahon's position as Donald Trump's head of the Small Business Administration. Congresspersons on both sides of the aisle called for WWE to cancel or postpone the event and not take Saudi money at this tenuous time. Trump himself was also pressed for the United States to halt trade and relations with the KSA, but the president demurred, citing an enormous amount of money that the Saudi government gave the United States in weapons trade. On the very day that Crown Jewel tickets were to go on sale, the Kingdom of Saudi Arabia confirmed that Khashoggi had been murdered inside the Saudi consulate in Istanbul. As the weeks went on and Crown Jewel got closer, it became clearer that the order to kill Khashoggi likely came from bin Salman himself, but there was just way too much money to potentially leave on the table. A week before the event, WWE confirmed Crown Jewel would go on as planned (although WWE stopped mentioning where the event was actually taking place when hyping the card on *Raw* and *SmackDown*). Two weeks after Crown Jewel, the CIA concluded—after studying audio recordings of the assassination—that the murder had been carried out on bin Salman's orders. Trump refuted that report, saying there was more investigation to be done. Bin Salman himself has denied being involved but accepted blame for the act since it happened "under his watch."

Speaking to Sky Sports about the decision to go ahead with the event despite all the scrutiny, Stephanie McMahon said on the day before Crown Jewel, "Moving forward with Crown Jewel in Saudi Arabia was an incredibly tough decision, given that heinous act, but at the end of the day, it is a business decision and, like a lot of other American companies, we decided that we're going to move forward with the event and deliver Crown Jewel for all of our fans in Saudi Arabia and around the world."

With each subsequent trip to the Kingdom, fewer members of the roster have signed up for the show. This reached critical mass with the 2019 Super ShowDown, which actually made headlines in mainstream circles for its abysmal aftermath, when the majority of the hundred-plus WWE employees who made the trip were held in the country for twenty-four hours, despite the fact that they needed to return to the States for that evening's episode of *SmackDown*. There continues to be full-throated opposition to the KSA partnership, but as long as it's making money for WWE (and at this point the Saudi money is pivotal to the continuation of the company), we can expect it to continue for the full ten years of that deal.

Back in the States, *NXT* continued to be the best-reviewed aspect of the WWE business model, showcasing nearly all its in-ring ability there week in and week out; it became the wrestling purist's oasis in the WWE desert. The brand split returned, along with a new top title, the Universal Championship. And WWE signed a billion-dollar deal to move *SmackDown* to Friday nights and to a new network—FOX— marking the first time regular WWE programming appeared on a broadcast network since the original *Saturday Night's Main Event* on NBC.

The great reversal was finally complete. Over the years, the fundamental business model upon which professional wrestling was built had completely inverted. The McMahons took advantage of an early television pro wrestling craze to launch and power the CWC and then the WWWF, but the adage had always been to "talk them into the building": the television served as a means to drive interest in the live events and reap the benefits of the live gate.

For a hundred years, pro wrestling promotions were focused on exactly that: promotion. Getting a live audience to pay money to get inside the building where the action was. But by the time WWE signed its landmark deal with FOX, the live event had become not exactly a relic, because they were (and are still) being run four or five days a week, crisscrossing the country and continuing to generate money (if not the massive profits they had for so many decades), but that was no longer where the bulk of the revenue came from.

WWE had stuck around long enough that it actually became an entertainment company and a content generator, invaluable to television networks because it is a self-contained, incessant machine that never takes a week off.

Television deals now power WWE, and it doesn't matter whether fans buy a ticket when the circus is in town. If you're familiar with the term "fuck you money," I think it definitely applies in this case. It's just an argument about to whom the company is saying "fuck you."

The current state of *Raw* and *SmackDown* is much the same as it has been in recent years: scripted promos, frenetic camerawork, treadmill story lines, and a focus on the WWE brand above individual stars.

Brock Lesnar has held the company's top title for the majority of the time since 2014, despite being a part-time performer. In 2016, following the brand split, a new Raw world title was introduced: the red strap–mounted Universal Championship. The title was loudly mocked upon its unveiling, both for its name and appearance, but as with all things in wrestling, we're all just used to it now. (But it was another adjustment when it turned blue after moving to *SmackDown*.) Lesnar was the fifth person to hold that title and held it for a whopping 503 days—making it the longest unbroken title reign in modern history, which *just so happened* to take that accolade away from WWE dissident CM Punk. The difference is that Lesnar only defended the title ten times during that reign, rarely appearing on *Raw*. Not surprisingly, it makes for less compelling or consequential television viewing if your world champion isn't around half the time. With two other Universal Championship reigns added in, Lesnar held the title for a total of 686 days as of November 2019—all other Universal Champions had held the title for fewer than 500 days combined in that span. (Oh yeah, you can add in a combined 300 days or so of Lesnar as WWE Champion from 2014 to 2019.)

That's not all just Lesnar's fault, of course. Both Daniel Bryan and Seth Rollins had to vacate the WWE Championship due to injuries since 2014. The Universal Championship has been similarly cursed since its introduction. The inaugural Universal Champion, Finn Bálor, was injured in the very match in which he won the title, tearing his shoulder to smithereens and vacating the championship the next night. An even more serious matter took place on October 22, 2018.

As we've covered, Roman Reigns has been a polarizing figure since Seth Rollins turned on the Shield. Despite headlining four straight WrestleManias from 2015 to 2018, he never appeared at the biggest show of the year with the live crowd's support and was 2–2 in those matches, with only one of those wins being in a world title match. By the time he won the Universal Championship in 2018, he'd held the WWE Championship three times, but only for a *combined* 118 days. He held the Universal Championship for only 63 days before surrendering it. For all the endless hand-wringing about Reigns being pushed down fans' throats and becoming the new Cena, he'd held world titles in the company for a grand total of six months over the course of four years of being in the main-event scene. Contrast that with John Cena, who—granted, in fifteen-plus years with the company—has held the WWE Championship a record thirteen times for a combined 1,254 days (fourth-most all-time), plus another three reigns as WWE World Heavyweight Champion.

But then something happened that immediately changed

the public's opinion of Reigns. Reigns's reason for relinquishing his Universal Championship after sixty-three days was one absolutely no one expected. He opened *Raw* on October 22, 2018, to address the WWE Universe not as Roman Reigns, but as Joe Anoa'i. He broke the news that he had battled leukemia before—and that the cancer had returned. He needed to take time off to undergo treatment and, as a result, was forced to surrender his title. He vowed to return as soon as he was able and left the belt (sorry—championship) in the ring. His Shield brethren (reunited after a couple of false starts in the previous year) emotionally embraced him. The majority crowd reaction and sentiment regarding Roman Reigns instantaneously flipped. With the stark light of real-life perspective being shined on Reigns for the first time, fans immediately realized what a special talent he is and that we're lucky he's around to entertain us.

Reigns, always a very private, reserved man regarding his life outside pro wrestling, had only told a select few people about his past battle with leukemia and only in the strictest confidence. It didn't define him, and it was nobody's business. For WWE's part—and quite out of character for the company, historically—they never once tried to cash in on Reigns's past cancer battle. It must have been the most tempting thing in the world, during Reigns's yearslong struggle to win the audience's approval, to portray him as a heroic cancer survivor. Who would possibly boo a cancer survivor? What's more universal or relatable or easier to root for than someone who has overcome *cancer*? A small but disgustingly vocal portion of the audience claimed his leukemia diagnosis was a hoax, merely part of a WWE story line to manufacture sympathy. (WWE also faced scrutiny for choosing to turn Dean Ambrose heel on Seth Rollins that same night, believing it to be crass timing for maximum effect.)

The cancer truthers only got louder when Reigns returned to in-ring action at WrestleMania 35 just a few months later. Weird creeps pointed out Reigns's lack of noticeable loss of hair or muscle mass while undergoing treatment. Enough dipshits chimed in on the matter that at least one actual, real-life leukemia association issued a lengthy statement about how no two cancers or cancer treatments—or reactions thereto—behave exactly the same. While Reigns returned to a prominent position on the card, his reactions have been much more welcoming. (It took several months for any boos to begin creeping back in during Reigns's entrances or matches.) It took Reigns the better part of a year since his return to get involved in any world title feuds, but (1) he doesn't need them and (2) there are many years left to go in his career. The world title reigns* are sure to come.

(Reigns also stepped away from the company once more following the COVID-19 pandemic, as he is immunocompromised due to his leukemia and wisely opted for safety over pro wrestling.)

In happier news on the recent main-event front, after two years of inactivity and a widespread belief that he would never again be cleared to compete in WWE, Daniel Bryan was finally able to become a professional wrestler full-time once again. Working a far less hectic schedule than he had maintained prior to his forced retirement, Bryan was cleared by WWE doctors to compete on March 20, 2018. A few weeks

---

*   I swear to you, the pun was not intended.

later, on April 8, 2018, Bryan and Shane McMahon defeated Kevin Owens and Sami Zayn at WrestleMania 34, with Bryan tapping out Zayn with the Yes Lock for the finish. Bryan worked a safer style while still retaining his inimitable panache and ability in the ring, having barely lost a step due to inactivity. As part of the deal struck when he was cleared to compete once again, Bryan is required to undergo concussion protocol testing after every one of his matches. So far, he has missed no time due to injury since his returning. And in true Bryan Danielson/Daniel Bryan fashion, he has managed to reinvent himself once again.

Drawing upon his own real-life outspokenness and convictions, Bryan declared himself "The New Daniel Bryan" after cheating to win the WWE Championship from AJ Styles on November 13, 2018. Every week, Bryan would deride fans for being fickle and returning to WWE every week despite claiming to hate the company, but he also fashioned himself an anticonsumerist and an eco-warrior. After enlisting award-winning vintner Erick Rowan as his muscle, the New Daniel Bryan threw the WWE Championship in the trash can because of his disgust at its being mounted on a leather strap (and made from a cow that he liked to think of as having been named "Daisy"). In its place, he unveiled a new version of the championship, made entirely of sustainable materials like hemp, canvas, burlap, and turquoise. As he has been at every step of his career, his work was sublime, taking fans to task for engaging in crass commercialism. For a long stretch of time, he wore a tasteful and granola-crunchy cardigan rather than merchandise advertising himself. Really, the only thing half-bad about his return was the expectation that fans would boo him simply for telling the god's honest truth about needing to save the planet and stop blindly following capitalism. (In 2020, he's once again a fan favorite and contenting himself by booking himself in feuds with some of the best and most underused wrestlers in the company, like Drew Gulak, Cesaro, Sami Zayn, and Shinsuke Nakamura.)

As has always been the case since he bought the company from his father, Vince McMahon is, in all instances, where the WWE buck stops. Despite having a creative team of dozens of writers, dozens more former wrestlers working as match and segment producers, executives of all stripes, and the most talented, diverse, and capable roster that any company has ever assembled, McMahon holds final say on 100 percent of decisions. It has perhaps happened more often in recent years, but it is not unusual for an episode of *Raw* or *SmackDown* to have a finalized and approved script, only for McMahon to change his mind, tear it up, and start over in the hours before the show goes on air.

McMahon's quirks are numerous and ever shifting. There is a long list of banned words, phrases, terms, and idioms that are forbidden from being spoken on WWE television. Those banned words famously include "wrestling" and "wrestler," despite WWE standing for "World Wrestling Entertainment." WWE doesn't have wrestling matches; it provides sports entertainment. WWE doesn't employ wrestlers; the performers are WWE Superstars. In fact, WWE doesn't employ them at all. For WWE taxation purposes, WWE Superstars are not employees; they are technically classified as independent contractors, and as such, have no legal protection or recourse afforded employees, in addition to having to foot the bill for their own health care. (If an injury occurs in the ring, WWE will pay for all surgeries, doctors' visits, and rehabilitation expenses. Routine checkups and other health concerns and issues are the wrestlers' responsibility. Certain very upper-echelon Superstars have health care included in their contracts, but those are rare exceptions.) Title belts aren't "belts," they're "championships." In that same vein, championships don't "change hands." Oddly, fans of the WWE product aren't "fans"—they're members of the "WWE Universe."

"WWE creative" gets blamed for many of the fans' least favorite aspects of the product, but "creative" really just means "Vince McMahon"—the man with the final word on everything. The creative team is comprised of passionate and talented wrestling fans, but everything that goes into five hours of *Raw* and *SmackDown* each week is fed into the same Vince McMahon sausage grinder. Of course, as Dave Meltzer has pointed out, that means McMahon deserves credit for the good things that happen on the shows—and every year, there are dozens (if not more) of unexpected, thrilling, wonderful moments, matches, promos, and stories. Good or bad, it's all Vince's baby—and will remain that way as long as he has control of the company.

23

NOBODY GETS OVER ON MY WATCH

If you asked the average wrestling fan what Vince McMahon's ideal pro wrestler (or Superstar, since he might not answer the question otherwise) looked like, perhaps the last name on the list would be Kofi Kingston. Lithe, slim, goofy in all the best ways. Talented and charismatic, but not intimidating or a traditional tough guy. And of course, there is also the fact that Kofi happens to be black, which historically is not a recipe for success in WWE.

Kingston had been tied to the future hopes and dreams of WWE fans for a long time. In December 2011, a single photo caused elation and daydreaming for a brighter future when it appeared a new "New Generation" might be afoot. That month, WWE gathered all its current champions for a posed photo that allowed fans to take stock of the wealth of talent on display—much of it with an independent pedigree. The world champions at the time were CM Punk and Daniel Bryan. United States Champion Zack Ryder was riding an unprecedented wave of self-created internet popularity. Intercontinental Champion Cody Rhodes was a cult favorite for his tremendous work as a smarmy heel. Divas Champion Beth Phoenix was one of the few "legitimate" women wrestlers in the company at the time (in the eyes of most smart fans). And the Tag Team Champions were the team of Air Boom: Kingston and Evan "Air" Bourne, a dynamic young performer who had cut his teeth in Ring of Honor and scores of other independent promotions as an innovative highflier under the name of Matt Sydal.

For a couple of years, that photo was a grim reminder of how quickly fortunes in WWE can turn and the best-laid plans and most hoped-for dreams can fall apart and disintegrate. Phoenix retired in 2012 and was inducted into the Hall of Fame in 2017. Bryan retired (for what many believed was forever) in 2016, two years after CM Punk left the company. Ryder was relegated to the lower card where— apart from brief reigns as Intercontinental and Tag Team Champion—he stayed for the next eight-plus years. Bourne was severely injured in a motorcycle accident in 2012 and only had one more match under contract before being released in 2014 and returning to the indies. And in 2016, Cody Rhodes—the son of Dusty Rhodes and brother of Dustin Rhodes (aka Goldust)—orchestrated his own release and eventually helped create a sea change in the American pro wrestling landscape.

Kingston's fate was to be more complicated. Kingston, who

signed with Deep South Wrestling less than a year after making his debut in 2006, has spent over a decade on WWE's main roster. He held many midcard championships during his time in the company, but his brief flirtation with the main-event scene was ended early on during a 2009 feud with Randy Orton. Kingston (who originally portrayed a character from Jamaica despite being born in Ghana) garnered immense fan support at this time (his feud with Orton and his performance at that year's Survivor Series bordered on runaway-train levels of crowds screaming for Kofi to emerge victorious), but the decision was made for Orton to overwhelmingly win the one-sided feud. Kingston's trajectory sputtered afterward—until 2014, when he joined the New Day.

The New Day came about when graduate student Xavier Woods recruited Kingston and Big E into a small faction after all three suffered losing streaks. Fans speculated that a new Nation of Domination was forming (which was an ironic sort of left-wing racism, as the New Day themselves would later point out: "Three black guys are teaming up, so it must be a rehash of the one black militant faction we can remember"). In November, WWE began running vignettes about the new faction, naming them the New Day and featuring a black choir. Stomachs sank; the New Day appeared to be stereotypical singing and dancing black pastors. The three men themselves were dismayed but vowed to give the gimmick their all. Although intended to be God-loving good guys, fans quickly began booing them and chanting "New Day sucks" whenever they appeared. WWE considered pulling the plug on the team almost immediately, but Woods had zero doubt in his team's ability to do anything, so he staked his career on it.

He pitched a heel turn. "I went to Vince McMahon," Woods told the Corridor Cast YouTube channel in 2019, "and said, 'If you give me a microphone for four weeks in a row, I *guarantee* you: they'll boo Kofi Kingston.' He [said], 'You really believe in this stuff that much?' and I said, 'Yes. I believe that I can do it.' And he goes, 'Four weeks? If you *don't* do it in four weeks, then what happens?' I said, 'If I don't do it in four weeks, you've got sixty dudes in developmental who deserve this spot more than I do.' 'So, I can send you home? Get rid of you?' I said, 'You should, if I can't do it.'"

The gambit worked. The New Day got free rein to be themselves on the microphone and in the ring and drove fans crazy. And as is the case 100 percent of the time, the New Day became *so* delightfully wonderful as heels that fans started to adore them. Throughout their run, the New Day were unabashedly proud of their blackness and let their personalities bleed through. Many black fans saw themselves in the New Day: three black men doing it for the culture, being fearlessly black not just on live national television every week, but on a television show and within a medium that rarely presented any black performers in a prominent position—and even more rarely presented black people as authentic and having agency.

It's nearly impossible to overstate the impact the New Day ended up having on black wrestling fans. David Dennis, a cultural reporter and critic for *The Shadow League, The Undefeated, Bossip,* and numerous other outlets, wrote, "[The New Day] showed us that we can dance without shucking and jiving. That we could be hilarious without being caricatures. That we could love each other without fear. They showed us that we could be unapologetically us no matter what.

"And we loved them for it. We sat our kids in front of TVs and showed them the New Day. We pointed at Kofi, Xavier, and Big E and allowed ourselves and our children to believe."

The New Day were goofy and incredible and unlike anything else in WWE. They became dominant tag team champions under the "Freebird* Rule"—the longest-reigning team in the history of the company. Eventually, they'll be the team with the most reigns. But it is against this backdrop of what the New Day and Kofi Kingston meant to fans of color and especially to black fans that made what happened in 2019 so special.

For at least a year beforehand, Big E and Woods had been saying in just about every interview that their ultimate goal was to get Kingston a reign as world champion. In their minds, Kingston had done everything else there was to accomplish in wrestling and no one in the world deserved it more. Thanks to an unfortunately timed injury, the stars finally aligned in 2019 on the Road to WrestleMania (that wonderful time of year spanning from the Royal Rumble in January to WrestleMania in late March/early April, when things actually happen, and fans actually have a good time). Heading into February's Fastlane PPV, the Elimination Chamber match—to determine who would be WWE Champion when WrestleMania rolled around—was set to feature six men: WWE Champion Daniel Bryan, AJ Styles,

---

* The Freebird Rule was named after the Fabulous Freebirds (ironically enough, a team of flamboyant Southerners who had a penchant for draping themselves in the Confederate flag), who set the precedent that any two members of a stable of three wrestlers could defend the title on any given night, regardless of which permutation was responsible for winning them. It's a *great* rule. Pro wrestling is the best.

Randy Orton, Jeff Hardy, Samoa Joe, and Mustafa Ali. Ali suffered an injury, so Kingston was inserted as his replacement. The go-home episode of *SmackDown Live*, on February 12, featured a show-long gauntlet match to determine which Superstar would earn the favorable position of entering the Elimination Chamber match last. Kingston started the gauntlet against Bryan. Over the course of sixty-plus minutes, Kingston managed to eliminate Bryan, Hardy, and Joe, but his gutsy effort came to an end when Styles eliminated him. Orton ended up winning the gauntlet, but the grassroots support for Kingston grew like wildfire during the gauntlet. It burst into full bloom during the Elimination Chamber match on February 17, as Kingston managed to survive long enough to eliminate his old nemesis Orton and boil the match down to just him and Bryan. As the match went past the thirty-minute mark and Kingston built momentum, fans dared to dream. Kingston ultimately fell short as Bryan pinned him to win the match and retain his title. The weight of Kofi coming so close and not winning fell like a ton of bricks on the fans as Elimination Chamber went off the air on a heartbreaking image: an inconsolable Kingston sitting on the steps of the Chamber, with his New Day brothers holding him tightly as the WrestleMania 35 sign loomed over them in the background.

The stage was set for Kingston to challenge for Bryan's championship at the biggest show of the year. It's anyone's guess what the original or tentative plans for the WWE Championship were prior to Ali's injury, but now the course was clear. The only thing left was to make the actual build for the match, with the maximum amount of drama and audience manipulation—in true pro wrestling fashion. Vince

McMahon appeared on television for weeks, screwing over Kingston seemingly out of spite, pulling the rug out from underneath both Kofi and the fans again and again. He said he would give Kingston a WWE Championship match at Fastlane, only to give Kevin Owens the title shot and put Kingston in a handicap match. He promised Kingston his WrestleMania match if Kingston would consent to another five opponent gauntlet match on *SmackDown*. After Kingston survived the gauntlet—by last defeating Orton, his forever-foe—McMahon announced one more participant, and Daniel Bryan handed Kingston the loss again. Bryan even threw in Kingston's face the same backhanded compliment the Authority had given to him prior to WrestleMania XXX, calling Kingston a "B-plus player" who didn't have what it takes to be the face of the company. In a spectacular reversal, it was now Bryan who was holding down the beloved and deserving underdog.

Kingston tried to hold his head up and remain the ever-loyal, good employee, but finally he had enough. The New Day confronted McMahon, with all three referring to the very real history of discrimination and underrepresentation that had nearly entirely prevented black wrestlers from ever truly reaching the top in WWE. Fans became extremely invested in the feud and the story line, mostly because it was all true. Kingston not only represented the fan-favorite, underappreciated "good soldier" WWE wrestler so often overlooked despite the overwhelming support of the audience, but, more important, represented the passionate WWE fans who were black or people of color, who longed to see a champion who looked like them. A Kingston world championship reign would never erase the company's awful history of failing to spotlight marginalized individuals, but it would be *something*. And that something is what fans clung to.

In a perfect bit of poetry, it was not Kingston himself who secured his place in the WrestleMania 35 WWE Championship match, but his New Day teammates. Big E and Xavier Woods outlasted five other teams in a tag team gauntlet to secure Kingston's spot—his brothers willing him to the promised land through unbridled love, solidarity—and of course, the power of positivity.

Kingston and Bryan put on a classic at WrestleMania 35, fraught with emotion and with the crowd hanging on every hold, move, and reversal. For many fans, the match provided the emotional high point of the night (and the year; and the decade; and for a good number of people, the emotional high point of their pro wrestling fandom) when Kingston managed to secure the pinfall victory and become WWE Champion. Big E and Woods cast aside Bryan's sustainable, eco-friendly championship and unveiled the restored, "real" version—complete with Kofi Kingston side plates—and presented their best friend with his hard-earned trophy. The New Day then celebrated in the ring with Kingston's children—and some new T-shirts touting Kofi as the new world champion.

While The Rock had become the first black WWE Champion in history years earlier (and still shamefully late in American history for that sort of color barrier to be broken), there was a not insignificant portion of the population who considered Kofi Kingston to be the first "real" black world champion. Some black wrestling fans—on the fringes, but loud in their dissent—never "claimed" The Rock as black, and many of that subset also felt strongly that WWE always presented The Rock as Samoan, first and foremost, despite his father's very visible status as a black former WWF tag team champion—in fact, Rocky Johnson and his partner, Tony Atlas, were the first-ever black men to hold those titles. (That color barrier was broken in the shockingly recent year of 1983, by the way.) Between 2017 and 2019, the debate about the "blackness" of The Rock intensified, with a good number of articles springing up around the topic. That debate finally provoked The Rock himself to tweet in response. "I identify as exactly what I am," Dwayne Johnson said. "Both. Equally proud. Black/Samoan. I transcended race in wrestling, so there was no 'booked [as the first black champion].'"

Fans—especially black fans—were surprisingly divided on the matter, and Johnson's claims that The Rock "transcended race" didn't really help put things to rest. But with Kofi, there could be no debate at all about his blackness—not just in the color of his skin and his original kayfabe billing from Jamaica and his actual birthplace and bloodline in Ghana, but in every facet of how the New Day conducted themselves at all times. The Rock seemed to transcend race—or at least apart from his time in the Nation of Domination, race never seemed to matter much to The Rock, his opponents, or his story lines. The New Day were black and proud, loudly and at all times. They wore Black History Month outfits accented with kente cloth. When Kingston finally captured the world title at WrestleMania, his ring attire was inspired by Basquiat.

To fans, especially those who felt they could never fully claim The Rock as "theirs," Kingston's championship meant something that Dwayne Johnson's many world titles never could. At the very least, representation is always important, and the significance of a world champion who looks like you can be great.

Kingston held the WWE Championship for six months, but his reign came to a pretty unfortunate end, as he lost to Brock Lesnar in five seconds on the first *Friday Night Smack-Down* episode in the new FOX deal. Kingston went for his finisher at the opening bell and was instead caught by Lesnar's finisher. As the first chapter in the story, it might not have stung so badly if there was any follow-up. Instead, Kingston never addressed the title loss on WWE television and instead rejoined Big E in the tag team division. After Xavier Woods suffered an Achilles injury, putting him out of action for the year, Kingston got another tag team championship reign, returning to the happy-go-lucky New Day member he was in 2018. The abrupt and unceremonious end of Kofi Kingston as WWE Champion was a bitter pill to swallow for many fans—especially the ones to whom his world championship win meant so much. To fans, it felt like WWE was saying he was in fact a B+ player all along, because the new FOX deal required a "real" star like Lesnar to anchor the SmackDown brand. Kingston had been a pivotal figure for so many fans and for so long. Now they'd have to look elsewhere for underdog heroes.

And that's where Cody Rhodes comes in—the man who decided he was done being ignored by the company.

Rhodes (birth name Cody Runnels) grew up in and around the pro wrestling business and excelled as an amateur wrestler in high school. He signed with WWE on a developmental contract in 2006, just a month shy of his twenty-first birthday. He was called up to the main WWE roster in 2007 and for the better part of the next decade, Rhodes (a lithe, shredded man who appeared to have gained no physical attribute of his father's apart from the famous lisp) bounced from gimmick to gimmick, fully committing to roles but never being viewed as more than a midcard stalwart. He was, at various turns, Hardcore Holly's protégé; Randy Orton's lackey in the Legacy stable; conceited "Dashing" Cody Rhodes who would place paper bags on rivals' heads and who wore a mask to protect his beautiful face after his nose got smashed; half of the arrogant "Rhodes Scholars" with fellow intellectual Damien Sandow; and finally, Stardust, an intergalactic traveler and a distortion of his brother's Goldust character.

The Rhodes brothers teamed and feuded at various points when Cody was "himself" and when he turned into Stardust. It seemed apparent to everyone that the familial rivalry would come to a head with a blow-off match at some WrestleMania or other—perhaps a career vs. career match that would serve as Dustin's well-earned retirement match. At least, it seemed apparent to everyone except WWE.* Despite continual lobbying from the Rhodes brothers—including in years when they were actively feuding with each other *during* the buildup to WrestleMania—it never happened.

The gimmick peaked at SummerSlam 2015, where a feud with *Arrow* star Stephen Amell led to one of the best celebrity matches in history, as Amell and Neville defeated Star-

---

* In an irony not lost on the longtime WWE fan, WWE is often reluctant to book story lines they feel to be overly predictable—even when dealing with story lines fans want to see, or where there's potential money to be made. Hornswoggle was the only midget wrestler (still the official term in English-speaking countries; that's not me being insensitive) on the WWE roster from 2006 to 2013. When Mascarita Dorada joined the roster as El Torito, Hornswoggle begged for a feud with him, only to be told for a year that the two little-person wrestlers on the roster wrestling one another would be "too obvious." They finally did have a series of matches in 2014 and their "WeeLC" match at Extreme Rules is still cherished by fans.

dust and (King) Wade Barrett, who had been granted the title of Cosmic King by Stardust during the angle. After that match, Stardust was rarely used until he finally asked for his release on May 21, 2016.

His request was granted the following day, and a week later, Cody posted a checklist of his dream opponents and promotions to work for once his noncompete clause was up in August. Over the next year, Cody (rarely using the last name Rhodes at first, out of fear of legal reprisal from WWE) fulfilled every item on his list, and over the next three years, he would eventually fuck up everything for all other wrestlers who asked to be let out of their WWE contracts early.

Cody traveled the world, breaking protocol by being so in-demand that the major non-WWE promotions didn't mind that he wasn't exclusive. Cody wrestled for Impact, Ring of Honor, and New Japan at the same time. He talked freely of his frustrations inside WWE during his ten years there, including mentioning that he continually pitched Stardust story ideas for at least six months, with all of them being ignored in favor of—just not using him at all, really. Cody quickly fell in with the Bullet Club in New Japan, kicking off a multiyear story line where he and Kenny Omega were supposed coleaders of the group and constantly at odds in their own personal pissing contest. At the same time, Cody became an integral part of the *Being the Elite* YouTube series along with Omega, the Young Bucks, Marty Scurll, Adam Page, and a host of others. With Cody in the fold, the inside jabs at WWE became more frequent and more pointed, carrying a good deal more weight coming from a former WWE lifer. Disgruntled wrestling fans ate it up and demanded more and more.

Bullet Club was already the hottest thing in pro wrestling, but the addition of Cody brought it up another notch. *Being the Elite* became a juggernaut of inside jokes, catchphrases, running gags, and T-shirt slogans. If you wanted to be cool and hip, you watched *Being the Elite* and you got a subscription to the New Japan World streaming service. Cody captured the Ring of Honor World Championship at the same time Kenny Omega was bringing New Japan its greatest exposure and acclaim of all time in the Western world, thanks mostly to his epic series of matches against IWGP Heavyweight Champion Kazuchika Okada. Bullet Club (or the principals who mattered—Omega, Cody, the Bucks, Page, and Scurll) was under contract to ROH in the States and to NJPW in Japan. *Being the Elite* also forged an invaluable relationship with Chicago-based on-demand print shop One Hour Tees, which had formed the Pro Wrestling Tees offshoot in 2013. Pro Wrestling Tees, for the first time ever, allowed any pro wrestler in the world to set up an online store and make money off T-shirt sales without having to put down money up front for screen-printing inventory. PWT storefront pages (like the Bucks') could offer literally hundreds of designs. Even if no one bought a single shirt of one of the designs on offer, wrestlers didn't lose money on the venture. Wrestling fans could finally support wrestlers directly, no matter where in the world either party was located. For decades, wrestling fans had to rely on the frail hope that a company would put their favorite wrestler on television, or maybe offer a shitty mail-order T-shirt that they'd be too embarrassed to wear out in public. Now, via podcasts, Patreon, internet webstores, YouTube channels,

Twitch streams, and so many other outlets, they could stay up to the second with the lives and careers of their favorite wrestlers and find ways to ensure that their monetary support went straight into their pockets, rather than paying a corporation and hoping they'd get their correct cut of the residual check.*

Even after Cody signed a one-year contract with ROH in 2017, he and the Bucks continued to take just about every independent date they could in the world. For the first time in his career, Cody cleared a million dollars from pro wrestling in the year after he left WWE. The Bucks likewise became millionaires off bookings and merchandise sales. WWE began sending out feelers to Cody, the Bucks, and Omega, well aware that they could make money off them. All four men were set to be free agents at the end of 2018.

Before that happened, though, Cody happened to make a significant bet with Dave Meltzer of the *Wrestling Observer Newsletter*. On May 16, 2017, a Twitter user asked Meltzer, "Do you think ROH can ever sell out an arena with 10,000-plus fans? Something like Madison Square Garden?"

---

* Revenue sharing in pro wrestling has always been weird as hell and extremely shady. Wrestlers used to make major paydays off PPV buys and being featured in the annual video game until WWE shifted away from PPV and toward the WWE Network. My personal favorite story of licensing rights fuckery is (naturally) from Hulk Hogan's time in WCW. At least one wrestler has said that when the first line of post-Hogan WCW action figures came out, Hogan or his agent (or WCW executives; no one is sure who exactly was responsible) had somehow orchestrated it so that every figure in the line rang up as a Hulk Hogan figure. That meant he got all the residuals there, even if someone bought a figure of the Giant or Ric Flair or Sting. Hulkster gonna Hulkster.

Meltzer offered a quick reply: "Not any time soon," he asserted. Eleven minutes later, Cody responded to Meltzer directly—and to the entire world.

"I'll take that bet, Dave," Cody tweeted. "I already gave [ROH] their biggest buyrate. Put the Bucks and I on the card and three months to promote." It took a bit longer than three months, but with Cody and the Bucks leading the charge, they were able to help create something that previously seemed impossible: a non-WWE entity selling out a 10,000-seat arena, devoid of any company branding.

On January 1, 2018, the men announced on *Being the Elite* that an independent supershow called All In would take place in September. In March, the venue was announced as being the 11,000 seat Sears Centre in the Chicago area. With only one match announced at the time, tickets went on sale on May 13—just three days shy of the anniversary of Cody taking Meltzer's bet. The show sold out in under 30 minutes. When the All In PPV finally rolled around on September 1, anchored by plenty of *Being the Elite* regulars and other Bullet Club, NJPW, and independent stars, the final attendance was 11,263. Although the event leaned heavily on Ring of Honor wrestlers, employees, and infrastructure (and featured a match for the ROH World Championship), it was not ROH-branded. All In was, at that time, a standalone, landmark event. It was a serious eye opener for absolutely everyone in the pro wrestling industry, and the *Being the Elite* crew immediately made plans for something even bigger.

ROH made plans for something bigger as well, even before All In took place. In a true coup, ROH managed to become the first non-WWE company to book a wrestling show at Madison Square Garden in fifty-nine years. What's more, they booked the show on the same weekend as Wrestle-Mania 35, which was also taking place in New York. On August 10, 2018, with Omega, the Bucks, Cody, Page, and Scurll all still under contract, Ring of Honor put tickets on sale for a G1 Supercard on April 6, 2019—a cobranded event with New Japan. The tickets sold out in minutes, without a single match announced.

ROH and NJPW had done the unthinkable. But for Ring of Honor, this was about to become the denouement. At the end of 2018, the entire *Being the Elite* principal crew, apart from Scurll, departed both ROH and NJPW en masse. The sold-out show still went on as planned, with New Japan getting the headline spot and half the time on the show. It was a show with a split personality, with all the ROH matches being panned and harrumphed about endlessly both in the arena and online, and with the NJPW offerings being praised. After the MSG show, New Japan began strategically distancing itself from ROH as they launched their own expansion plans in the United States.

Throughout 2019, in a company now largely devoid of the Bucks, Cody, the *BTE* crew, or New Japan, ROH struggled to routinely draw 500 fans to shows, just months after selling out Madison Square Garden. Ring of Honor, by now owned by massive syndicate Sinclair Broadcast Group, is in no danger of going under unless Sinclair someday decides to pull the plug for whatever reason, but it seems to enjoy having regular wrestling content on its channels. But the company that shaped current pro wrestling (including WWE) more than arguably any other not owned by Vince McMahon has never been less hip or cool, and its crowds continue to dwindle. The roster will also likely continue to thin now that there are two true alternatives for larger exposure.

Oh, yeah: about that . . .

The *BTE* crew of Cody, the Bucks, Omega, Scurll, and Page were courted from all sides, including big-money offers from WWE, ROH, and NJPW. The five men publicly vowed to stay together no matter their final destination (although with the caveat that Scurll's ROH contract ran out approximately one year after the others') and they further teased fans about their upcoming decision with a running bit about a count-down timer for months on *BTE*.

The group's ultimate decision was to take none of the offers on the table. Instead, they launched a new national wrestling promotion, joining with Tony Khan, a lifelong wrestling fan and son of billionaire Shad Khan, the owner of the Jacksonville Jaguars and English Premier League club Fulham F.C. Building on the existing infrastructure and the Jacksonville offices of the Jaguars, this new group announced on January 1, 2019, the birth of a new promotion called All Elite Wrestling. Tony Khan was installed as president, CEO, and head of creative, while Cody, the Young Bucks, and Kenny Omega all took positions as executive vice presidents as well as wrestlers and integral parts of the creative team. Cody's wife, Brandi Rhodes, became chief brand officer, in part because the wordplay of "chief Brandi officer" was too good to pass up. As their top big-name star to the casual fan, AEW signed Chris Jericho. In early 2019, Goldust finished up with WWE and Dustin Rhodes signed with his brother's company as well. (Scurll, long believed to be AEW-bound, instead re-signed with Ring of Honor in January 2020—and was given head booker duties to boot.)

AEW's first official show was a PPV called Double or Nothing on May 25, 2019 (before another sellout audience of 11,000), which was as well received as All In (if not more so) and featured the kinda-surprise debut of Jon Moxley, who had finished an eight-year WWE run as Shield member Dean Ambrose* a month earlier. (The show also featured a bloody, Southern-style showdown between Cody and Dustin Rhodes—a passionate and dramatic reckoning that finally gave the brothers a semblance of their WrestleMania blow-off match that never happened.) After courting various television networks over the summer—because the viability of a national wrestling promotion in the twenty-first century lives and dies with whether there's a weekly television deal in place—AEW secured a prime-time, two-hour slot on TNT, making it the first time wrestling would air on the network—and the biggest non-WWE television deal, both in terms of

---

* Ambrose's departure was the most high-profile WWE resignation since CM Punk left the company in 2014. Ambrose was a Grand Slam Champion and one of the most popular characters in the company, despite constantly being given some of the goofiest and outright stupidest material of anyone in the roster since the dissolution of the Shield. Ambrose always did what was asked of him despite vehemently objecting most of the time, since he knew the material would make him look like an idiot and the fans would shit on stuff like him beating up a mannequin with a pair of tongs, feuding over a potted plant, and commandeering a hot dog cart. In an appearance on Chris Jericho's podcast after leaving WWE, Ambrose explained how his interactions with McMahon would inevitably go whenever he objected to the material he was given. "I go in and talk to Vince," Ambrose said. "I'm like, 'Yo, I can't say all this stuff. It's ridiculous.' And he's like, 'Oh! It's such good shit! Oh, this stuff! This is the reason people like you! . . . This is you!'" In short order, "such good shit" became a meme and shorthand for awful, cringe-worthy content on WWE television that almost certainly came directly from McMahon—like Baron Corbin mocking Roman Reigns by bringing out a guy wearing a dog costume. You understand; it's such good shit.

scale and profitability—since WCW went under in 2001. AEW's weekly show, *Dynamite*, debuted on October 2, 2019.

And WWE was ready for it. Sort of.

Fans had long pined for a second, viable alternative to come along ever since WWE bought out WCW. Not just for the, you know, alternative of it all, but operating under the idea that historically, Vince McMahon and his company had always produced their best content when there was a true national rival to go head-to-head with. Iron sharpens iron, and all that. The hope was that not only would AEW give fans some high-level, well-produced wrestling that wasn't created by WWE, but that its mere existence might goose some life back into the McMahons' product.

While AEW didn't seem interested in making this a head-to-head war, WWE was happy to proactively oblige. Once it was clear that *Dynamite* would air on Wednesdays, a night when neither *Raw* nor *SmackDown* aired, WWE began shopping *NXT* as a program to networks that might be interested in a Wednesday night wrestling program of their own. It didn't take long to find a match, as USA Network reversed course about not wanting two nights of its prime-time lineup devoted to WWE programming and snapped up a two-hour live version of *NXT* to more or less replace the loss of *SmackDown* to FOX.

NXT moved to USA Network (with a video-on-demand version of the show available the next day on WWE Network) on Wednesday nights two weeks before AEW's first episode aired on TNT. The Wednesday Night Wars kicked off on October 2 and fans were prepared. The expansion to two hours and the addition of commercials for *NXT* just meant more of the same for fans who already loved the product. Prior to the move to USA, there was rampant fear that Vince McMahon would take a hands-on approach because of the AEW competition and the relocation of the show to cable. And of course, "Vince McMahon hands-on approach" is just a synonym for "ruin" in the minds of the most vocal and most online wrestling fans. All that hand-wringing was for nothing, as it turned out.

NXT continued being the same product it always was, AEW offered plenty of what the *BTE* crew promised (heavy on action-packed matches, postmodern metatextual irony and goofiness, and light on sketches and promos; when Cody and inaugural champion Chris Jericho were on-screen, the show also tended to be heavy on Dusty Rhodes channeling old-school pathos-filled Southern wrestling drama), and fans continued to be treated to more options on a weekly basis than ever before. The same month *Dynamite* debuted, a relaunched NWA (the trademark to the name having been purchased by Smashing Pumpkins frontman and onetime would-be Impact Wrestling buyer Billy Corgan and run by former WWE writer David Lagana) debuted a throwback-style studio show that aired on YouTube, called *NWA Powerrr*.* And of course, since what is dead may never die, the new owners of Impact Wrestling, Anthem Sports & Entertainment, purchased AXS TV (the American home network of New Japan), giving Impact its biggest network since leaving Spike TV in 2014.

---

* One is forced to assume that "Power" spelled with three *r*'s was a consideration related to something capable of being trademarked, and not simply Corgan inadvertently leaning on the keyboard when they were building the chyron for the show.

The birth of AEW led, inevitably, to fans passionately taking sides. The return of two wrestling shows in head-to-head battles on prime-time television led to the return of websites, journalists, and especially fans studying and scrutinizing the weekly overnight ratings—possibly the worst artifact left over from the Monday Night Wars; a wretched vestigial tail that a plurality of fans is convinced means something. While AEW consistently won the head-to-head ratings battles in those initial months,* no one seemed to understand that both networks and both companies were extremely happy with how everything played out each week, largely because ratings mean an entirely different thing now than they did twenty years earlier, in the days before widespread DVR use and ease of broadband streaming. In this new television landscape, television is only the starting point. Thanks to digital and social media, networks and wrestling companies have already sold the product to the television company, the company has already sold the product to advertisers, and there are five different social media platforms that allow monetization of clips, streams, and video on demand. In 2020, money comes

---

* The initial belief and hope for AEW's TNT show was that there was a vast ocean of lapsed pro wrestling fans—the ones who stopped watching when WCW went under—who would return to watching wrestling now that there was a new show from a new company. Instead, a completely stable 700,000 to 1 million fans watched both shows live every week. When *NXT* lost viewers in a given week, AEW didn't grow by the same amount of viewers. The television-watching pool in 2020 is precisely what it is. (And we don't know what it is, since we aren't given DVR and streaming and illegal stream numbers, which from all indications are sizable.) If those WCW and disgruntled WWE fans who aged out of wrestling are ever coming back, it isn't for anything that's currently on either channel.

in from all angles; live television viewers are just icing on a very lucrative cake. Much as the very nature of the wrestling business flipped from live events to television as the end-all, be-all, the exponentially fragmented and balkanized nature of television and online viewership has led to a model where content is king. Channels need programming above all else, and pro wrestling guarantees a fifty-two-week-a-year consistent program with consistent viewership. Pro wrestling probably *should* have an off-season, but its lack thereof is a feature, not a bug, to the people counting the money.

"There's no off-season," Roman Reigns said on Corey Graves's official WWE podcast, "and you know, the real way to show your value nowadays is consistency. I think that's in everything, not just in this business. People can complain and say that it's tough; the schedule's tough—but any deep level of success is an everyday job. You have to be on it and working at all times; constantly thinking about it." Yes, that's true, but there's sort of a difference between people running startup businesses and people getting dropped on their head for money.

The sudden existence and instant viability of a second major wrestling promotion led to a combination of restlessness and prosperity for pro wrestlers across the board. Many wrestlers unsatisfied with their spot in WWE either requested their release or began laying the groundwork for when their contracts would eventually expire, knowing they could land safely at several other destinations. WWE didn't grant any releases, even when the Superstar in question went public with the news that they'd requested one, but they did immediately begin working to lock up wrestlers with long-term deals—at massive increases in pay. Jake Hager, who was briefly WWE World Heavyweight Champion in 2010 under the name Jack Swagger, requested his release in 2017 after over a decade in the WWE system.

"I valued myself at a certain price," Hager said. "[WWE] valued it at another. I've gotta move forward." He admitted to being frustrated with his role in the company toward the end of his run there. "For the longest time, I felt like I was literally the toughest guy in the locker room," he said. "Yet I would go out there and have two-minute matches with guys who couldn't hold my jock. It even got to the point where I pitched to them, I was like, 'Look: I got something to prove. Let me prove it. Pick the fighter; I'll fight anybody [in a shoot fight]. Put them on your show and I'll fight them.' They didn't really want to go down that route." Hager eventually got his wish after WWE, signing with MMA promotion Bellator and going 2–0–1 through his first three professional fights. (Hager also ended up in AEW as part of Chris Jericho's Inner Circle faction.)

Plenty of WWE stars were happy to get pay hikes to stick around. (Randy Orton was also happy to publicly suggest that he wanted to go to AEW in 2020 when his contract was up, only to use that as leverage for a new five-year deal with WWE.)

Proceeding on the theme that had been building for years, 2019 continued to be the best era ever for pro wrestling fans and pro wrestlers alike. Unparalleled access, options, variety—and money and opportunity for those performers who continue to find an audience, no matter what company they worked for.

AEW, Cody, Omega, and the Young Bucks expressed in a mission statement that they wanted to change the world.* At the end of the day, *Dynamite* just ended up being another wrestling show. It's nothing revolutionary in terms of content or production—but it is an alternative.

NXT may have been an indie-pleasing quasi-alternative to *Raw* and *SmackDown*, but it was still a WWE product. AEW may not have changed the world, but it did provide a *true* alternative for the first time in nearly twenty years. Fans have gladly taken that alternative, even if AEW hasn't been able to snap up all those millions of WCW fans who just stopped watching from 2001 on.

It's a golden era of wrestling and a golden era of being upset about wrestling. Is it any surprise we wrestling fans are always at each other's throats online? After all, we're obsessed with fake fighting.

---

* Both Cody and the Young Bucks talked often about the benefits of a potential wrestlers' union prior to AEW officially forming, then walked back those comments after the company was announced, saying it's more complicated than fans realized. Perhaps not coincidentally, all employees at the executive level receive health care through the Jacksonville Jaguars' corporate infrastructure. If you need reminding, Cody and the Young Bucks are executives.

AFTERWORD

All Bets Are Off for What Comes Next

As much as fans love to complain that nothing ever happens or ever changes in WWE, an awful lot has transpired since I began writing this book. When I started, I had no idea that AEW would launch and then dominate the Wednesday Night Wars, or that Bray Wyatt would reinvent himself with his "Fiend" persona and become the hottest thing in wrestling (and then, of course, face the inevitable backlash for being popular). I didn't know WWE would run three concurrent cuckold story lines, or that Erick Rowan would carry a cage to the ring for months before revealing it contained a comically unconvincing "giant spider." And of course, I never predicted that the entire world would be turned upside down by the COVID-19 novel coronavirus in 2020, leading to the cancellation of all live sporting events and to the strangest WrestleMania we'll ever see.

WrestleMania 36, which had been slated to run at the Tampa Bay Buccaneers' Raymond James Stadium on April 5, was in jeopardy for over a month as the pandemic spread. In March, Tampa city officials left the decision to run the event up to WWE, although that became a moot point as more and more bans against public gatherings and "shelter in place" orders became the norm. In the weeks prior, WWE scrambled to tape episodes of weekly television—and for the first time ever, to present WrestleMania as a two-night, pretaped affair. Recording the in-ring matches at the Performance Center in Winter Park, the Superstars wrestled their matches in front of zero fans, setting an all-new attendance record, although not the one that WWE likes to tout every year at the event.

The viewing experience of WrestleMania happening in front of no one was bizarre, but as it has done many times in dire situations before, WWE managed to innovate. Featuring pro wrestling visionaries like Wrestling Society X, Lucha Underground, and Matt Hardy's Broken Universe, each night of WrestleMania 36 featured a "cinematic" match. (If you want to be charitable and consider the Randy Orton vs. Edge Last Man Standing Match a third cinematic offering, knock yourself out.) On Night One, the main event was a "Boneyard Match" between the Undertaker and AJ Styles, which was a three-act, nineteen-minute brawl in and around an abandoned cemetery and barn that was delightful fun, filled with explosions, one-liners, and supernatural happenings, and played like the best Halloween episode of *Sons of Anarchy* that never existed. The match appeared to end with Styles's literal murder and being buried alive before the Undertaker's weird-old-man magic made a barn turn into a Goth rave and then explode as he drove his chopper into the night as heavy metal music blared. It was peak

Undertaker, and the perfect, escapist way to end the first night.

The cinematic match on Night Two was a "Firefly Fun House Match" between Bray Wyatt and John Cena, which saw Cena get teleported to Bray Wyatt's nightmare pocket universe, where he had to face his toughest opponent: himself. The thirteen-minute masterpiece—where Wyatt confronts Cena with visions of his past iterations like they're the stages of the cross before defeating him without issue and causing him to disappear right off the screen—might just be the most creative and ambitious single thing ever produced by WWE, and essays have already been written about just what it all means.

A week or so after WrestleMania 36, Linda McMahon's Super PAC to reelect Donald Trump donated $18.5 million to the state of Florida. By a fall-over-backward stunning coincidence, within days, WWE was declared an essential business in Florida, allowing the company to continue broadcasting live episodes of *Raw*, *NXT*, and *SmackDown* from the Performance Center during the nationwide pandemic shutdown. That same week, WWE bragged about its capacity to weather the storm of the COVID-induced recession, divulging that they had over half a billion dollars in cash on hand. They then immediately started releasing wrestlers and furloughing office employees, producers, and writers. Among those released were Zack Ryder, who had the audacity to use the internet to get himself over during his fifteen-year run with the company; senior referee Mike Chioda, who had been employed by the McMahons since 1989; and Heath Slater, whose only official solo T-shirt in his fourteen-year run in WWE said I GOT KIDS on the front and I NEED THIS JOB on the back—an inside joke turned character arc about his tenuous standing in the company after his teammates in 3MB had been released as part of a mass cut in 2014.*

Granted, the coronavirus mini-era of WWE television is an unprecedented stretch but has given us glimmers of untapped potential about how even a promotion that fans purport to be stale and stagnant can continue to find ways to push the medium forward. It's possible for WWE to still create art—and at times, art that is important.

The past couple of years have brought truly unprecedented times in professional wrestling across the board. WWE has allowed Superstars and performers to appear for other promotions while still remaining under contract. They've fully partnered with independent companies like EVOLVE and PROGRESS. The performers have continued to get smaller and better at pro wrestling, with longer histories of indie credibility.

While WWE continues to frustrate fans to no end with its Vince McMahon–filtered weird proclivities, awful humor, overly scripted promos, and scores of other sticking points, it also produces a thoroughly crowd-pleasing product in *NXT*; and it also must be noted that there *is* a large section of the fan base—probably the largest section, in fact—that actively enjoys the WWE product and continues to tune in every week.

With the advent of All Elite Wrestling, the abundance of promotions that offer a streaming service, and the steady popularity and expansion into the United States of New Japan Pro-Wrestling, fans of the sport have actual, tangible,

---

* The week after his release, Slater opened up a Pro Wrestling Tees storefront where fans could buy his first post-WWE merchandise offering: a parody of his I GOT KIDS shirt that reads, simply, I GOT FIRED.

true alternatives. They can enjoy anything they want, at any time, and there is truly something for everyone.

One of the biggest parts of the sea change is that, for the first time, the overwhelming majority of pro wrestlers are unabashed fans of pro wrestling and have been for their entire lives. They've always wanted to be professional wrestlers—and not for money or fame (although those things are wonderful if they're part of the deal), but for sheer love of the art of wrestling.

For decades, pro wrestling was a haven of strongmen, body-builders, former football players, amateur athletes, Olympians: some of the biggest stars of the 1960s, like Ernie Ladd and Wahoo McDaniel, were NFL players who wrestled in the offseason—and made more money doing it. For the majority of the existence of pro wrestling, most pro wrestlers were in it for the prestige of being a professional athlete or, far more common and overwhelmingly, for the money. Certainly, most wrestlers prided themselves on being good at their craft, but the minority really considered themselves artists. Pro wrestlers now, especially on the independent scene, have something to say or express, and they convey it via their chosen medium, inside the squared circle.

That love and dedication and expression is why more wrestlers than ever before are either getting disgruntled at not being able to ply their trade in the way *they* want to and are asking to get out of WWE so they can be unfettered in their art—or are forging their own path without WWE being part of the equation.

It's an exciting time to be a wrestling fan—probably the *most* exciting time to be a fan in my lifetime, if not ever. Anything feels like it can happen at any moment, even in the largely predictable WWE. Right when you're least expecting it, something mind-blowing happens.

Like CM Punk coming back.

As part of the new FOX partnership, a studio recap-and-analysis show was created on FS1 called *WWE Backstage*. This was done in part to replace the previous FS1 UFC studio show that went away when UFC moved television networks to ESPN (thus opening the door for the FOX partnership in the first place). The show was conceived as a pull-no-punches, kayfabe-busting program, the type of which wrestling fans had never seen before. On November 12, CM Punk appeared on the show in the closing seconds, a surprise to everyone but host Renee Young and a handful of other backstage people. Fans immediately freaked the hell out as Punk said he'd see them next week. In backstage videos and the following week during a sit-down interview with Young, Punk stressed repeatedly that he was working for FOX, not for WWE, and that while he didn't have any plans to return to WWE or to pro wrestling, he was open to the conversation for the first time, admitting that there would be a whole lot of bridges that would have to be repaired along the way if that sort of thing were to become a possibility.

But the very presence of Punk on a show that has "WWE" in the title was unthinkable just last year, much like the return of Daniel Bryan was unthinkable in 2016 and the idea of Cody Rhodes and the Young Bucks creating a viable alternative to WWE and bringing pro wrestling back to TNT was unthinkable in 2017. The unthinkable happens all the time now and, as it should, catches us unaware again and again.

Unthinkable is the new normal. The average quality of pro wrestling matches has never been higher. There's never been more volume of pro wrestling happening at once. Pro wrestling is everywhere. Even if the average person isn't as aware of Roman Reigns and Seth Rollins as they were of Steve Austin, The Rock, or Hulk Hogan, pro wrestling has never been more passionately loved, defended, and debated by the fans who keep coming back for more—even when they proclaim to just be hate-watching.

Everything is pro wrestling, and to the people who perform it, pro wrestling is everything. That's exciting.

No one knows what's going to happen next. The McMahon family has not shot down the idea that they might sell the company if a wild enough offer comes along. Triple H may fully take over the reins one day and bring *Raw* and *SmackDown* closer in line with his vision for *NXT* that has worked out so well. Maybe WWE will end up buying out AEW. Maybe Tony Khan's dad will end up buying WWE in a bizarre reversal of WCW's fate.

But if you're a pro wrestling fan, you're going to keep watching. You're going to keep hoping it gets better, not just in terms of story lines and content, but for the performers as well. You're going to keep getting your hopes up, and getting them dashed, and getting fed up, and nearly giving it up altogether because you can't stand the discourse. Even when you hate it, you're going to keep loving it. We came to this fandom and this life because there is absolutely no other thing in the entire world like pro wrestling, and nothing else in the world fills that void.

WWE has shaped modern pro wrestling, for good or ill, more than any other company. But the same is true for WWE as it is for every other practitioner of this fucked-up, larger-than-life art form: When it's bad, it's bad. When it's good—brother, there ain't nothing better.

Let's keep watching, together. You never know what's next.

ACKNOWLEDGMENTS

This book has shifted and changed as I have written it, but it absolutely could not have been written without the bedrock of important work and research done by the elite wrestling historians who have been doing this for decades. It is only through the exhaustive, fastidious, and indispensable work of historians Tim Hornbaker, Steve Yohe, Scott Teal, J. Michael Kenyon, many at Crowbar Press, Mike Mooneyham, and Steven Johnson, and the contemporaneous reporting of Dave Meltzer at the *Wrestling Observer Newsletter*, Wade Keller and others at the *Pro Wrestling Torch*, and Mike Johnson at *PWInsider* that we have any records at all of the actual inner workings of the sport. There are too many historians for me to list and I would never insult them by claiming that I am one of their illustrious number, but I would like to specifically thank Steve Yohe and Tim Hornbaker for taking the time and showing me the kindness to assist me with a few of my questions. I hope I have not embarrassed you too badly with my work here.

Thank you to Kevin Kleinrock, Roy Lucier, and Ron Funches for taking the time to talk to me and provide much-needed context and perspective. All my love, respect, and appreciation to my colleagues at SB Nation, Cageside Seats, and FOX Sports, and to Martin Rickman, Chris Mottram, Robby Kalland, Bill DiFilippo, Ryan Nagelhout, Danielle Matheson, Justin Donaldson, Scott Heisel, and Elle Collins.

Immense thanks to Eric Nelson at Harper and Tim Wojcik at Levine Greenberg Rostan Literary Agency for making this all happen.

Gargantuan and heartfelt credit must be given to my editor at Harper, Hannah Long. In twenty years of writing, she's only the second person to give me good notes. If you enjoyed this book at all, raise a glass to Hannah for making it as good as it is. Sorry Thanos vanished you.

Thanks to David Dennis Jr. and Emily Pratt for offering their thoughts and feedback on portions of the book that I would never be qualified to write about on my own.

Thank you to David Bixenspan for his assistance, as he is the only person in the world I would trust to fact-check any book about professional wrestling. I appreciate him taking the time to fact-check significant passages of this book for me.

My unending gratitude and awe go out to Lauren Moran, who not only graciously agreed to provide the illustrations for this book, but knocked my dang socks off from the moment she showed me the rough layouts. I couldn't have hoped for better.

Thank you to the many performers, promoters, bookers, announcers, writers, and personalities who have taken the time over the years to not completely dismiss me as a run-of-the-mill mark (not to my face, at least) and who have let me into your fraternity, even briefly or tangentially. I won't name names in print (kayfabe, brother), but I'll seek you out in person to let you know how much I appreciate you.

Perhaps most important, thank you to all professional wrestlers, past and present, for putting your well-being on the line in the name of art every single time you step in the ring. I am grateful for every ounce of pain you have suffered, and I hope this book helps in some small way to legitimize the importance of what you do and why you do it.

INDEX

ABOUT THE AUTHOR

Bill Hanstock is an Emmy-winning producer, screenwriter, editor, and journalist. He has covered and interviewed countless WWE and independent wrestling personalities and events for SB Nation; has contributed to Polygon, The Athletic, and *Inked*; and has penned nearly a dozen stories for the official WWE comic book. He lives in Los Angeles with his wife, son, and two cats.